R.K. Narayan

JOHN THIEME

Manchester University Press

Manchester and New York

distributed exclusively in the USA by Palgrave

Copyright © John Thieme 2007

The right of John Thieme to be identified as the author of this work has been asserted by him in accordance with the Copyright, Designs and Patents Act 1988.

Published by Manchester University Press
Oxford Road, Manchester M13 9NR, UK
and Room 400, 175 Fifth Avenue, New York, NY 10010, USA
www.manchesteruniversitypress.co.uk

Distributed exclusively in the USA by
Palgrave, 175 Fifth Avenue, New York, NY 10010, USA

Distributed exclusively in Canada by
UBC Press, University of British Columbia, 2029 West Mall, Vancouver, BC, Canada v6t 1z2

British Library Cataloguing-in-Publication Data
A catalogue record for this book is available from the British Library

Library of Congress Cataloging-in-Publication Data applied for

ISBN 978 0 7190 5926 1 *hardback*
ISBN 978 0 7190 5927 8 *paperback*

First published 2007

16 15 14 13 12 11 10 09 08 07 06   10 9 8 7 6 5 4 3 2 1

Typeset in Aldus
by Koinonia, Manchester
Printed in Great Britain
by Bell & Bain Ltd, Glasgow

for Barbara

Contents

Acknowledgements

This book has been eight years in the writing and this makes it difficult to be sure one is acknowledging all those who helped. So I apologise in advance to anyone I may have forgotten and, as always, those whose ideas have influenced me without my being conscious of it.

In Chennai and Mysore in 1997–98, Mini Krishnan, N. Ram and C.D. Narasimhaiah were very generous to me, both in sharing their own time and ideas and also in putting me in touch with others. These included R.K. Narayan himself, who was equally kind, not to mention good-humoured, when I met him. In the US in 2000, I was grateful to staff, who assisted me with my work on the Narayan holdings in the Mugar Memorial Library at Boston University and the Harry Ransom Humanities Research Center at the University of Texas in Austin and on Graham Greene's papers in the John J. Burns Library at Boston College. John Atteberry at Boston College, Sean D. Noël at Boston University and Shanon Lawson at the Harry Ransom Humanities Research Center all deserve special mention. I am also grateful to David Higham Associates for permission to photocopy material from the Narayan material in these collections.

I owe particular thanks to students at the Universities of Guyana, North London (now London Metropolitan), Hull, London South Bank, East Anglia and Turin, who taught me much of what I know about Narayan; and I am particularly grateful to London South Bank and Jeffrey Weeks for funding that facilitated my visit to Chennai and Mysore and my work on the Narayan papers in Boston and Austin.

Ranga Rao introduced me to gunas comedy and helped me understand the role of asramas in secular Hinduism, a topic that I also discussed with Hyacinth Cynthia Wyatt. Robert McGill's work on Alice Munro made me think about small towns in illuminating ways and Sean Matthews and other colleagues at the University of East Anglia helped me develop my ideas about heterotopias. Maria-Sabina Alexandru stimulated my interest in the *Natya Shastra*. Ira Raja was a fund of information on numerous aspects of Indian culture and answered my often ill-informed queries with alacrity and accuracy. I owe her a particular debt.

Looking along my shelves as I was completing this study, I realized with some embarrassment just how many people have given me books and information that have been influential in its shaping. They include Silvia Albertazzi, Matthew Frost, Kaiser Haq, Tabish Khair, Mini Krishnan, Alan McLeod, Ira Raja, Ranga Rao (who also shared his unpublished work with me) and Cynthia vanden Driessen. If there are others, I have forgotten, I can only apologise, partly excusing myself on the grounds that the book *has* been a long time coming.

As always it has been a great pleasure to work with Matthew Frost and I am grateful to Matthew and his colleagues at Manchester University Press for their support, both for this book and for the Contemporary World Writer Series more generally.

Series editor's foreword

Contemporary World Writers is an innovative series of authorita-tive introductions to a range of culturally diverse contemporary writers from outside Britain and the United States or from 'minority' backgrounds within Britain or the United States. In addition to providing comprehensive general introductions, books in the series also argue stimulating original theses, often but not always related to contemporary debates in post-colonial studies.

The series locates individual writers within their specific cultural contexts, while recognising that such contexts are themselves invariably a complex mixture of hybridised influences. It aims to counter tendencies to appropriate the writers discussed into the canon of English or American literature or to regard them as 'other'.

Each volume includes a chronology of the writer's life, an introductory section on formative contexts and intertexts, discussion of all the writer's major works, a bibliography of primary and secondary works and an index. Issues of racial, national and cultural identity are explored, as are gender and sexuality. Books in the series also examine writers' use of genre, particularly ways in which Western genres are adapted or subverted and 'traditional' local forms are reworked in a contemporary context.

Contemporary World Writers aims to bring together the theoretical impulse which currently dominates post-colonial studies and closely argued readings of particular authors' works, and by so doing to avoid the danger of appropriating the specifics of particular texts into the hegemony of totalising theories.

Abbreviations

BA	*The Bachelor of Arts*
DR	*The Dark Room*
ET	*The English Teacher*
FE	*The Financial Expert*
Gods	*Gods, Demons and Others*
GT	*The Grandmother's Tale*
Guide	*The Guide*
M-E	*The Man-Eater of Malgudi*
MrS	*Mr Sampath – The Printer of Malgudi*
MyD	*My Days*
PS	*The Painter of Signs*
RG	*Reluctant Guru*
Swami	*Swami and Friends*
Talkative	*Talkative Man*
Tiger	*A Tiger for Malgudi*
VS	*The Vendor of Sweets*
WM	*Waiting for the Mahatma*
WN	*The World of Nagara*

Chronology

Every person is so much a part of his background – take him away from it and he becomes limp and featureless.

(R.K. Narayan, *The Painter of Signs*)

The identities of places are always unfixed, contested and multiple.

(Doreen Massey, *Space, Place and Gender*)

Contexts and intertexts

In a typically whimsical 'Self-Obituary', written in the middle of his life, R.K. Narayan imagines himself, 'On a certain day (towards the close of the twentieth century)' being interrogated by 'four grim men' from the 'I.T.F.K.E.O.N' ('INTERNATIONAL TRIBUNAL FOR KEEPING an [sic] EYE ON NOVELISTS') and charged with various offences.[1] These include: writing too much (exceeding his allotted weight limit of 60 pounds of books); inventing an 'imaginary town', with 'false geography' that is bad for the tourist industry; and leaving his 'characters in mid-air, their destinies unresolved.'[2] The second and third of these charges highlight central characteristics of Narayan's fiction. His invented South Indian town of Malgudi, which is the setting for virtually all his fiction, has been seen by many of his readers as a site that represents quintessential Indianness. Graham Greene's oft-quoted comment, 'Without him I could never have known what it like to be Indian'[3] is the most famous of many testimonials to Narayan's supposed grasp of essential Indianness, but it is only one; and it is mirrored in remarks made by numerous Indian critics, such as the highly respected C.D. Narasimhaiah, who, despite a preference for Narayan's contemporary, Raja Rao, says of him, 'Few writers have been more truly Indian'.[4] Such critics have, often nostalgically, invoked Narayan's fictional town as a microcosm of the nation, sometimes tempering this by an acknowledgement of the extent to which it is representative of a particular region of India and a particular segment of Indian society. Thus a commentator such as the following emphasizes the South Indian specificity of Narayan's world, but has little difficulty in reconciling this with the nation as a whole in his appeal to Indian 'authenticity':

> Of all the Indian writers in English, R.K. Narayan is surely the finest and most authentic in his representation of the national ethos, the scenery, the sights and sounds, the ambience of the nation – or at least of South India, which he has made his special domain under the name of Malgudi. There is hardly ever anything that is unreal in his picture of peoples and places alike; we are constantly aware that what he depicts is what we are accustomed to, what we know from experience or from report.[5]

Similarly, in a passage which uses a Gandhian analogy to suggest the extent to which Narayan's language functions as a means for articulating a local subjectivity through an imported medium, K.R. Srinivasa Iyengar, author of a ground-breaking history of Indian writing in English, says:

> He is of India, even of South India: he uses the English language much as we used to wear dhoties [sic] manu-factured in Lancashire – but the thoughts and feelings, the stirrings of the mind, the wayward movements of the consciousness, are all of the soil of India, recognizably autochthonous.[6]

In such readings Malgudi becomes a metonym for a tradi-tional India, a locus that exists outside time and apart from the forces of modernity, a site that the complicitous 'we' used in both passages will immediately recognize as 'authentic'. However, for readers from early twenty-first century urban India, more accus-tomed to the pluralist vision that dominates the writing of most of the post-Rushdie generation of Indian writers in English, the claim that Narayan captures 'the ambience of the nation' often rings hollow, an expression of a dated Hindu-centred version of Indianness, which is no longer acceptable as a national meta-narrative, because it fails to address the multiplicity of discourses that have constituted India, as it exists both today *and* yesterday. A consequence of such readings has been that Narayan's 'false geography' has begun to seem quaint, a mythologized version of the national imaginary which runs the risk of being dismissed by those alert to the multiplicity of India then and now.

However, the very reasonable charge that Narayan leaves his characters in mid-air is an index of a more general indeterminacy in his mode of writing, an elusiveness which is the antithesis of fundamentalist thinking; and his habitual use of irony frustrates unitary interpretation. Furthermore the actual, as opposed to the perceived, Malgudi of his fiction is always a fractured and transitional site, an interface between older conceptions of 'authentic' Indianness and contemporary views that stress the ubiquitousness and inescapability of change in the face of modernity. Malgudi is also seen from varying angles of vision and with shifting emphases at different points in Narayan's career. In his early novels his perennial fascination with place and space is less concerned with the public countenance of the small town than with interiors, domestic and otherwise, while in his middle-period and later novels characters frequently go beyond the parameters of Malgudi and, as they do so, find their beliefs challenged by values previously undreamt of in their philosophy. In early novels such as *The Dark Room* (1938) and *The English Teacher* (1945), the room is a central trope and more generally the novels of this period engage with buildings, notably schools, colleges and temples. It is only as he moves into his middle period, with novels such as *Mr Sampath* (1949) and *The Financial Expert* (1952), that Narayan seriously embarks, albeit in a meandering way, on the project of mapping Malgudi, creating the vivid 'false geography', which to his amusement enabled the University of Chicago to place it on the map of India and an academic to produce a plan of the town.[7] Subsequently the geographical field of reference expands further in more picaresque works, such as *Waiting for the Mahatma* (1955), *The Guide* (1958) and *The Painter of Signs* (1976), in which the protagonists' travels outside Malgudi open up perspectives on village India, which belie the notion that the 'imaginary town' represents the whole of India.

The charge that Narayan leaves his characters in mid-air also goes to the heart of his often-elusive fiction and directs attention to its apparent resistance to narrative closure. Although the method of his novels is more indebted to the comic conventions of a certain kind of social realism than an anticipation of postmodernist deferral, Narayan's open endings are the logical conclusion to works written in a discursive mode that is as hard to place generically as Malgudi is cartographically. The passage in which he ironically levels the charge of open-endedness against himself goes on to relate this to the moral indeterminacy of his writing. Answering his inquisitors' complaint that he should be taking more pains '"to make virtue triumph and evil suffer"', he replies:

> 'How can I?' [...] when God himself seems unable to arrange things that way. In any case I can't undertake it because I do not understand what is evil and what is good in my various characters. They interest me only as individuals and not as symbols or embodiments of this or that.[8]

I have begun with these references to Narayan's 'Self-Obituary' because they relate to one of the central concerns of this study. With reference to Michel Foucault's thinking on heterotopias, it attempts to reassess exactly what Malgudi can be seen to represent, arguing that far from serving as a metonym for a settled, secure India, the town is the product of a particular coming together of social, religious and above all psychic forces, which undergo transformations as they interact with one another. In varying ways in the different novels, it is seen to be at a cultural crossroads, transforming itself in response to a range of incursions, many of which are associated with aspects of modernity. Malgudi also emerges as a liminal location, because of the seemingly discrepant admixture of genres which its creator draws upon. Built on the fault-lines, where classical Hindu discourse and the more 'realistic', supposedly Western form of the novel collide, it ushers new forms of fiction into being. So this study endeavours to identify the range of discursive intertexts, as well as some of the social and personal contexts that inform Narayan's novels, with a view to pinpointing what constitutes their uniqueness.

In Narayan's tenth novel, *The Vendor of Sweets* (1967), the protagonist Jagan finds his settled way of life challenged by the advent of outside forces. It is a pattern that recurs in the middle period of Narayan's fiction, in which the action is frequently structured around a small businessman's encounter with modernity. In this case modernity is personified by Jagan's son, Mali, who goes to America with a desire to become a writer. Prior to Mali's going, Jagan misunderstands what he intends. Jagan makes a distinction between literature, which he associates with classical Hindu texts, and writing, which he associates with clerical activities of the kind introduced into India during the period of colonial rule. Consequently he thinks that Mali is planning to become a clerk. When he is corrected, he feels his son would do better to stay home: after all, Valmiki, the legendary author of *The Ramayana*, did not need to travel to America to learn his craft and, he says, Mali could learn more about storytelling from a village grandmother. Fairly clearly, then, 'writing' means different things to different people in South India in the third quarter of the twentieth century. But Jagan and Mali agree on one thing: both lament the dearth of contemporary Indian writing and the novel seems to be investigating the problematics of the situation of a writer like Narayan. Mali's answer to the problem of contemporary authorship is to manufacture story-writing machines! Jagan turns to classical literary models, as mediated by the oral storytelling figure of the grandmother. Given the starkness of this choice, Narayan fairly obviously sides with Jagan.[9] There is no real dialectic involved in the binary of Jagan and Mali's contrasted attitudes to narrative, but the opposition serves to point up the possibility of alternative attitudes to writing and implicitly at least directs attention to the mode of fiction Narayan is employing. It is a mode that pays its dues to classical Hindu discourse, both Sanskrit and Tamil, while more obviously working within the conventions of certain kinds of Western fiction. Its most obvious affinities are with the kinds of social comedy written by novelists such as Dickens and Wells, but to locate Narayan's novels in such a tradition is as reductive as seeing them as twentieth-century reworking of classical Hindu myths.

For all its apparent immersion in comic realism, *The Vendor of Sweets* is, as Jagan and Mali's contrasted attitudes to writing suggest, as much a metafictive text as an attempt to transcribe an observed social reality onto the printed page. Narayan's discursive universe is a space where the tectonic plates of ancient and modern narrative come together and when these move, as they frequently do in his novels, new forms of expression emerge. Narayan's fiction is centrally concerned with the life of writing and this study views his sixty-year career as a uniquely individual instance of a novelist's struggle to forge a distinctive fictional practice from disparate discursive traditions *and* as a fascinating barometer of the changing possibilities available to Indian writers in English during this period. Beginning in the 1930s, his career spanned some of the crucial moments in the formation of modern India as a nation-state before and after Independence. It also bridged a period that saw Indian fiction in English coming of age and achieving recognition both inside and outside the country.

At the time when Narayan published his first novel *Swami and Friends* in 1935, there was only a very small readership for English-language writing in India and his South Indian brahmin contemporary, Raja Rao, gave voice to the concerns of the late colonial Indian writer who chose to use English, in the frequently quoted Preface to his novel *Kanthapura* (1938):

> The telling has not been easy. One has to convey in a language that is not one's own the spirit that is one's own. One has to convey the various shades and omissions of a certain thought-movement that looks maltreated in an alien language. I use the word 'alien', yet English is not really an alien language to us. It is the language of our intellectual make-up – like Sanskrit or Persian was before – but not of our emotional make-up. We are all instinctively bilingual, many of us writing in our own language and in English.[10]

Today such a comment seems dated, since despite its emphasis on bilingualism and the way languages reflect different aspects of Indianness, the reference to 'the spirit that is one's own' still effectively articulates an essentialist view of Indianness and obscures the extent to which supposedly competing languages interact. Arguably, though, this datedness is not just a matter of the extent to which later novelists, in a line of descent that runs from G. V. Desani's *All About H. Hatter* (1948) to Salman Rushdie's *Midnight's Children* (1981) and Arundhati Roy's *The God of Small Things* (1997), have sensitized readers to the nuances and multiple possibilities of Indian English, but an index of Rao's failure to see the limitations of his position as a writer trying to communicate a supposedly 'pure' Vedantic Hinduism through what he initially calls the 'alien' medium of English. The truth, as he goes on to say, is that English is not an alien medium to him – simply another language that he is able to write in with some fluency – even if he feels it is more suited to the expression of certain aspects of his 'make-up'.

Narayan's situation was, if anything, more complex, since he was trilingual. Born in Madras in 1906, from 1921 he lived most of his life in Mysore, becoming fluent in Kannada, as well as Tamil and English. One of his earliest influences was his grandmother, who was an oral storyteller of the kind that Jagan sees as a repository of narrative tradition in *The Vendor of Sweets*, and retellings of ancient myths and legends were an important part of his early socialization, though as he grew older and aspired to become a writer, he aspired to realize his ambition in English. In his autobiographical memoir *My Days* (1974) he recalls agreeing to his uncle T.N. Seshachalam's deathbed advice that he should study Kamban's *Ramayana*, but only doing so 'out of consideration [and] with no conviction that I would or could ever be interested in Kamban; we were poles apart. I was a realistic fiction-writer in English and Tamil language or literature was not my concern'.[11]

After his move to Mysore, he attended the Maharaja's Collegiate High School, where his father was headmaster, subsequently moving on to the Maharaja's College, which was a part of the recently founded University of Mysore; and his own education was very close to that of the heroes of his early trilogy, *Swami and Friends*, *The Bachelor of Arts* (1937) and *The*

English Teacher. Although it allocated some time to the study of Tamil writing and Indian history, it was founded upon a colonial curriculum in which the study of English literature and history predominated. From an early age, then, two particular sets of contexts and intertexts were determining the direction his future career as a writer would take. In *My Days* he says that he 'started writing, mostly under the influence of events occurring around me' (*MyD* 64), but immediately prior to this he gives an account of the reading he was privileged to enjoy as a headmaster's son. It included numerous authors from the canon of English literature, with Scott and Dickens being given particular pride of place;[12] influential romance writers such as Mrs Henry Wood and Marie Corelli, an author for whom his enthusiasm subsequently waned; and various prominent contemporary or more recent figures, among them Arnold Bennett, P.G. Wodehouse, Conan Doyle, H.G. Wells, George Bernard Shaw and Thomas Hardy. Along with the books in the school library, he had access to many of the leading English journals of the day, including *The Spectator*, *The Times Literary Supplement*, *The Strand*, *John O'London*, the London *Mercury* and *The Bookman*. And amid this eclectic mix he also read *The Boy's Own Paper*, a magazine that seems to have influenced *Swami and Friends*, where details from his own South Indian schooling are shaped within the genre of English schoolboy fiction.[13] And '[t]hrough '*Harper's*, the *Atlantic*, and *American Mercury*', he also received 'glimpses of the New World and its writers' (*MyD* 63–4). Perhaps the most surprising aspect of the account that Narayan gives of his early reading is the comment that he 'loved tragic endings' and 'looked for books that would leave me crushed at the end' (*MyD* 61). This is amplified by details of his response to the endings of Mrs Wood's *East Lynne*, which he says 'left me shedding bitter tears' and to 'stories in which the heroine wasted away in consumption', an area in which he found Dickens particularly satisfying (*MyD* 62). This maudlin attraction to the tragic seems significantly at odds with his later practice in which most readers have felt the comic takes precedence. Perhaps it is best just seen as an expression of an adolescent sensibility – he refers to his admiration for Marie Corelli's 'overcharged romanticism' (*MyD* 62) – but from another point of view it could be seen to anticipate the extent to which comedy is subsumed in more sombre and reflective responses to experience, in novels as different from one another as *The Dark Room*, *The English Teacher*, *Waiting for the Mahatma*, *The Guide* and *A Tiger for Malgudi* (1983).

Given this reading and his education it was not, then, surprising that English became Narayan's language of choice; and he seems to have turned to it instinctively as the medium most suited for the kind of fiction he saw himself as writing. Years later, in a 1978 radio talk, he said that he wrote in English rather than Tamil or Kannada out of 'personal preference', adding that when he began his career 'no one questioned it, language had not become a sensitive issue. People spoke and wrote any language suited to their needs or circumstances'.[14] More self-conscious at the time of the talk, he spoke of the need for Indian writers 'to evolve a brand of English which keeps close to our own idiom of thinking. I am not suggesting what is disparagingly termed Indian English, I mean a real brand of English language suited to our needs just as the Americans have evolved their own idiom and usage.'[15] In many ways this is how Narayan's English functions throughout his career, as a supple medium that never attempts the regionally specific registers of Nissim Ezekiel's 'Very Indian Poems in Indian English',[16] not the later verbal pyrotechnics of a Salman Rushdie.

However, while English was the language in which Narayan felt most at home as a writer, using it had implications for his choice of subject-matter and his notions of audience. V.S. Naipaul's view that he wrote 'in English for publication abroad'[17] is mistaken if taken to mean that he wrote exclusively for an overseas readership, but initially Narayan did look to England. Thanks to the assistance of his friend, 'Kittu' Purna, who introduced his work to Graham Greene, and Greene's help in getting *Swami and Friends* accepted for publication in England, he was influenced by the need to meet the perceived demands of the English reading public. Subsequently World War II would prove a period when paper shortages and other related factors meant that English publication was denied him and he had to find local outlets for English-language writing, becoming a magazine editor and publisher himself, but in the years before and after the war his English mentor and publishers exercised a considerable influence on his writing. His name was changed to make it more manageable for the English reading public. So, too, were the titles of his first novels; and Greene amended his English in ways intended to make it more correct, while still retaining what he saw as a distinctive Indian inflection (see Chapter 2 for details of these changes). Later, in the 1950s and 1960s, when Narayan's work attracted attention in America, at a time when notions of Indian mysticism were becoming fashionable, he found himself subjected to similar pressures to minister to perceived American tastes (see the opening of Chapter 4). However, in both cases he can be seen as simply adjusting the balance of elements that had gone into his discursive formation in one direction or the other; and paradoxically his American 'reinvention' licensed him to make more of the Hindu aspects of his background that had hitherto been subordinated to meet the perceived demands of the English reading public. Meanwhile his foray into magazine publishing in World War II had alerted him to the potential English readership in India and by 1945 he had published three volumes of his short stories and reprints of *Swami and Friends* and *Mysore*, a travel-book originally commissioned and published by the state government of Mysore.[18] These appeared under the imprint 'Indian Thought', which took its title from the short-lived journal he had edited in the early years of the war. He would continue to publish Indian editions of his books under this imprint for the rest of his life.

Tamil intertexts become more prominent in the second half of Narayan's career, but they occur in a dialectical relationship with his Western influences and novels such as *The Guide*, in which a tourist guide is assumed to have been transformed into a spiritual guide, are less concerned with expounding Hindu philosophical wisdom than with asking questions about its applicability in contemporary situations. Older values *are* presented sympathetically, but with a quizzical, non-committal attitude with regard to their efficacy. In mid-life Narayan began to re-read ancient texts, 'going to their Sanskrit origin with the help of a scholar'.[19] In *Gods, Demons and Others* (1964),[20] he retold a selection of ancient myths and he subsequently produced his own versions of *The Ramayana* (1972) and *The Mahabharata* (1978). At this point, then, it is as if he had heeded his uncle's advice that he should study Kamban's *Ramayana* – his *Ramayana* was based not on Valmiki's Sanskrit text, but on Kamban's Tamil version of the epic.

In one sense this was simply the acknowledgement of a strand that had been present in Narayan's writing from its inception. He may have chosen to write in English and for the most part turned his back on Tamil *intertexts*, but Tamil brahmin *contexts* are omnipresent in his work. In the early novels they provide the values by which his protagonists live; subsequently at the very least they serve as the backdrop against which their enterprises and struggles are set. As Lakshmi Holmstrom indicates, Narayan's protagonists' development is usually related to the four *asramas* (or stages) of the ideal Hindu life and although the fact that his novels have travelled well attests to their cross-cultural valency, it is as reductive to see them as expressive of universal human characteristics as it is to see them as representing quintessential Indianness. Holmstrom's concise exposition of the 'commonplaces of Indian [for which one should perhaps read 'Hindu'] thought' that inform early Indian novelists' representations of character and action identifies beliefs in

> varnasramadharma or a man's [sic] role and duties according to his place in a scheme of castes and also according to his stage of life; karma or the principle of deeds and consequences which is worked out both in this life and in successive births until the ultimate release; a hierarchy of values, generally classified as dharma or right action, artha or worldly interest and kama or human love; and a cyclically ordered time and universe which encompasses these values.[21]

This summary outlines time-honoured tenets and Holmstrom, whose pioneering monograph was published in 1973, is quick to point out that the extent to which individual Hindus hold these beliefs and apply them in particular situations is variable. Adherence to them has, of course, suffered further attenuation since the time when she was writing, but then most of Narayan's work predates this. Holmstrom also suggests that professional responsibilities may weigh more heavily than attitudes to *varna* (or caste) and many of Narayan's novels centre on figures whose identities, as indicated through the novels' titles, are first characterized by their occupations (*The English Teacher*, *The Financial Expert*, *The Guide*, *The Vendor of Sweets*, *The Painter of Signs*). Nevertheless the notion of *varnasramadharma* (right action, particularly as determined by one's caste and stage in life) is centrally important, albeit in varying degrees, and is particularly associated with their caste identity as brahmins (the highest of the four castes) and their progression through the various *asramas* or stages prescribed in the *Manusmriti* (laws of Manu), the classic exposition of the doctrine.[22] Again it needs to be emphasized that the *asramas* involve behavioural ideals and Narayan's protagonists are men contending with the day-to-day pressures of lived social experience. Nevertheless the schema of the four-fold progression prescribed in the *Manusmriti* does inform their response to their secular worlds and the existential problems with which they wrestle. Holmstrom's outline goes on to explain that the second *asrama* is the lynch-pin of the whole system:

> Asrama ideally divides a man's life into studenthood or apprenticeship, the status of a householder and finally renunciation of the world, with a shadowy intermediary stage of withdrawal before the last. In practice the chief place belongs to the householder and youth is a training and preparation for it; nevertheless there is a vague but strongly felt ideal of falling away from the married state towards non-attachment in old age. Few men renounce the world in the classical style at the appointed time; yet the ideal of renunciation has a strong hold on the Hindu imagination.[23]

Narayan's fiction is underpinned by these four stages, respectively known as the *brahmacharya, grihastya, vanaprastha* (the 'shadowy' third stage in which the householder becomes a forest-dweller or hermit prior to the final renunciation) and *sanyasa*. His first two novels, *Swami and Friends* and *The Bachelor of Arts*, have protagonists who can obviously be located in the first *asrama*, though their colonial education implicates them in a process of double socialization and Tamil and 'English' strands interact in their coming-of-age process. Subsequently several of his protagonists (such as Sriram in *Waiting for the Mahatma* and Raman in *The Painter of Signs*) are bachelors of an age, at which they might reasonably be expected to have entered into the second *asrama*, while others (such as Nataraj in *The Man-Eater of Malgudi* [1961] and Jagan in the *Vendor of Sweets*) are very definitely adult householders and men of affairs. Renunciation is a major trope in the texts and Narayan protagonists, like Chandran in *The Bachelor of Arts* and Raju in *The Guide*, are attracted to the withdrawal of the fourth *asrama* at an early age, while the third *asrama* is 'shadowy' in his work, appearing only occasionally, as in the character of a hermit encountered in *The Painter of Signs*. Putting this simply, hints of the *dharma* associated with particular *asramas* are omnipresent in Narayan, but there is seldom a straightforward progression from one stage to the next, nor are characters able to inhabit any of the four stages in a settled and uncomplicated way.

The complications and tensions that recur from novel to novel have much to do with their unstable geography – Malgudi is a world in flux – but in addition to attesting to a broader social experience of change, they can be seen as a product of Narayan's own personal and professional experience. As a schoolboy and student, he received an education that divided him between colonial and Tamil influences. As a writer, he drew on a similarly disparate range of intertexts and despite his choice of English as the preferred medium of his fiction and his early adaptation of his material for an English audience, there are classical Hindu (particularly Tamil) elements running through all his work. And as a *grihastya*, he found himself in an equally split situation, when his wife Rajam, whom he had wed in a 'love marriage' and to whom he was devoted, died of typhoid in her early twenties. Like Krishna in his most autobiographical novel, *The English Teacher*, a seminal work for any account of his development though by no means his best fiction, Narayan was distraught, only finding relief from his trauma in his relationship with his little daughter, Hema. He subsequently remained single for the rest of his life – more than six decades – and so in one crucial sense his situation as a *grihastya* was untypical. And as a writer in English, interpreting the lives of protagonists who mostly pursue twentieth-century equivalents of traditional brahmin scribal professions, he was also venturing into territory that was largely uncharted. He was not, of course, the first Indian novelist to write in English, but in much the same way as Pope's proudest boast was that he lived by his pen, Narayan could lay claim to having been the first fully professional Indian-English writer, partly because of his international popularity, but also because of his Mysore publishing ventures. His involvement in the business of authorship means that he followed a profession that had much in common with the occupations followed by several of his heroes – Srinivas in *Mr Sampath* seems to be particularly closely modelled on Narayan in this respect – but from the time when *Swami and Friends* was published his horizons were broader and the need to appeal to both a Western and a local audience also made him an untypical *grihastya*.

Narayan's protagonists' scribal professions represent a version of brahmin life, adapted to the print culture that had taken hold in South India in the late nineteenth century. Characteristically, and this is often assumed rather than explicit in the novels, they search for a *dharma* appropriate to their situation in a changing world. This is frequently the unifying element in what may seem to be loosely structured narratives. They also, especially in the early novels, demonstrate a brahminical fear of being polluted by contact with the impure, a phobia which comes across particularly strongly in *The English Teacher*, where it is legitimized by a sequence of events closely based on Narayan's own experience: the protagonist's young wife is taken ill and dies after visiting an unsanitary location. In short, even when Narayan appears to be transparently accessible to an overseas readership, his fiction is predicated upon layers of social experience that are often hidden to outsiders. It is, however, mistaken to see it as exhibiting what Iyengar refers to as 'thoughts and feelings' and 'wayward movements of the consciousness' that are 'all of the soil of India, recognizably autochthonous'. Narayan's brahmins are also colonials: their subjectivity is in transit and they live in a world of flux that is best understood in relation to the kind of thinking about space that has displaced older essentialist ideas.

In one sense literary topographies are always *other* worlds, since they are brought into being through acts of composition and can never offer unmediated access to an external social reality. Moreover, place is never a constant since it always exists in a dialectical relationship with time. And arguably postcolonial geographies are subject to additional ruptures as a consequence of the intersection of the different forces that have gone into their making. In any case the 'false geography' of Narayan's 'imaginary town'[24] of Malgudi forms the epicentre of his work. With the exception of his last extended work of fiction, the autobiographical novella 'Grandmother's Tale' (1992), all his novels are set in Malgudi and to understand its cultural and psychic geography is to understand the cognitive mapping that is central to the fictional project that he undertook over six decades – from *Swami and Friends* to *The World of Nagaraj* (1990).

Malgudi is a highly local environment and, bearing in mind Narayan's 'Self-Obituary' comment on his resistance to his characters' being seen as 'symbols or embodiments of this or that', one should be wary of reducing his fictional world to a microcosm of India. Nevertheless from the moment when its contours are first outlined in *Swami*, Malgudi offers a series of pictures of South India in transition, which relates to Narayan's recurrent concern with the situation of the Indian writer. Although he has been widely discussed, in fairly straightforward terms, as either a 'realistic' or 'mythic' writer, the issue of *how* to write India, *what kind of* discourse is appropriate for the task, recurs again and again in his fiction, to a point, where although his writing is a world away from the self-consciousness of Western postmodern novelists, it has a distinctive metafictive ring to it. This becomes prominent in his middle-period novels, such as *The Vendor of Sweets* and his masterpiece, *The Man-Eater of Malgudi*, but it is present from the outset in *Swami*, and it assumes major importance in his late work, such as *Talkative Man* (1986) where the act of tale-telling is in many ways the central subject. And at the very end of his career, in 'Grandmother's Tale', a narrative based on his family history, which revisits material previously recounted in *My Days*, Narayan addresses the problematics of personal historiography, foregrounding the act of storytelling and prefacing the work with a cautionary note about the porousness of '[t]he borderline between fact and fiction'.[25] In short, despite the apparent transparency of his writing, Narayan often includes metafictive references to his chosen modes of narration and arguably such passages emanate from an instinctive awareness of his situation as a writer drawing on different literary inheritances and refashioning them to produce a mode of fiction that is distinctively his own. In novels such as *Mr Sampath*, *The Vendor of Sweets* and *The Painter of Signs*, there is an overt metaliterary dimension, because representational practices are central to the theme, but more generally all of Narayan's novels wrestle with the need to find an appropriate fictional mode to give voice to the fractured world that is Malgudi.

Malgudi has been compared with such fictional landscapes as Hardy's Wessex and Faulkner's Yoknapatawpha County,[26] both of which can be seen as mythologized versions of the social worlds they construct that verge on elegy, because they dramatize the conflict between the old and the new: the rural past and the increasingly mechanized present in Hardy; the conservative Sartorises and the parvenu Snopseses in Faulkner. In both cases the old is preferred and the opposition involved is predicated on the nostalgic assumption that the old offers stability. Putting this another way, pre-industrial Wessex and pre-Snopes Yoknapatawpha County are what Michel Foucault has termed heterotopias, *other* places that exist as alternatives to familiar, everyday spaces. Like Wessex and Yoknapatawpha County, Malgudi offers the illusion of a recognizable transcribed reality, but in fact is an imagined world that ministers to fantasies of what India has been or should be like; and like Wessex and Yoknapatawpha County, it is a site where the old and the new join battle.

Foucault's notion of the heterotopia was developed in relation to his views on the history of space in *Western* societies, but it proves a useful framework for a consideration of Narayan, perhaps because Narayan's choice of English as the medium for this fiction meant that he was metaphorically moving between cultures at a time when travel was far less common than today. Long before he began to undertake physical journeys (initially to the United States via Britain) in the second half of his life, he was effectively negotiating the terms of his project by inventing the heterotopia of Malgudi. In an interview originally published in 1982, Foucault offers a succinct explanation of what heterotopias are, identifying them as 'those singular spaces to be found in some given social spaces whose functions are different or even the opposite of others'.[27] He is not referring to literary space here, but one might develop his thinking on the subject to say that fictional sites are always defined in contradistinction to 'given social spaces', since signifying practices, the act of rendering them in *language* inevitably renders them 'other'. This is the sense in which literary topographies are always *other* worlds; by definition the writerly imagination creates its own places – it is impossible to realize the actualities of a location in words.

Earlier, in a 1967 talk, 'Of Other Spaces', Foucault had expressed the view that:

> The present epoch will perhaps be above all the epoch of space. We are in the epoch of simultaneity: we are in the epoch of juxtaposition, the epoch of the near and far, of the side-by-side, of the dispersed. We are at a moment. I believe, when our experience of the world is less that of a long life developing through time than that of a network that connects points and intersects with its own skein.[28]

These remarks represented something of a Pauline conversion for a theorist who had earlier privileged time over space. Moreover, since they were developed in relation to space-time configurations in European discourse and in one sense at least they were born out of a particular moment in French intellectual history – 1960s structuralism – they might seem inapplicable in a South Asian context. They do, however, have particular resonance when applied to a writer like Narayan, again because his fiction is centrally concerned with constructing a version of a *place*, 'Malgudi', which is not allowed to exist outside of history (though many commentators have seen it in this way while others have felt it exists in a time-warp), but in which space seems to be more important than time. More generally, Foucault influenced cultural geographers such as Edward Soja, who have argued that until recently space continued to be the poor relation of time. Soja subtitles his influential 1989 study *Postmodern Geographies* 'the reassertion of space in social critical theory' and quotes Foucault's comment that 'space was treated as the dead, the fixed, the undialectical, the immobile. Time, on the contrary, was richness, fecundity, life, dialectic'.[29]

At the same time such a 'reassertion of space' cannot be isolated from its relationship with time. In Doreen Massey's words, 'social relations are never still; they are inherently dynamic' and so it is necessary to 'move beyond a view of place as bounded, as in various ways a site of authenticity, as singular, fixed and unproblematic in its identity'.[30] In her view, 'the identities of places are always unfixed, contested and multiple' and so 'attempts to institute horizons, to establish boundaries, to secure the identities of places' are no more than 'attempts to get to grips with the unutterable mobility and contingency of space-time'.[31] This has immediate relevance to Narayan, whose Malgudi has frequently been seen as a timeless zone, where traditional Indian values are being preserved in amber, in much the same way as Vasu, the taxidermist antagonist of *The Man-Eater of Malgudi*, seeks to preserve the animals he stuffs. Certainly space is central to Narayan's project, which involves a mapping of both the human and physical geography of Malgudi, but it is always in flux, changing with the passage of time, whether this be historical eons or fleeting minutes. In *The Financial Expert*, the protagonist Margayya lives in a street that is bedevilled by poor sanitation, but it is also a location with an alternative and enduring spiritual presence, since it is the site of an ancient temple. In *The Guide*, a drought uncovers a submerged ancient temple, which in one sense it is a trope for the *past*, but it opens up alternative contemporary possibilities for this spot. In each case history and geography interact *in the present*.

Foucault's talk continues with a potted history of European space. He argues that:

> [I]n the Middle Ages there was a hierarchic ensemble of places: sacred places and profane places: protected places and open, exposed places: urban places and rural places (all these concern the real life of men [sic]). [...] There were places where things had been put because they had been violently displaced, and then on the contrary places where things found their natural ground and stability. It was this complete hierarchy, this opposition, this intersection of places that constituted what could very roughly be called medieval space: the space of emplacement.[32]

Again this has striking resonance when applied to Narayan's fiction, where one finds places that seem to be founded on some kind of 'natural ground and stability' challenged by sites that indicate displacement. Thus in an early novel such as *The Bachelor of Arts*, the protagonist Chandran is clearly displaced when he goes to Madras, but even within Malgudi there is a sense of shifting tectonic plates as the forces of modernity begin to destabilize traditional value-systems. Similarly in *The Dark Room*, *Waiting for the Mahatma* and *The Guide*, the brahmin protagonists spend periods in the seemingly sacred site of a temple, a location which promises spiritual fulfilment, but fails to provide any uncomplicated resolution in a world where conflicting discourses interact under the impact of secular modernism. Again, as Foucault puts it:

> The space in which we live [...] is also, in itself, a heterogeneous space. [...] We do not live inside a void that could

be colored with diverse shades of light, we live inside a
set of relations that delineates sites which are irreducible
to one another and absolutely not superimposable on one
another.[33]

and one of the 'principles' that Foucault ascribes to the heterotopia
is that it is 'capable of juxtaposing in a single real place several
spaces, several sites that are in themselves incompatible'.[34]

This is a view of space that has general relevance to literary
representations of place, but it is arguably one which, like much
recent work in cultural geography, has particular resonance for
spaces that have been affected by the ruptures of colonialism.
Displacement, whether social or caused by the process of
rendering space in language, may be a facet of all discourses
of place, but colonial epistemic violence generates particularly
abrupt discontinuities. However, Foucault himself does not take
this position when, towards the end of 'Of Other Spaces', he
briefly addresses the issue of colonial space. Talking about the role
of what he terms the heterotopia of 'compensation' in creating 'a
space that is other, another real space, as perfect, as meticulous,
as well arranged as ours is messy, ill constructed, and jumbled',
he says that he wonders if 'certain colonies have not functioned
somewhat in this manner'.[35] As examples he cites Puritan New
England and Jesuit Paraguay. These seem a far cry from South
India, but if one pays attention to those responses to Narayan's
fiction that have seen Malgudi as a settled site, arguably it, too,
is a colonial space that offers the 'compensation' of apparent
meticulousness and perfection. As always the 'other' place offers
its appropriator an opportunity for achieving self-definition
through contradistinction and in the heterotopia of compensation, alterity supposedly takes the form of a promise of stability
and familiarity. This model seems to fit perceived versions of
Malgudi better. Certainly many of Narayan's Western readers,
from Graham Greene onwards, have looked to Malgudi for just
such a consoling vision of apparent permanence. This study will,
however, dismantle such views by demonstrating that Narayan's
town proves to be 'messy, ill constructed, and jumbled' and that
the tearing-point of many of the novels is the protagonists' wish

that it were otherwise.

But where exactly is Malgudi and what exactly does it signify? Although it is an invented place, Malgudi has frequently been identified with Mysore.[36] In fact it is a mythic construct which draws on aspects of a number of South Indian cities to create its own discursive space, a space which Narayan has cherished as a liberation from reality.[37] Narayan once said that Malgudi is 'nowhere'[38] and that in inventing it he was creating a symbolic milieu for the exploration of some of his preoccupations. Over the years he sometimes stressed the universality of Malgudi characteristics:

> [...] I am often asked, 'Where is Malgudi?' All I can say is that it is imaginary and not to be found on any map (although the University of Chicago has published a literary atlas with a map of India indicating the location of Malgudi). If I explain that Malgudi is a small town in South India I shall only be expressing a half-truth, for the characteristics of Malgudi seem to me to be universal.[39]

More often, though, he preferred to emphasize the other side of the 'half-truth' by insisting on the *South* Indian specificity of Malgudi. His invented town draws on aspects of Mysore, the Purasawalkam area of Madras, where he grew up, and Coimbatore, while its name appears to be an amalgam drawn from Lalgudi (near Trichy) and Mangudi (near Kumbakonam).[40] However, despite all these possible identifications and the temptation to universalize this very particular place, the suggestion that Malgudi is 'nowhere' should perhaps be taken most seriously, as it liberates the 'imaginary town' from fixed definition and allows it to take up a place in the heterogeneous world of heterotopias. In a passage in which he anticipates more recent cultural commentators, among them novelists such as Rushdie who have argued against essentialist definitions of India,[41] Narayan likens generalizations about the country to the attempts of the five blind men of a traditional Hindu fable to define an elephant. Each describes the particular part that he has touched, a situation that Narayan sees as analogous to writers' implied claims that their piecemeal versions of the 'jigsaw puzzle' that is

India represent the whole and a salutary warning against trying to present one's own world as 'typical'.[42] Malgudi is a composite discursive formation born from Narayan's own highly individual sensibility and his distinctive hybrid upbringing. As such its only existence is on the printed page and yet it is a construct with which generations of readers from varied backgrounds have felt able to identify and which absorbed Narayan's own imagination from the moment when, as he puts it in *My Days*, 'Malgudi with its little railway station swam into view, all ready-made, with a character called Swaminathan running down the platform peering into the faces of passengers, and grimacing at a bearded face' (*MyD* 79–80).

Early novels

Narayan's 1950 comment, quoted at the beginning of the previous chapter, on his inconclusive endings in his 'Self-Obituary', continues by providing examples of his supposed crime of leaving his characters in mid-air. He particularly focuses on the open endings of his first four novels, grouping them together in a single paragraph.[1] His interrogators from the 'I.T.F.K.E.O.N' ('INTERNATIONAL TRIBUNAL FOR KEEPING an [sic] EYE ON NOVELISTS') tell him:

> [...] You have left Swami (of Swami and Friends [sic]) standing on a railway platform watching a departing train, you have left Chandran (of the Bachelor of Arts [sic] cycling down the road, you have left Savitri (of The Dark Room [sic]) sitting at a window and moping; is your English Teacher dead or is he dreaming of wool-gathering in the last page of that book?[2]

Three of these novels – *Swami and Friends* (1935), *The Bachelor of Arts* (1937) and *The English Teacher* (1945) – are often grouped together as a kind of loose trilogy[3] about the coming-of-age of the male protagonist, a figure whose name changes from novel to novel, but whose main characteristics and situation as a young brahmin experiencing various stages of the English-oriented colonial educational curriculum and gradually making the transition from the first to the second of the four *asramas* of the *Manusmriti* is a constant. *The Dark Room* (1938), a novel focused on the plight of a mistreated wife, is ostensibly the odd one out of the four. I hope, though, to show that a commonality of concerns runs through the early novels, and that in some ways *The Dark Room*, though by no means the strongest of the four, is a pivot on which the others can be seen to turn, particularly since its focus on domestic interiors is important for any consideration of Narayan's representation of space. In all four novels, Western and Tamil forces interact, both in the formal constituents of the text and in the social and psychic milieux depicted. Arguably, though, these early novels are Narayan's most 'English' work. In the fiction of his middle and later periods he would draw on the Tamil elements in his upbringing more extensively. These are not completely ignored in the first four novels, but they are not accorded a central role in the fiction that was published in England and was partly tailored to suit the perceived tastes of its British readers.

Graham Greene's patronage of Narayan, which began with his finding a publisher for *Swami and Friends*, also operated in other ways. In addition to convincing the publisher Hamish Hamilton to accept *Swami* in 1935[4] and also helping him to place the novels that followed, Greene acted as his mentor, offering suggestions and providing corrections for all Narayan's manuscripts[5] up to *The Vendor of Sweets* (1967).[6] Where *Swami* was concerned, Greene and Hamilton persuaded Narayan to change the title he had originally envisaged for the novel; and they also decided to re-christen their distant Indian author, with the consequence that Rasipuram Krishnaswami Narayan Swami became 'R.K. Narayan',[7] and the author's affiliations with his family's village and his paternal ancestry that were respectively contained in the first two elements of his full name disappeared at a stroke. It would be wrong to make too much of this. The use of initials for the first two elements was, and is, not uncommon in South India,[8] and in any case Narayan had been writing to Greene and Hamilton as 'R.K. Narayan Swami'. However, his acquiescence in this English make-over, which resulted in the loss of 'Swami' from his own name,[9] suggests that he was willing, at least in part, to allow his identity to be trimmed to fit perceptions about the reading public in England in the 1930s.[10] This said, like all his fiction *Swami and Friends* and the novels that followed in the 1930s blend Western and Hindu – specifically Tamil brahmin – elements in a variety of ways, to produce fiction which on one level locates itself in an extremely particular environment, but on another succeeds in speaking to an international readership.

Narayan's original title for *Swami and Friends* was 'Swami the Tate'.[11] In the closing chapters of the book the eponymous schoolboy hero becomes obsessed with an imminent cricket match, which promises, in the fashion of the best English schoolboy fiction of the late nineteenth and early twentieth centuries, to bring the action to a climax. Swami's talent as a fast bowler leads to his friends nicknaming him 'Tate', after Maurice Tate, the cricketer best known to posterity as Harold Larwood's fast bowling partner on England's infamous bodyline tour of Australia in 1932–33, a defining episode in the sporting history of the late colonial period. The novel's attitude to cricket is complex,[12] but at least on the surface Narayan's original title would seem to suggest a degree of colonial filiation[13] likely to find favour with English readers and there is no hint of the hostile reaction that England's departure from 'fair play' aroused in Australia. Swami simply identifies with Tate and his friends do not question his absorption in the role.

However, Graham Greene and Hamish Hamilton proposed a different title, perhaps feeling that Narayan's intended one was too specific and in any case looking for a more *literary* identification that would locate what might otherwise have appeared to be an unusual item in Hamilton's list within the recognizable subgenre of English schoolboy fiction. So the title *Swami and Friends* was chosen to echo Kipling's *Stalky & Co.* (1899),[14] a book that had retained its popularity as a juvenile classic and whose influence had already found its way into other titles. For example, the year before *Swami* was published, K.M. MacLeod's account of a group of village lads who are recruited into a company of 'Life Boys' by their new schoolteacher had been published with the title *Derry and Co.* The teacher Miss Stanley explains that '"A Life Boy is loyal to his home, his Sunday School, and his team. He is a total abstainer. He is truthful in word and deed. He follows the Great Leader."'[15] And the link between Christianity, the team ethic and the colonial mission becomes overt when Miss Stanley falls in love and leaves her English Life Boys to convert young Africans to the cause. Though by no means the first novel of its kind, *Stalky & Co.* had by this time become a blueprint for such fiction, having gone further than its predecessors in the genre in demonstrating the interpenetration of the public school and apparently far-flung corners of Empire.[16] While it is ostensibly concerned with the adolescent escapades in which Stalky and his friends engage in their very English boarding school, based on Kipling's own experiences at the United Services College at Westward Ho in Devon, it repeatedly demonstrates the extent to which the imperial ethic pervades the school. In the final chapter it becomes explicit that the school is a breeding-ground for the future guardians of Empire, but long before this, sections such as the two-part 'Slaves of the Lamp' story, in which Stalky and his fellow 'empire boys' stage a pantomime version of Aladdin, have demonstrated ambivalent linkages between the school and an imagined, Orientalist version of Empire.[17]

So how does *Swami* fit into the genre of English schoolboy fiction? Is Swami himself an ambivalent 'empire boy', imagining the specular relationship between supposed centre and periphery from the other side of the colonial looking-glass? The novel is loosely autobiographical and Narayan's early education certainly suggests the possibility. Not only did he finish his school education at the Mysore Maharaja's Collegiate High School,[18] where his father was the headmaster and where the medium of instruction was English, he also grew up reading a diet of English literature and magazines such as the *Boy's Own Paper*,[19] a journal that was the brainchild of the Religious Tract Society who promoted it as an antidote to the Penny Dreadfuls that had become popular reading for boys after Forster's 1870 Education Act brought about a massive increase in literacy. Typical of its contributors was Talbot Baines Reed, author of the paper's first cover story and later famed for the classic public school novel, *The Fifth Form at St Dominic's*, which was serialized in the *Boy's Own Paper* in 1907.[20] Reed's fiction was characteristic of the B.O.P. in that it linked team games and a sporting ethic of fair play with Christian morality and charitable work in the Empire. *Stalky* belongs to this genre, though Kipling's ambivalence and incursions into adult characterization stretch the conventions employed by a writer such as Reed, but does *Swami*?

At first glance *Swami* may appear to be a fairly innocent portrait of the escapades of the protagonist and his friends after the manner of Reed and, rather later, Richmal Crompton.[21] So one is left wondering just how much of the novel derives from Narayan's own experience as a schoolboy in Madras, as it then was, and Mysore and how much is drawn from his reading. The petty quarrels of the boys, their rivalries and their skirmishes with their schoolmasters lack obvious cultural specificity. The use of the cricket match as a unifying site that brings the various narrative elements together provides a more specific colonial inflection; and looked at more closely, it becomes clear that *Swami* is far from politically innocent. Although it occupies very different geographical terrain from Kipling's *Stalky*, it shares that novel's ambivalent response to Empire, with the boy protagonist once again becoming the tearing-point for a consideration of cultural interaction. Although in one sense Swami accepts the adult world into which he is being socialized as given – and in this case this involves indoctrination into the school's primarily, but not exclusively, colonial curriculum – hints of alternative ideological positions inform the text from the outset. In the very first chapter, the fanatical scripture master, Mr Ebenezar, engages in a tirade against Hinduism that makes Swami's 'blood boil[ ]',[22] leading him to challenge Ebenezar and having his ear pulled in consequence.

In fact, the Mission School that Swami attends has a curriculum that includes lessons in Tamil as well as the Christian scriptures and, like the protagonist, the novel's mode draws on both Hindu and Western discursive codes. When Swami takes his Tamil exam, he writes his address on the paper's flap in a passage that is reminiscent of Joyce's Stephen Dedalus's boyhood positioning of himself in the universe:[23]

Tamil   Tamil
W.S. Swaminathan
1st Form A section
Albert Mission School
Malgudi
South India
Asia. (*Swami* 62)

Significantly, unlike Stephen, he stops short of universalism or even attempting to locate himself in the *world* at large. Malgudi, *South* India and Asia are the geographical co-ordinates provided and tellingly Swami's act of self-positioning occurs under the heading 'Tamil'. Narayan was familiar with Tamil classics from an early age,[24] but he seldom draws on this in his early fiction, paradoxically making rather more reference to ancient myth and legend in his middle phase, at a time when, despite his amusement at the American belief that 'all Indians are spiritually preoccupied',[25] he became a reluctant guru. In *Gods, Demons and Others* (1964), a work from the middle period in which he provided his own version of a number of Hindu myths, he retells the story of Harischandra, a king who loses his throne, wife and child as a consequence of his desire to be true to himself.[26] He had, however, begun to tell this story much earlier in his writing career: Swami's grandmother – as always in Narayan the grand- mother is a repository of the oral tradition – tries to tell him this tale, only to find her young grandson, who is altogether more interested in the exploits of his class-mates, falling asleep half way through (*Swami* 22).[27] And this typifies the weighting of the balance of the two elements in *Swami*: the Hindu fable is effectively ousted by the English-based schoolboy narrative. The latter is subtly subverted and the inherent irony of employing such a convention to encapsulate *Malgudi* experience is inescap- able. Nevertheless Narayan still uses it as a way of narrowing the distance between his South Indian world and his English reader- ship, accommodating his material in a sub-genre that provides a comforting degree of sameness, along with the fairly obvious appeal of an insider's view of difference. Graham Greene's often-quoted remark, 'he has offered me a second home. Without him I could never have known what it is like to be Indian',[28] typifies such responses, which seem to fit Foucault's model of the heterotopia of compensation.

In *Swami and Friends*, Malgudi is, then, far more than an anglicized version of South India and it provides Narayan with a locus that enables him to stage some of the conflicts and conjunctions that characterized the social world in which he had come of age during the latter days of the Raj. Although the author of a study of nationalism in 'Indo-Anglian' fiction refers to Narayan's 1955 novel *Waiting for the Mahatma* and a single short story as his only treatments of the Gandhian freedom struggle,[29] a central chapter in *Swami*, Chapter 12: 'Broken Panes' (*Swami* 94–107), *very* clearly dramatizes a microcosmic juvenile version of the struggle, as the boys shout Gandhian slogans and break window panes on a day of national protest. With typical ambivalence, Narayan frames this within the conventions of the pranks and escapades of the schoolboy fiction genre and consequently diffuses the episode's potential for heavy-handed political statement, but when Swami is beaten by the headmaster for his part in the vandalism and rushes away muttering '"I don't care for your dirty school"' (*Swami* 107), these '*political* activities' (*Swami* 108; my italics) lead to his leaving the school. In short, his behaviour goes beyond the bounds of the kind of youthful exuberance that is condoned and even celebrated in most British schoolboy fiction. Despite his lightness of touch, Narayan renders the school a site of struggle and subtly subverts the codes of English schoolboy fiction, while ostensibly operating within its conventions.

Subsequently Swami attends Malgudi's Board School, where he becomes involved in a similar confrontation with the headmaster, when he seeks to be let out early in order to attend cricket practice with his friends, who have formed the 'M.C.C.', the Malgudi Cricket Club. And in many ways the ending of the novel is very dark. Swami runs away, misses the match and the team lose. 'Cricket' and the ethic of participation in team games fail to resolve the plot's complications, as they might be expected to do in a filiative colonial contribution to the schoolboy fiction genre. Moreover, the novel ends in anti-climax in another respect, as Rajam, the most 'English' of Swami's friends leaves Malgudi and there is no comfortable healing of the rift that has opened up between the two boys as a result of Swami's letting the side down. The novel is aptly titled, *Swami and Friends*: it is centrally about friendship, but its treatment of the theme is again unsettling, suggesting the difficulties of finding common ground and sustaining relationships, not simply because the boys are at an awkward age, but more specifically because of the conflicting codes to which they are subjected in their colonial situation. Again Narayan's conclusion moves in an opposite direction from the resolutions that characterize the endings of most English schoolboy fiction. These involve a reaffirmation not only of the English social order, but also of the colonial ethic, with which it was twinned.

So Greene and Hamish Hamilton may have given *Swami* and its creator a make-over to render the novel more suitable for its British readership, but, although the original manuscript appears not to have survived, it seems likely that representing the ambivalent nature of the South Indian colonial situation was an integral part of the novel from the outset. Certainly this survives in the published text. Narayan may not have been consciously responding to his hybrid situation, but the dilemmas in which Swami finds himself – and parallel tensions in the narrative mode – make it difficult not to read *Swami and Friends* as a subversive response to the colonial ethic and particularly to the educational curriculum that was one of its lynch-pins. This view of the curriculum is carried over into *The Bachelor of Arts* and *The English Teacher*.

Greene also helped Narayan with the publication of *The Bachelor of Arts*, placing it with Thomas Nelson, a more established English publisher than Hamish Hamilton. By now he had also found Narayan a literary agent, David Higham, and mentor, publisher and agent all felt the need to find a title for the second novel that would again be more suitable for the English market than Narayan's original working title, which was *Chandran*, the name of the novel's protagonist.[30] So, with Greene also correcting his grammar, once again Narayan found his work being reshaped in a manner designed to make it more acceptable to his overseas readership. He suggested an alternative title from the *Rubaiyat of Omar Khayyam*, but eventually agreed to Nelson's preferred title, *The Bachelor of Arts*, in preference to what he referred to as his own 'gushing Omar Khayyam title'.[31] According to Susan and N. Ram, who cite a 1993 conversation with Narayan as the source for their information, Narayan's suggested alternative was *Wind Along the West*.[32] It would seem more probable, though, that he actually proposed *Wind Along the Waste*, since 'waste' not 'west' appears in the wording Narayan wished to borrow from Edward Fitzgerald's translation of the *Rubaiyat* and he would later allude to this correctly in *The Dark Room*.[33] So perhaps Narayan was remembering this inaccurately over half a century later. If not, taking his early co-optation into Western preconceptions into account, the change to 'west' – if indeed this was what he suggested – could be seen as Freudian slippage.

Whatever Narayan said originally, it is interesting to find the young Indian author proposing an 'Eastern' title and his Western mediators regarding it as too poetic – the stuff of Orientalist cliché – and favouring the more prosaic *Bachelor of Arts*. The *Rubaiyat*, in Fitzgerald's translation, was a firm favourite with early twentieth-century English readers and when Greene wrote to Narayan informing him that he had provisionally accepted the publisher's suggestion for the change of title on his behalf, he pointed out that references to it had been very widely used in Britain. It would seem, then, that in Greene's eyes the alternative titles did not represent a simple East-West opposition. *Both* would have had the effect of helping to make Narayan's Indian milieu more familiar to English readers, but the more straightforward *Bachelor of Arts* appears to have been perceived as better suited to the mood of a decade in which social realism was becoming the dominant mode in fiction. Additionally, emphasizing that the protagonist is a bachelor of arts must have had the effect of locating him in an academic context that would have been familiar to the majority of the coterie British reading public that was consuming novels in the 1930s.

Meanwhile Narayan's own scepticism about this public was being held in check. A 1933 *Punch* article, entitled "How to Write an Indian Novel" makes it clear that he was alert to market pressures prior to his correspondence with Greene and his publishers over *Swami* and *The Bachelor of Arts*. In this article he offers ironic advice on how to avoid mistakes when writing about India, pointing out that, 'Bombay is not governed by a Raja, nor is Calcutta, nor Madras, nor a great many parts of India' and informing the would-be writer on India:

> You are likely to feel the greatest difficulty with the names of persons. [...] In a recent Indian novel, the author has given the name Chattophadhyay to a Tamil coolie of Madras. A blunder like this will give you a black mark that will stick to you like a mole. It is something like naming a native of Southern France, Von Epp, or a pure Russian, Angus McBride, or a red-blooded German, Scott O'Connor.
>
> Of course these slips will not matter to a large number of your readers, who, you can safely assume, will not have heard of India.[34]

So, as with *Swami*, Narayan found his work being reshaped in a manner which, it was hoped, would strike a chord with his intended readership. With his consent, Greene tidied up his prose, while still in his own mind leaving a distinctive Indian '"twang"'[35] in his English. In a 1978 introduction to the novel, he singled out a passage that begins as follows as an instance of the local 'charm' of Narayan's style that 'Kipling would have detested':

> 'Excuse me, I made a vow never to touch alcohol in my life, before my mother,' said Chandran. This affected Kailas profoundly. He remained solemn for a moment and said: 'Then don't. Mother is a sacred object. It is a commodity whose value we don't realise as long as it is with us. One must lose it to know what a precious possession it is. [...]'[36]

Local charm still suggests the fascination of the provincial and Greene does not consider that Narayan's English may be a distinctive medium in is own right.

Despite its apparent transparency, Narayan's use of English is arguably more complex than Greene seems to have realised and it is no coincidence that his first novels are about the products of an English-derived system of education. His accounts of colonial school and college life are shot through with the ambivalence of his particular colonial situation. Readily lending itself to being read as a sequel to *Swami and Friends*, *The Bachelor of Arts* takes the South Indian portrait of a young man to the threshold between adolescence and adulthood and has consequently been seen as a *Bildungsroman*[37] that speaks across cultures with a universalist appeal.[38] However, such a reading misses the cultural specifics that inform Narayan's second novel and these are tangled and difficult to pinpoint, as is the tone of the novel. From one point of view, his account of the rite of passage from adolescence to adulthood is a modern-day version of the progression from the first to the second of the four *asramas* prescribed in the *Manusmriti*, but the hero Chandran is also very much the product of the late colonial educational system as it operated in South India. Additionally, *The Bachelor of Arts* debates the relative merits of 'Custom and Reason' (*BA* 118–19), employs a romantic love plot, which has affinities with Western examples of the genre, and challenges 'Custom' by suggesting the possibility of questioning the ways in which caste and sub-caste determine the *dharma* of individuals.[39] In short, the novel's hotch-potch of motifs and styles involves an eclectic mélange of Western and orthodox Hindu elements.

Whether Narayan's alternation between Western and Hindu codes generates complexity or confusion is another matter. What is certain is that *The Bachelor of Arts* operates across a continuum of discourses and this generates considerable ambivalence in its tone. And this is perhaps the most interesting aspect of the novel. Seemingly unaware of the metafictive possibilities of narrative at this stage in his career,[40] Narayan nevertheless produces a text that reads as a blueprint for the problem of writing a novel in English during the late colonial period. *The Bachelor of Arts* shares the indeterminacy of his later, more obviously comic novels and yet it is a text that for all the apparent simplicity of its coming-of-age theme frustrates attempts at neat pigeonholing in generic terms. While *Swami and Friends* has a skewed relationship to the English school novel, *The Bachelor of Arts* holds a distorting mirror up to the Western romance novel, partly by virtue of its lopsided, uneasy use of its conventions, but more obviously because of it failure to commit itself to any genre fully. It moves between this and an exploration of the protagonist's progress from the first of the four *asramas*, the *brahmacharya* (the stage of bachelorhood, in which the student seeks knowledge) to the *grihastya* (the stage of married householder and man of affairs), but this orthodox progression is complicated by the forces of modernity and it is as unsatisfactory to see this as a structure that codifies the novel's overall meaning as to see this as emerging from the romantic elements of the plot.

The Bachelor of Arts is divided into four sections and at first sight the relationship between them seems to be fairly casual, at best loose picaresque. In the first part Chandran is a student, aspiring to become a Bachelor of Arts, but just when this narrative element seems to be moving towards climax with the approach of his exams, the story breaks off. When Part II begins, this potential moment of climax is six months in the past. Chandran has graduated and his family are busy talking about what career he should pursue. In this section he is mainly seen as a love-struck adolescent, smitten with thoughts of a girl he has barely seen and pleading with his parents to stretch the bounds of Hindu custom to allow him to marry her. When the object of his romantic fantasy is married off to another man, Chandran is disconsolate and a further disjunction in the narrative occurs. Chandran develops a high fever and departs for Madras, frequently an actual or potential alternative to Malgudi in Narayan's fiction,[41] though the move does not represent a flight to a positive heterotopia.

In Madras he falls into company with Kailas, an 'aggressive' bigamist, who 'occasionally descended on Madras in order to have a good time' (*BA* 159). On this occasion the 'good time' in question involves alcohol, which the teetotal brahmin Chandran refuses,[42] followed by a taxi-ride to a prostitute's house, which Chandran runs away from in a fit of terror:

> Chandran fled from Mint Street. He had escaped from Kailas. This was the first time he had been so close to a man in drink; this was the first time he had stood at the portals of a prostitute's house. He was thoroughly terrified. (*BA* 166)

At this point the novel, like Chandran, may seem to be wandering without any central focus. It is, however, possible to read it in terms of a coherent, developing patern, if one relates Chandran's vicissitudes to the *varnashramadharma*, or prescribed roles for various stages in the orthodox Hindu life-cycle. His going to Madras involves a temporary abnegation of any attempt at progress into the second *asrama*. The episode with Kailas shocks him into recognition of his delinquency, while Madras functions as what Foucault calls a 'crisis heterotopia':

> [t]here are privileged or sacred or forbidden places, reserved for individuals who are, in relation to society and to the human environment in which they live, in a state of crisis: adolescents, menstruating women, pregnant women. the elderly, etc. In our society, these crisis heterotopias are persistently disappearing, though a few remnants can still be found. For example, the boarding school, in its nineteenth-century form, or military service for young men, have certainly played such a role, as the first manifestations of sexual virility were in fact supposed to take place 'elsewhere' than at home.[43]

Displaced from Malgudi and his romantic dream of entry into the stage of the *grihastya* through a love match, which represents a modest challenge to his orthodox mother's belief in 'Custom', Chandran's brahminical sensibilities are nevertheless revolted by the side of Madras to which Kailias introduces him. In a state of turmoil, he briefly contemplates going 'home' to

Malgudi, but at this point in the novel it has become an ambivalent site, a place to which he feels unable to return, and in this
state of mental exile, he resolves to enter the fourth stage of the
varnashramadharma and become a *sanyasi*:

> Chandran realized that he had definitely left his home.
> Now what did it matter where he lived? He was like a
> *sanyasi*. Why 'like'? He was a *sanyasi*; the simplest solu-
> tion. Shave the head, dye the clothes in ochre, and you
> were dead for aught the world cared. (*BA* 167)

His response to 'home' is particularly interesting here. Although
critics have often read Malgudi as an uncomplicated version of
the home place, a trope for an imagined homogeneous India
of the mind, it is a location, which from its first appearance in
Swami and Friends is seen to be riven with internal divisions.
It is particularly contrasted with the heterotope of Madras, in
a small town/big city pairing that may appear to suggest an
opposition between the secure, demarcated values of the town
and the threatening challenges of modernity represented by the
sprawling metropolis. However, this apparent contrast is an illusion. Both places are heterogeneous.

Chandran's decision that his loss of 'home' makes him a
sanyasi is, of course, unusual. As with the protagonist of V.S.
Naipaul's *The Mimic Men* (1967),[44] his espousal of the role of
an elderly mendicant, who has renounced active life is out of
keeping with the progression expected in the *varnashramadharma*. As Shirley Chew points out,[45] the admonition of the
barber who shaves his head, '"Master, at your age!"' (*BA* 171)
highlights the incongruity of his donning this role at a point
in his life when he has yet to make the transition from *brahmacharya* to *grihastya* successfully. For a brief interlude, which
anticipates the more extended treatment of the same theme in
relation of the behaviour of Raju, the protagonist of *The Guide*,
he wanders from town to town, enjoying the hospitality offered
to him because of his assumed role. A role is all it is and, for once
in Narayan, the narrative voice is unambiguous about the difference between his behaviour and that of a real *sanyasi*:

> He was different from the usual *sanyasi*. Others may renounce with a spiritual motive or purpose. Renunciation may be to them a means to attain peace or may be peace itself. [...] But Chandran's renunciation was not of that kind. It was an alternative to suicide. [...] His renunciation was a revenge on society, circumstances, and perhaps, too, on destiny. (*BA* 176)

Like Raju in *The Guide*, he eventually finds himself among a group of villagers who take his 'ascetic's make-up at its face value' (*BA* 179). However, while *The Guide* remains subtly ambiguous and allows for the possibility that the roguish Raju has actually been transformed into a holy man,[46] *The Bachelor of Arts* is explicit about the fraudulent nature of Chandran's role, presenting him as all too aware of his deceit: 'He felt a cad, a fraud, and a confidence trickster. These were the gifts of a counterfeit exchange' (*BA* 179). Subjecting his behaviour to self-scrutiny, Chandran comes to the conclusion that he has arrived at this situation as a consequence of his belief in the discourse of romantic love, which he now comes to regard as 'a foolish literary notion'. He abandons his *sanyasi* role and decides to 'do the most decent and practical thing that he could do' (*BA* 181), return to Malgudi.

The fourth and final part of the novel appears to involve another disjunctive shift. Back in Malgudi, Chandran is persuaded by his poet friend, Mohan, to try to become an agent for the Madras-based newspaper, *The Messenger*. A second and very different visit to Madras helps him to secure this position, partly thanks to the mediation of his uncle and he quickly sets about devising strategies for increasing the newspaper's Malgudi circulation. In many ways this is the most surprising shift of all in the novel, as it has Chandran metamorphosed from aimless drifter and romantic idealist into a shrewd practical businessman at a single stroke. Readers are left to ponder whether this represents inconsistent character development, Chandran's capacity for picaresque role-play which he has demonstrated during his *sanyasi* phase, or something that can be seen to form part of a consistent and coherent structure. One possible solution to this problem can to be found in Pankaj Mishra's account of the world of Narayan's protagonists:

> Chandran is one of the first in Narayan's long gallery of young restless drifters who, hungry for adventure, very quickly reach the limits to [sic] their world and then have to find ways of reconciling themselves with it. The reconciliation itself can never be complete. You can see again and again in Narayan's novels how the encounter with the half-baked modernity of colonialism has deracinated Indians like Chandran; has turned them into what Narayan, in an unusually passionate moment in *The English Teacher*, describes as 'strangers to our own culture, and camp-followers, feeding on leavings and garbage.'[47]

In a passage that recycles the Chekhovian cliché that Graham Greene frequently used to characterize Narayan for his English readership,[48] Mishra goes on to identify this 'part-feudal, part-modern setting of inchoate longing and vague dissatisfaction and intellectual impotence' as the aspect of his work that 'reminds one of Chekhov'.[49] However, he underestimates the extent to which Tamil brahmin culture underlies the text in saying that 'only a few, easily missed domestic details hint at the fact that Swami and Chandran, along with many other Narayan protagonists, are Brahmins marginalised by a fast-changing world'.[50] The forms of *puja* described in the novel make this fairly clear and more centrally the marital possibilities open to Chandran depend not just on caste, but also on sub-caste. Both Malathi, the girl with whom he becomes infatuated in the second part of the novel, and Susila, the girl he eventually marries, are not just brahmins but also, like Narayan himself, Iyers.[51] So even Chandran's rebellion against brahmin 'Custom' is conducted within the confines of what is possible for a particular sub-caste. Later Narayan novels move beyond such heroines, but at this point in his career the romantic possibilities open to Narayan's hero are strictly defined by caste and sub-caste parameters.

Chandran's period as a *sanyasi* is anticipated by an earlier episode, where a man who has been stealing flowers from the family garden is revealed to be a *sanyasi*. In Chandran's mother's view, this transforms him in an instant, from a thief to a worshipper who should be revered. Additionally, the various occupations of Chandran and his friends and family are those which have traditionally been the prerogative of Tamil brahmin scribal culture. Collectively, all of this amounts to far more than 'easily missed domestic details'. Narayan's representation of brahmin culture is all-pervasive in the novel, the bedrock on which its whole edifice is built, and yet from another point of view Mishra's emphasis goes to the heart of what the novel is about and what generates its apparent inconsistencies in a way that very few other commentators have managed. The novel *is* about 'the encounter with the half-baked modernity of colonialism' and the crisis facing brahmin culture in a fast-changing world.[52] Its apparent formal disjunctions are a manifestation of this.

The kind of modernity introduced by colonialism also figures prominently in the opening sections of *The Bachelor of Arts*, where Chandran is a diffident college student, responding in various ways to demands made on him by 'History'. The novel opens with his being approached by the College Union secretary to be the Prime Mover of a debating society motion that 'in the opinion of this house historians should be slaughtered first' (*BA* 13). Reluctantly persuaded to undertake this role, he success-fully carries the motion, though initially he can only think of one persuasive argument to support the early extermination of historians, 'namely, that they might not be there to misrepresent the facts when scientists, poets, and statesmen were being killed in their turn' (*BA* 15). It may be mistaken to read too much into the idea of history as *mis*representation, since the novel's treat-ment of the subject is fairly whimsical, but 'History' is certainly the main subject of the first part and it is a troubling subject for the would be Bachelor of Arts. Despite his best efforts to apply himself to his studies, Chandran finds himself thwarted by 'a few impossible periods in History, like the muddle that was called the mediaeval South Indian History, early Christi-anity with warring popes and kings, and feudalism' (*BA* 78). The 'muddle' here may be as much in his mind as in the curriculum, though again this does seem to be inflected with a colonial bias, but the novel's emphasis is, as usual in Narayan, on the mental state of the protagonist. Tellingly, after his debating society success in proposing the summary execution of historians, he finds himself pulled in an opposite direction, when the Professor of History, Ragavachar, a man who feels that the country's most urgent need is for 'a clarified, purified Indian history' (*BA* 67) tries to enlist him as a founder member of a college Historical Association. Torn between these competing attitudes to history, Chandran leaves Ragavachar's room feeling 'that he was on the verge of losing his personality' (*BA* 53–4).

Narayan's ironic approach sidesteps overt political engagement, but when the college principal, Professor Brown, opposes Ragavachar's proposal for a Historical Association with a light-hearted monologue about the uselessness of linear historiography and scientific factuality, the case against 'History', and in particular its place in the colonial curriculum, seems to have been made. As a genial ironist and teacher of literature, Brown[53] seems to personify those aspects of Raj culture that Narayan admired from an early age. However, a darker side of his character emerges when Chandran is told that he monopolizes the activities of the Literary Association, debarring the reading of original creative work in favour of rehashes of his own lectures on Wordsworth and eighteenth-century prose. Read as a trope for the English-oriented education that Narayan and his peers received, this suggests that superficial benevolence masks the paternalistic cultural imperialism of a system which demands the collusion of its infantilized colonial charges. Like Brown, though, the novel operates through irony and indirection and only implies such criticism at certain points. Its representation of Chandran's encounters with 'History' suggests the muddle that the curriculum generates in the colonial student's mind, but there is no overall indictment of the kind of education that Narayan received in Maharaja's College and the ambivalent characterization of Brown leaves the issue delicately poised.

Written between traditions, *The Bachelor of Arts* remains ambivalent to the last. At the end, having suggested that Chandran is on the verge of becoming a *grihastya* through his work as a newspaper agent, this pattern looks close to completion when a marriage is arranged for him. Horoscopes match, the girl is of the right caste and sub-caste and the one possible remaining obstacle to a successful union is removed when Chandran sees her and finds her more beautiful than the girl with whom he has previously been infatuated. Neatly – rather too neatly, one is tempted to say – everything seems to be moving towards a happy ending that will resolve all the entanglements of the plot and, when the couple are united in marriage, the social order that they represent seems to have been reaffirmed for another generation. Earlier, in the very first chapter, Chandran has viewed an American film version of just such a happy ending, in a Western movie that he has gone to see in the local cinema[54] and on this occasion Narayan's comments suggest the perfunctory, contrived nature of happy endings that purport to resolve all of life's dilemmas:

> [I]n the end the good man [...] always came out triumphant; he was an upright man, a courageous man, a handsome man, and a strong man, and he had to win in the end. Who could not foresee it? And yet every day at every show the happy ending was awaited with breathless suspense. [...] There was a happy moment before the end, when the lovers' heads were shown on an immense scale, their lips welded in a kiss. Goodnight. (*BA* 35–6)

As it approaches its conclusion, *The Bachelor of Arts* seems to be moving towards a happy ending that will offer this kind of resolution in a Tamil brahmin context. However, there is no reaffirming close-up of the united lovers to suggest that they and the social world they represent will live happily ever after. On the contrary, they are separated at the end. Western representational conventions, of the kind purveyed in the film that Chandran has gone to see, prove ill-suited for Narayan's more inquisitve vision of society. Like its hero, the novel has wandered between a variety of positions and evasiveness remains the dominant note to the very last page. This finds Chandran separated from Susila and wondering why she is not writing to him. Just as Part I has ended with the issue of whether he will pass the exams he is dreading left open, the novel as a whole concludes in an enigmatic manner, leaving the mystery of why Susila is not writing unexplained. One might attribute this to what V.S. Naipaul refers to as Narayan's appearance of being 'speculative and comic, aimless and "Russian"',[55] but arguably it is the logical culmination of a novel which dramatizes the tensions in Tamil brahmin culture during the late colonial period. The dénouement has moved towards an endorsement of traditional beliefs, with Chandran, as an agent for a newspaper, succeeding as an employee in the contemporary scribal medium of the print culture and finding a bride who meets all the expectations of 'Custom'. Significantly, though, *The Bachelor of Arts* undermines the possibility of a conventional happy ending, by continuing beyond the moment of the marriage without investigating the possibility that the couple will subsequently come together in the best Hindu fashion. It ends with Chandran bemoaning the fact that Susila has not written for six days to his friend, the poet Mohan, whose 'obscure statements' (*BA* 84) have earlier fascinated him; and Mohan's writer's response, in the final two sentences, seems to refract back on the novel's fictional practice: 'Mohan [...] turned in, throwing his arms up in despair. But then, it is a poet's business only to ask questions; he cannot always expect an answer' (*BA* 265). Narayan, too, leaves questions unanswered and they are questions that particularly revolve around the problems of writing a novel in English and the breakdown of consensual narratives in his social microcosm of Malgudi.

One might have expected Narayan's next novel to continue the *Bildungsroman* aspects of *Swami and Friends* and *The Bachelor of Arts*, with the young male protagonist completing the transition from the *brahmacharya* into the *grihastya* (the stage of the householder and man of affairs). His 1945 novel *The English Teacher* does follow this pattern up to a point, since it deals with a further phase in the coming-of-age of a Tamil brahmin protagonist, and it has been published along with *Swami and Friends* and *The Bachelor of Arts* as a loose trilogy.[56] It is, however, a very different kind of novel from *Swami* and

The Bachelor of Arts and ultimately resists classification as a *Bildungsroman* about progression into the second *asrama* – and it was not Narayan's next novel after *The Bachelor of Arts*.

In 1938 he published *The Dark Room*, a work which moved away from the male viewpoint of his first two novels and in doing so also demonstrated considerable ambivalence about gender roles in Tamil brahmin society. *The Dark Room* takes a mistreated wife as its protagonist and main focalizer and is in many ways the most surprising, though by no means the most accomplished, novel in Narayan's whole oeuvre. *The Bachelor of Arts* ends ambivalently, suggesting that marriage may not provide a comfortable resolution to all the entanglements of the plot, as it does in many English novels of manners. The implication would seem to be that this form of narrative closure, which not only generates a romantic happy ending, but also serves to reaffirm the social order, cannot easily be transferred into Narayan's social world, even when the marriage in question is a love-match. *The Dark Room* takes this further, venturing into incipiently feminist territory, in its concentration on the situation of a wronged wife. Critics writing from a variety of backgrounds have been quick to comment on this aspect of the novel.[57] William Walsh, conveniently choosing to ignore the first wave of twentieth-century Western feminism and, more importantly, the Gandhian ethic's championing of women's roles in the independence movement, has seen it as projecting an image 'of the Indian woman as a victim [...] some thirty-five to forty years before the current talk of women's liberation'.[58] Usha Bande sees it as Narayan's first major work on 'woman's predicament', a text which dramatizes 'two alternatives' open to women, both of which are rejected as 'unsatisfactory'.[59] Nilufer E. Bharucha refers to it as his 'most woman-centred novel'[60] and, discussing its attack on patriarchy with reference to a number of Western gynocritics, sees it as progressive for its period and setting. Arguably, though, the most pertinent comment on Narayan's putative feminism comes from the novelist himself. In a letter to Graham Greene, he outlined his intentions in terms of a view of 'Woman' which was as much metaphysical as social:

I was somehow obsessed with a philosophy of Woman as opposed to Man, her constant oppressor. This must have been an early testament of the 'Women's Lib' movement. Man assigned her a secondary place and kept her there with such subtlety and cunning that she herself began to lose all notion of her independence, her individuality, stature, and strength. A wife in an orthodox milieu of Indian society was an ideal victim of such circumstances. My novel dealt with her, with this philosophy broadly in the background. (*MyD* 119)

A concern with gender relations informs every aspect of *The Dark Room*. It is central to the novel's main story of the protagonist Savitri's marriage and her husband Ramani's adulterous affair with another modern brahmin woman. It also appears in accounts of conversations between the family's servants and in details of Savitri's children's behaviour, which show how they are being socialized according to prevalent gender norms; and it is also present in a contrastive pairing of Savitri's two closest friends – Gangu, who aspires to a place in the wider world, whether it be as a film star, professional musician or political activist, and Janamma, a woman who prefers to stay at home and stresses the importance of women's submissiveness in marriage – and in a vignette of a non-brahmin couple's marriage. Marriage and more specifically women's roles inside and outside of marriage are, then, ubiquitous in *The Dark Room*, to a point where the novel *may* seem to be a manifesto for women's rights. However, the incipient feminism of *The Dark Room* proves to be distinctly limited. Although Savitri's plight is compassionately portrayed, sympathy for her predicament is achieved through contrasting her with Ramani's mistress, Shanta Bai, who can equally well be viewed as a type of the modern brahmin woman, as her situation and aspirations also dramatize the struggle of educated, independent women of her class and caste.[61]

Interviewing candidates for positions as trainee agents to be employed to attract women to take out policies with the insurance company for which he works, Ramani's initial response to the applications he receives is informed by his usual dismissive

attitude towards '"the fair sex"' (*DR* 62). However, his attitude
changes in an instant when he is struck by the beauty of the
final applicant, Shanta Bai. He plies her with intrusive personal
questions, pleading the excuse that head office will need to be
reassured that family commitments will not prevent her from
carrying out the duties of the position. She tells him her life-
history, a story of marriage at the age of twelve to a cousin who
was a drunkard and gambler, of leaving this husband when she
was eighteen, of being disowned by her parents and of having
turned to education, which she has hoped will help her to find
fulfilment. Narayan's depiction of her character is far from subtle,
but it locates her as a type of the 'new woman', endeavouring
to find a niche for herself in a society in which the workplace
remains a male-dominated domain. During this initial interview
she tells Ramani:

> '[...] I passed my B.A. three years ago. Since then I have
> been drifting about. I have had odd teaching jobs and I have
> also been companion to a few rich children. On the whole
> it has been a very great struggle. It is all nonsense to say
> that women's salvation lies in education. It doesn't improve
> their lot a bit [...]. We struggle hard, get our B.A., and think
> that we are the first of our kind; but what happens? We find
> that there are thousands like us.' (*DR* 66–7)

In short, Shanta Bai is very explicitly presented as a type of the
modern brahmin woman, whose intelligence and education leave
her displaced within the transitional world of Malgudi, where
the orthodox basis of traditional gender relations is less settled
than previously. However, unlike Savitri, she is represented
negatively: as a character who has no real interest in or aptitude
for her work, but is adept at staging temporary breakdowns and
affecting 'the perfect Garbo manner: the temperamental heroine
and the impending doom' (*DR* 88); and her modernity and independence are further compromised by the depiction of her as a
woman dedicated to achieving her ends through feminine wiles
rather than feminist self-sufficiency.

The contrast with Savitri is fairly stark and, although
Narayan is clearly also intent on presenting Savitri as a type of

the modern brahmin woman who has been rendered a victim by changing social mores, the choice of her name points in an opposite direction: in the *Mahabharata* Savitri is a model of wifely devotion. Narayan retells the mythic Savitri's story in *Gods, Demons and Others,*[62] where he relates how she confronts Yama, the personification of Death, and saves her husband's life, partly by suggesting that if she is widowed she will be left without a role in life and partly by persuading Yama he is 'king of dharma' (*Gods* 188). Narayan glosses *dharma* in a footnote:

> Dharma may be defined broadly as the ultimate code in thought, word and deed for each individual – that which alone is right for him [sic]. The word also carries the meaning of duty, as well as the code, at all levels. Evil arises when one deviates from the path of dharma. All stories and parables taken together illustrate the eternal importance of dharma. Although it varies from one individual to the next, according to birth and mental equipment, there is a dharma for everyone, whether he be a king or a Chandala [member of the lowest caste], and he must live according to it. (*Gods* 188)[63]

Although Savitri's reference to *dharma* in Narayan rendition of the encounter specifically relates to Yama and the gloss is male-inscribed, the suggestion is that it applies to every human being. Earlier in his version of the mythical Savitri's story, Narayan has her say: '"Married life is the highest goal attainable by me, as taught to me by my elders; and so I have nowhere to go except where my husband goes" (*Gods* 187) and she seems to fulfil her *dharma* as a wife in an exemplary fashion.

The narrative action of *The Dark Room* is played out against this mythic backdrop and the concept of wifely *dharma*. The suggestion that *The Dark Room*'s Savitri may be a contemporary reworking of her archetypal namesake is first introduced by Ramani, who comments early on in the novel, '"You are really like some of the women in our ancient books"' (*DR* 14), while resisting any such epic analogue for himself, saying, '"you'd have to write a new epic if you wanted anyone like me in an epic"' (*DR* 15). The implication is that women continue to be defined in terms of traditional roles, while modernity allows men to elude such stereotypes, even though Ramani's name echoes that of the hero of *The Ramayana*. Later in the text Savitri is more explicitly linked with her mythic namesake, particularly in a passage which invokes the epic Savitri's encounter with Yama. This passage occurs at a moment in the action when Narayan's heroine has left her home and husband and asks herself whether, in so doing, she has assumed another identity: '"Am I the same old Savitri or am I someone else?"'(*DR* 115). The clear suggestion is that leaving home involves a repudiation of the traditional role of a 'Savitri', that she effectively becomes a new woman through this transgressive act; and the text underscores the extent to which she has broken with the *dharma* that consigns women to be victims in a patriarchal society:

> 'One definite thing in life is Fear. Fear, from the cradle to the funeral pyre, and even beyond that, fear of torture in the other world. Afraid of a husband's displeasures, and of the discomforts that might be caused to him, morning to night and all night too. […]' Afraid of one's father, teachers and everybody in early life, afraid of one's husband, children and neighbours in later life – fear, fear, in one's heart till the funeral pyre was lit, and then fear of being sentenced by Yama to be held down in a cauldron of burning oil. … (*DR* 116)

Crude though the feminist sentiments expressed here may be, they nevertheless contribute to a polemic against women's subjugation, which employs a classic Hindu intertext. *The Dark Room* seems to be attacking such subjugation by suggesting the possibility of a transformation that would allow the heroine to escape from the role assigned to her by her mythic name. So, in part at least, the novel interrogates the fixed roles assigned to women in classic Hindu discourse. Modernity has unsettled the basis of gender relations in 1930s Malgudi and Narayan's novel responds to this by pleading the case for a reworking of the mythic archetype of Savitri.

The Dark Room seems, then, to be undermining the stereotype of wifely devotion that Savitri's name evokes and in its early sections, where Ramani's domineering behaviour leads her to withdraw into the eponymous dark room in the family home, this retreat seems to be a physical expression of her sense of psychic alienation. However, seen as an expression of Savitri's mental condition, the dark room is an ambivalent space. If one compares it with classic Western uses of the room as a trope for either the repression or empowerment of women's desires, it seems to leave her poised somewhere between, say, the attic imprisonment of Charlotte Brontë's Bertha, seen by critics such as Gilbert and Gubar as a metaphor for the situation of nine-teenth-century women,[64] and Virginia Woolf's room of one's own. As so often, though, Western parallels can be misleading, at the same time as they are partially illuminating. The dark room *is* a refuge in which Savitri is able to escape from Ramani's tyrannical authority, but such a room was a traditional space in older Indian homes,[65] in which it offered little by way of a creative alternative. This said, the novel presents Savitri's with-drawal into the room as a defining moment in her attempt to liberate herself from her husband and the gender codes he embodies. So, rather like the seamier side of Madras, to which Kailas introduces Chandran in *The Bachelor of Arts*, the dark room acts as a catalyst for a change in the protagonist's state of mind. The house seems to be a trope for the established ortho-doxies of Malgudi, a *supposedly* timeless, patriarchal South Indian world, where traditional values are maintained and affirmed; the presence of the dark room as a traditional space inside its walls suggests that such a world sanctions moments of separateness for women, but only within the domestic sphere and only as a temporary retreat. Savitri's occupancy of it does, however, suggest the possibility of transforming it into a more permanent site for female autonomy.

In fact, far from presenting Malgudi as a timeless site, the novel emphasizes the particular moment in which the action is set. Thus, its comments on film and the coming of a new cinema are precisely located in the early years of the sound era, a period associated with modernity:

Malgudi in 1935 suddenly came into line with the modern age by building a well-equipped theatre – the Palace Talkies – which simply brushed aside the old corrugated-sheet-roofed variety hall, which from time immemorial had entertained the citizens of Malgudi with tattered silent films. (*DR* 26–7)

'Time immemorial' suggests a very short memory for a society which in other respects prides itself on the antiquity of its living narrative traditions and, although Hollywood is seen to be making inroads into Malgudi – Savitri's son, Babu, is an admirer of Shirley Temple and *Frankenstein* (*DR* 31)[66] and Shanta Bai models her manner on Greta Garbo – the two films that actually figure in the text are products of the Madras-based Tamil film industry. They serve as vehicles for contrasting the two main female characters and underscoring the main themes of the novel. At different points in the action Ramani takes both Savitri and Shanta Bai to see modern-day South Indian reworkings of stories from the ancient epics. He takes Savitri to *Kuchela*,[67] the story of a 'classmate' (*DR* 27)[68] of Krishna, who neglects his longsuffering wife to devote himself to a meditative, spiritual life. Ramani comments on the wife as an exemplar of patience; Savitri sympathizes with her misfortunes, but not to the extent of allowing her enjoyment of the film's 'superhuman splendours' (*DR* 29) to be spoiled by this aspect of its theme or its many irrelevant episodes. He takes Shanta Bai to see a film based on an episode from the *Ramayana* and her response to this modern version of an epic story is completely different. She criticizes the film's poor production standards, saying she would '"have given [her] life to see a Garbo or a Dietrich"' (*DR* 90) and expressing the view that there is no hope for Indian cinema until it moves beyond '"mythological nonsense"'(*DR* 91). The contrast is, once again, fairly clear-cut. The cinema is a metonym for the modernity which has come to Malgudi and which has unsettled the society's traditional gender codes, leaving intelligent women such as Savitri disempowered, but without the sustenance that tradition has supposedly accorded women such as her mythological avatar. Mistreated by *her* husband and left unfulfilled by her education, Shanta Bai is also a victim of modernity, but Narayan's representation of her as the seductive 'other woman', who prefers Western cinema, cultivates movie star poses and is delinquent over her work, is altogether less sympathetic.

In short, *The Dark Room* addresses the problem faced by brahmin women in a changing society and is, at least superficially, progressive in its concern with feminist issues, issues which on two occasions are related to the larger context of the 'All-India Women's Conference' (*DR* 18 and 141). Yet, despite its apparent challenge to the gender codes prevalent in Malgudi society, it only goes part-way towards questioning such norms. Its focus on Savitri's predicament has the effect of privileging the wifely devotion personified by her mythic namesake over the westward-leaning modernity represented by Shanta Bai: the latter is never seen from the inside and eventually disappears, without any account of her eventual fate being given. Narayan's critique is more concerned with the forces that are destabilizing the traditional balance of gender relations within the society – forces such as the advent of women into the workplace – than a plea for a sympathetic view of the emancipated modern woman.

Despite shifts in focalization, which allow Ramani to become the centre of consciousness for certain sections of the text, Savitri's plight remains central. When she eventually leaves Ramani, the novel dramatizes alternative possibilities open to a woman of her caste and background. They prove to be very limited. She is saved from an attempt at suicide by Mari, a locksmith-cum-burglar, and offered refuge in the lower-caste household he shares with his wife, Ponni. Food taboos discourage her from accepting this offer: it would involve transgressing caste divisions as well as the gender codes of her background and so it is never really a viable possibility for her. Given her brahmin background, the avenues open to her as a woman alone are very few; and the novel seems similarly limited in its attempt to step outside Narayan's customary brahmin world to provide credible representations of other areas of South Indian social life. Ponni and Mari are presented as a practical, well-suited couple and as such their union provides a foil to Savitri's marital situation, but they are sentimentalized to a point where the text's apparent attempt at a progressive portrayal of lower-caste life falls as flat as the putative feminism. One further avenue is explored as a possible escape-route for Savitri. Mari suggests she could become an attendant at an old village temple and, after some hard bargaining with its priest, Savitri is assigned this role. A single terrifying night in a second dark room, a shanty attached to the temple which again functions as an index of her psychic state, is sufficient to convince her that, as with the mythical Savitri, spiritual renunciation is not a possible alternative for her. Her *dharma*, it would seem, is that of a wife.

The novel ends with Savitri back in the marital home, having reached an impasse. True to her name, she has returned to the role of wife and the pessimistic conclusion is that this is the only option available to her. One afternoon, she hears Mari passing by in the street, plying for trade, and asks her servant to call him, but then thinks better of it. Meaningful contact with the wider world and those from other social groups now seems to be pointless. The ending is low-key to a point where it is almost anti-climactic. In one sense this is typical of Narayan's habitual resistance to closure. However, in another respect it is at odds with the method that will later characterize his major works. Their apparent narrative aimlessness and a lack of definitive closure go hand-in-glove with a comic elusiveness that has the effect of opening up multiple perspectives on the action. Here comedy is conspicuously absent and the tone is finally far from ambivalent. *The Dark Room* ends as it begins, as a *roman à thèse* about the predicament of sensitive, intelligent brahmin women in a rapidly modernizing society. Like other Narayan novels, it negotiates the middle ground between myth and modernity, but its lack of comic ambivalence leaves it unable to do more than bemoan the impact that social change is having on women in Malgudi society.

Seven years elapsed between the publication of *The Dark Room* and *The English Teacher* and it has been suggested that the tragic death of Narayan's wife, Rajam, to whom *The English Teacher* is dedicated, from typhoid in 1939 was an obstacle that prevented him from writing during this period. Clearly Narayan was very deeply distressed by the loss of Rajam. Shortly after her death he was in touch with Graham Greene, saying he was finding it difficult even to write a letter and wondering how long this state would last;[69] and his younger brother, the cartoonist R.K. Laxman, has spoken of the depression into which he subsided at this time.[70] In the two years that followed the death of Rajam, his attempts to come to terms with the bereavement included trying to establish contact with her through the intercession of a medium and regular conversations with the English 'mystic' Paul Brunton, who was resident in Mysore at this time.[71] At the same time other factors appear to have contributed to Narayan's silence as a novelist during this period. His first three novels had been published in England,[72] where book publication was severely curtailed during World War II and so this outlet was now effectively closed to him. He did, however, continue to produce a steady stream of work for local publication. By 1939 he was contributing regular fortnightly stories to the leading Madras newspaper, *The Hindu*, and he continued to send stories to the paper at the time of Rajam's death.[73] Then, in late 1940, he turned his attention to editing and publishing and three issues of a quarterly magazine, *Indian Thought*, to which he also contributed, appeared in 1941. These were followed by a delayed fourth issue in 1943, before the magazine, too, fell foul of wartime newsprint and printing-ink shortages.[74] So the seven-year hiatus in Narayan's career as a novelist can be attributed to a variety of factors. Nevertheless Rajam's death *was* the most traumatic event of his life and eventually his attempts to come to terms with it found expression in *The English Teacher*.

In *My Days*, Narayan describes *The English Teacher* as 'autobiographical in content, very little part of it being fiction', saying that 'the dedication of the book to the memory of my wife should to some extent give the reader a clue that the book may not be all fiction' (*MyD* 134–5); and its most moving section, the conclusion to the first half which details the hero Krishna's response to Susila's death in a poignantly understated diary-format is closely based on a personal record that Narayan wrote at the time of Rajam's death.[75] More generally, Narayan saw the novel as an attempt to 'attain a philosophical understanding'.[76] So, although *The English Teacher* initially seems to be a continuation of the story of Chandran in *The Bachelor of Arts*, it takes a different direction in its second half, where the autobiographically based account of the protagonist's attempts to establish contact with his deceased wife lead to encounters with the paranormal. It is less obviously related to *The Dark Room*, but its concern with spatial dynamics, particularly evident in the parallels that it draws between mental states and houses and rooms, also has much in common with that novel.

In the opening chapters *The English Teacher*'s links with *The Bachelor of Arts* are so pronounced that it does seem to be a sequel to the earlier novel. The protagonist's name, Krishna, has been changed, but his wife is still 'Susila' and his colleagues include Professor Brown and Mr Gajapathy, both figures that had previously appeared in *The Bachelor of Arts*. At the outset Krishna is living apart from his wife in a hostel and his situation, as a married man yet to enter the second *asrama* as a householder, also suggests a continuation of Chandran's story. The opening pages moot the possibility of progression into the role of *grihastya*, when Krishna's father-in-law proposes that his wife and young daughter should join him and that he should 'set up a family'[77] and most of the remainder of the first half of the novel takes the form of a gradual movement towards this situation, with the young couple's search for a home of their own assuming a central importance. Mundane though this subject is on one level, Narayan's use of the trope of the house relates Krishna and Susila's quest for a house to ancient thinking on the progression into the second *asrama*, but when Susila contracts typhoid and dies half way through the novel, this is abruptly terminated. However, just as marriage does not provide a happy ending in *The Bachelor of Arts*, Susila's death, an event that might have terminated a Victorian novel, does not provide an ending here, despite the sense of closure and the feeling of existential emptiness that pervade the text when it occurs. Instead it offers an entry-point into a very different kind of narrative, a work in which secular themes, underpinned by traditional Hindu beliefs, are replaced by a more philosophical line of inquiry and in which the mood of gentle comedy is overtaken by sombre reflections on the meaning of existence and the possibility of contact with the after-life.

From its earliest reviewers onwards, many of *The English Teacher*'s readers have seen it as a broken-backed novel. The anonymous reviewer of the London *Times* saw it as changing 'for the worse' after Susila's death and felt there was 'a weak and disappointing conclusion to a tale of unaffectedly light and delicate texture'.[78] Compton Mackenzie took a rather more generous view, but still concluded that Narayan 'just fails to secure for the second part the glow of reality that illuminates the early part'.[79] Another British reviewer who commented on the divergence between the two halves speculated that the problems faced by Westerners reading across cultures might account for the apparent decline: 'The latter part of the book may be less convincing to the Occidental reader'.[80] Later critics have generally agreed: K.R. Srinivasa Iyengar sees the attempts at psychic communication as introducing 'a whimsical or fantastical element into a story that has so long been transparently true to life', with the consequence that 'it is difficult to feel that the first and second halves of *The English Teacher* blend naturally and make an artistic whole';[81] Lakshmi Holmstrom concedes that the 'psychic experience [...] is treated seriously and in detail', but finds that 'it contradicts the most moving and most credible parts of the rest of the novel'.[82] Perhaps most significantly of all, in *My Days* Narayan himself summed up the change of direction and the responses it occasioned:

> That book [*The English Teacher*] falls in [sic] two parts
> – one is domestic life and the other half is 'spiritual'. Many
> readers have gone through the first half with interest
> and the second half with bewilderment and even resent-
> ment, perhaps feeling that they have been baited with the
> domestic picture into tragedy, death, and nebulous, impos-
> sible speculations. (*MyD* 135)

However, despite its bipartite structure, change in tone and movement from 'domestic life' to the '"spiritual"', *The English Teacher is* the most thematically unified novel of Narayan's first period.

Formally it represents a new departure in Narayan's fiction. Written in the first person, it is his first sustained attempt to explore his brahmin protagonist's psychology from the inside. Its chapters are longer, making for more continuity in the narrative, and there are less of the seemingly abrupt shifts of emphasis and the lacunae that characterize the previous three novels. A self-reflexive passage in which Krishna is talking to his little daughter Leela bears an interesting relationship to the way in which the novel shapes its disparate and seemingly discrete materials into a patterned, sequential 'story'. When Leela asks him to read to her from her favourite book, Krishna comments:

> It had illustrations in green, and a running commentary of a couple of lines under each. It was really not a story, there was not one in it, but a series of illustrations of tiger, lion, apple, and Sam – each nothing to do with the other. But Leela would never accept the fact that they were disconnected. She maintained that the whole book was one story – and always commanded me to read it; so I fused them all into a whole and gave her a 'story' – Sam ate the apple, but the lion and the tiger wanted some of it …' and so on. (*ET* 101)

Something very similar occurs in *The English Teacher* itself: metonymy gives way to metaphor, as Narayan shapes contingent details from apparently unrelated areas of experience into a narrative which, despite the shift of tone and focus that appears to occur half-way through, is 'an artistic whole'. At the same time *The English Teacher* is a dialogic text, which juxtaposes and assesses the rival claims that various approaches to life make on the individual.

Once again location is central: the particular properties of rooms and buildings link the social themes of the first half of the novel, which not only centres on 'domestic life' but also Krishna's place in Malgudi's colonially oriented educational system, with the second, which moves into psycho-spiritual terrain. A concern with the dialectics of space runs through the whole novel and Narayan introduces a series of sites that allow him to debate the competing claims of the social, political, psychological and spiritual. So, despite the apparent change of direction and shift in mood that occurs when Susila dies, *The English Teacher* has a greater coherence than the other novels of Narayan's first period. Krishna, who in the opening paragraph presents himself as feeling 'some sort of 'vague disaffection' (*ET* 5) with life as he nears the age of thirty, develops from being another of Narayan's drifters to become a man forced by circumstances to ponder fundamental existential questions and to take responsibility for Leela. There is a similar movement in the novel itself and by the end, where Krishna feels 'grateful to Life and Death' (*ET* 184),[83] it is clear that the apparently meandering structure embodies a debate about the relative merits of issues connected with location, social change, family life and ultimately existence itself.

This debate is particularly conducted through a focus on the physical and psychic properties of space. As in *The Dark Room*, houses and rooms are accorded a central prominence and they become the sites for both a brahmin-based view of cleanliness and pollution and for an exploration of the individual's quest for an appropriate *dharma*. Early on in the novel Krishna presents himself as a lecturer who performs his duties in a perfunctory manner and whose primary interest in his position is mercenary. However, teaching a class on *King Lear*, for which he readily admits he is ill-prepared, he suddenly finds himself deeply moved by Lear's 'poor naked wretches' speech[84] and his previous ironic self-deprecation gives way to a more compassionate tone as he contemplates the plight of 'helpless humanity' (*ET* 13). As in *A House for Mr Biswas* (1961), V.S. Naipaul's classic study of a Hindu protagonist's quest to become a householder, where there is an allusion to the same *Lear* passage,[85] the reference seems to connote far more than the physical situation of 'unaccommodated' man. It also relates to the protagonist's progression into the second *asrama* and the sense of psychic accommodation that comes with it.

As such the *Lear* passage provides a curtain-raiser to the novel's engagement with the properties of specific locations, particularly houses and rooms. When Susila rejoins Krishna and they are taking their first tentative steps in living together, their desire to find a home of their own expresses their felt need for both physical and psychic accommodation. Krishna feels that the setting and ambience of the house they choose will be crucial to their well-being and, commenting in a vein that anticipates the gentle social comedy of the novels of Narayan's middle period, caricatures the inhospitable characteristics of several of the houses that he is considering renting:

> 'The builder of this house must have been dead-drunk while doing the latter portion of the house. This is a house evidently intended for monkeys to live in. This house must have been designed by a tuberculosis expert so that his business may prosper for the next hundred years. This house is ideal for one whose greatest desire in life is to receive constant knocks on his head from door-posts. A house for a twisted pygmy.' (*ET* 23)

Throughout such passages the main focus of attention is not on Malgudi at large, but on domestic interiors.

The possibility of Krishna's genuine entry into the role of *grihastya* comes when his father offers to advance him the money to buy or build his own house rather than have to rent. This leads the couple to explore the possibility of buying a house in Lawley Extension, which takes them into an environment that plays a crucial role in both the narrative and the symbolic cultural geography of the novel. Lawley Extension, a section of Malgudi that Narayan will return to again and again in his novels, is a highly significant location for the young couple's attempt to find a house. As an addition to the old town, which in Narayan's cosmos is closely, though not exclusively, associated with orthodox Hinduism, it represents the changing face of Malgudi. The impulse to 'extend' is itself a challenge to the parameters of Malgudi's tightly circumscribed old town, which seems to comprise little more than the few streets clustered together around its focal point, Market Road. The 'moving spirit' behind the extension is Krishna's colleague, Sastri, a logician whom he describes as 'a most energetic "extender"'. In Krishna's view Sastri is 'a marvellous man – a strange combination of things, at one end "undistributed middle" [sic], "definition of knowledge", "syllogisms", and at the other he had the spirit of a pioneer. His was the first building in the New Extension [...]' (*ET* 56). And, as Krishna and Susila venture into this new section of the town, they do so with optimism that a similar 'strange combination' will provide them with a home of their own and the sense of autonomous selfhood that comes with it.

The tragic sequel frustrates this. They eventually arrive at a house, which Krishna sees as both attractive and propitious, because of the perfume thrown off by its jasmine creepers.[86] He is impressed by its pleasant garden and its view of Mempi Hills, another site that will come to assume a central role in Narayan's mapping of Malgudi and its environs. Rousing himself from his self-preoccupation, he notices that Susila, who has gone off to look at the backyard, has been absent for rather too long and the mood begins to darken. She has undergone a deeply disturbing experience, but Narayan's understated, circumstantial style and apparent immersion in domestic issues initially obscure this. Susila has locked herself in an unclean outside lavatory, which she has entered barefoot in the expectation that its interior will be as clean as its brightly coloured door. Krishna's insensitive account initially views this as no more than 'a sad anti-climax to a very pleasing morning' (*ET* 62) and it is easy to read the episode as commentary on the discrepancy between the housing developers' versions of properties they are trying to sell and their underlying shoddiness. But far more is involved here. Susila is thoroughly traumatized by her experience. She emerges from the lavatory filled with disgust and, although Krishna is slow to realise it, the auspicious promise of the house has been completely negated.

Susila's illness, which leads to her subsequent decline and death from typhoid appears to stem from this moment, though with characteristic ambivalence Narayan stops short of categorically identifying the experience as responsible for her death – he subsequently suggests that she may have contracted her illness in a restaurant. However, reading beyond the naturalistic surface of the novel and irrespective of whether the New Extension lavatory has provided the physical cause of her terminal illness, this experience with a crisis heterotopia seems to be as traumatic for Susila as, say, Adela Quested's experience in the Marabar Caves. Underpinning it is a brahmin-based fear of pollution and, read as an allegory about spatial economies, both physical and mental, the novel suggests that it is the development of Lawley Extension that is responsible. While Susila has been undergoing her ordeal, Krishna has been busy debating the sanitation of the house's surroundings and the clear inference is that the 'strange combination' that it represents – the challenge represented by the coming of modernity to Malgudi – is the cause of the tragedy.

Narayan's technique leaves all this implicit, but later references to the psychic and spiritual properties of place establish a pattern, which makes it hard to resist the conclusion that it is the transgression of brahmin codes of cleanliness that causes Susila's death. Read like this, *The English Teacher* is a far cry from the 'domestic' novel of manners that it may initially appear to be. Krishna teaches his students *Pride and Prejudice (ET* 45), but, as in *The Bachelor of* Arts, the novel's account of married life is a world away from Jane Austen's comforting conclusion which reaffirms the conventions of her middle-class social world. Narayan's apparent shift of direction in the second half of the novel is in fact a movement which raises questions that relate to the mode of the novel. As in *The Dark Room,* where Savitri's room of her own finds a later parallel in the dark room of the temple, the closet is complemented by another space with similar connotations. The sickroom, to which Susila is confined when she falls ill and in which she eventually dies, is another heterotopian place that disturbs the values by which Krishna has hitherto lived his life and the possibility of his achieving a normal progression into the role of *grihastya*. It is contrasted with his own room, a study into which Leela is allowed, while being banned from the forbidden space in which her mother has died. The second half of the novel sees childhood innocence as one possible antidote to the feeling of existential futility that overtakes Krishna after Susila's death and Leela has to be protected, not simply from the fact of her mother's death, but also from entry into a location that is a metaphor for the violation of brahmin identity.

The closet and the sickroom are not, however, the only sites that Narayan invests with symbolic properties. In the second half of the novel, Krishna encounters two figures who provide him with possibilities for overcoming his despair: a medium through whose offices he hopes to contact Susila and a headmaster whose educational thinking challenges colonial norms. Both are associated with heterotopian sites which are crucial tropes in the novel's debate about the relative merits of different approaches to life. His initial visit to the medium is very precisely related to the place where this man lives. This is in a secluded spot, 'out of town, but near enough to be able to run into it' (*ET* 110), while his actual house is situated in an idyllic setting, on a lot which has a casuarina tree, a lotus-pond and a ruined temple. As an exponent of a supposed pseudo-science, the medium is clearly a suspect figure and much of the tension of the second half of the novel revolves around the issue of whether he is a genuine conduit to the spirit world or a charlatan. There is evidence to support both views, but gradually the balance is tipped in his favour and when at the very end Krishna 'sees' Susila, the novel comes out in favour of a belief in the paranormal. This raises the issue of *who* the medium is and, more importantly in the spatially focused dynamics of the text, what the site he inhabits represents. The medium is certainly no *sanyasi*, nor an other-worldly guru. When he disappears from Malgudi for a short period, it is because he is 'up to [his] ears in litigation' (*ET* 151). He is, then, it would seem a particular kind of *grihastya*, a man who has a gift for communing with the spirit-world. The lot on which he lives is arguably more interesting in locating his identity and his place in the novel's scheme. In addition to its auspicious natural elements, it contains a ruined temple, dedicated to '*Vak Matha*, the mother who came out of a syllable' (*ET*

109–10). So the paranormal elements of the novel, which are effectively endorsed by the ending are associated with ancient spiritual beliefs,[87] but the ruined nature of the temple and its location outside Malgudi suggest that these are marginalized in the present and no longer integral to the transitional site of the small town.

The other character, who figures prominently in Krishna's regeneration in the second half of the novel, is the headmaster of the school that Leela attends, an establishment that is a foil to Albert Mission College where Krishna teaches. On one level this opposition functions as a device for criticizing the colonial educational curriculum. Despite Narayan's allegedly apolitical stance and his own 'English' education, his early trilogy offers an implicit indictment of colonial education and in *The English Teacher* the criticism is more overt than in *Swami* or *The Bachelor of Arts*. Though Krishna's disaffection with his position as a lecturer may seem to be another version of the Narayan protagonist's inability to commit himself to the responsibilities of the second *asrama*, it also relates to the particular nature of the English-oriented curriculum of the college. The opening episode casts Professor Brown in an unsympathetic light, when his discovery that an English Honours student is spelling 'Honours' without a 'u' prompts him to deliver a forty-five minute tirade on 'the importance of the English language, and the need for preserving its purity' (*ET* 6). The point is obvious enough, but lest it be missed and despite the fact that he is writing for publication in England, Narayan underscores it by having Krishna say to his colleague, Gajapathy, '"Ask Mr Brown if he can say in any of the two hundred Indian languages: 'The cat chases the rat'. He has spent thirty years in India"' (*ET* 6).

Subsequently the novel moves away from Krishna's professional life and political commentary of this kind, but the final chapter, in which he gives up his job as a lecturer, provides closure where this possible *dharma* is concerned. He articulates his disillusion with the college in an uncompromising letter of resignation to Brown, which can be read as a response to the language policy inaugurated by Macaulay's Minute of 1835.[88]

Krishna writes: '"I am up against the system, the whole method and approach of a system of education which makes us morons, cultural morons, but efficient clerks for all your business and administrative offices"' (*ET* 179). Again the nature of the political statement is more than usually direct for Narayan, even if it is mediated through the mouthpiece of Krishna. Yet it may seem to be a somewhat perfunctory and over-obvious return to the subject-matter of the novel's opening, which has subsequently been left aside. Once again, though, *The English Teacher* proves to be more unified than may initially appear to be the case, in this instance because the introduction of the unconventional primary school headmaster and the details of the locations *he* inhabits have prepared the ground for Krishna's resignation and attack on the educational curriculum.

The headmaster's educational philosophy is a complete contrast to that of Albert Mission College: he attacks schools that have 'sold [their] soul to the Government for [a] grant', sees the 'worship' of sports as apish colonial 'copying' (*ET* 135)[89] and encourages his charges to develop their abilities through play. Subsequently, when an astrologer predicts he is about to die, he enlists Krishna as a successor, asking him to ensure that the school's children are protected. The day on which he is supposed to die comes and goes without his death and so the astrologer's claims to paranormal knowledge are discredited, unlike those of the medium, to whom he is an obvious foil. So again Narayan juxtaposes two related approaches, without any heavy under-scoring of the point. In so doing, he seems to be setting up some kind of dialectic, even if he begs as many questions as he answers.

The headmaster reacts to the shock of finding himself still alive by declaring himself 'dead' to the duties of domestic life. In another rejection of important aspects of the role of the *grihastya*, he deserts his wife and family, telling them to treat him as 'dead or as one who has taken *Sanyasa Ashrama*' (*ET* 168) and goes to live in his school. So, like Chandran in *The Bachelor of Arts*, he turns his back on one aspect of the second *asrama* in favour of a premature entry into the spiritual detachment of the fourth phase of life, but he still remains within the second stage as an active educationalist, promulgating an alternative system. Again the emphasis is on the psycho-spiritual dimensions of physical space and the headmaster is fleeing from an environment, which the novel presents as tainted. His home is in a lane of artisans and traders and when Krishna first visits him there, he sees it as another unclean environment, a place beyond the pale which ministers to his brahminical fear of pollution:

> Carpenters, tinsmiths, egg-sellers and a miscellaneous lot of artisans and traders seemed gathered in this place. The street was littered with all kinds of things – wood shavings, egg shells, tin pieces and drying leaves. Dust was ankle deep. I wondered why my friend had selected this of all places. I was afraid to allow my daughter to walk here. I felt she would catch all kinds of dreadful diseases. Unkempt and wild-looking children rolled about in the dust, mangy dogs growled at us, donkeys stood at attention here and there. (*ET* 142)

This lane is only a furlong from Krishna's house, but, he says, it is 'a locality we had never visited' (*ET* 141–2), which not only suggests the narrowly circumscribed nature of the physical space he inhabits, but also the exclusiveness of his cognitive geography. His ignorance of the lane is not, however, simply an aspect of his own insulation from non-brahmin space. The novel adds, 'There was every sign that the municipality had forgotten the existence of this part of the town' (*ET* 142).

Unlike the medium's house and lot, the lane is close to the centre of Malgudi and yet it represents a location that has much in common with Lawley Extension. Its name, 'Anderson's Lane', would seem, like Lawley Extension,[90] to have a British provenance, though Narayan is typically evasive about this. The headmaster says, '"I have often tried to find out who Anderson was. But nobody seems to know. Perhaps some gentleman of the East India Company's days!"' (*ET* 143). So there is a suggestion that the disease-ridden site may be a product of British interference, but this remains unconfirmed and the municipality's neglect points to shared post-Independence responsibility. All that is certain is that, irrespective of who is to blame for the lack of sanitation, Krishna sees the lane as a heterotopia that rekindles the traumatic memory of Susila's illness and death.

The headmaster's house is represented as similarly squalid and his children as wild and dirty. He blames the house's condition and his children's unruliness on his wife's ability to turn any place she inhabits into a hovel. Krishna remonstrates with him, suggesting that his wife deserves to live in a better environment, and the headmaster's reply expresses his belief that place is malleable, a construction of the mind which can be transformed through the attitude one brings to it: '"if we have any worth in us the place will change though our presence. [...] You see, the trouble is not external."' Krishna remains unconvinced at this point, saying, 'The river flowed on against the night. I listened to him; he appeared to me a man who had strayed into a wrong world' (ET 147). The subsequent action vindicates this view. When the headmaster finds himself still alive after the day predicted for his death, he deserts this 'wrong world' and goes to live in his school. Earlier the main hall of the school has been seen as an altogether more positive heterotopia: a site of childhood innocence. Its partition screens are 'filled with glittering alphabets and pictures drawn by children – a look at it seemed to explain the created universe' (ET 124). Again physical spaces, particularly rooms and houses, find their correlatives in states of mind; and, as with the redemptive power through which Leela helps Krishna overcome his sense of existential futility, childhood is presented as the alternative to the disease and pollution that appear to have caused Susila's death. When Krishna resigns from the college, he says he is seeking an 'inner peace', which can only be attained through withdrawal '"from the adult world and adult work into the world of children"' (ET 183). Again the disparate strands of the novel begin to come together.

The headmaster's progressive educational philosophy is, then, a clear alternative to the British system, which is rejected at the end of the novel. However, the political contrast involved finally comes across as less important than the novel's assessment of the competing claims of political and psycho-spiritual views of life. On a secular level Krishna is denied the role of house-holder, but he becomes a different kind of teacher, choosing a form of education which is at odds with colonial practices, as the novel's conclusion moves beyond everyday concerns. Its closing pages make the psychoanalytic dimensions of the distress he feels explicit, when he tells himself:

> 'Wife, child, brothers, parents, friends. ... We come together only to go apart again. It is one continuous movement. They move away from us as we move away from them. The law of life can't be avoided. The law comes into opera-tion the moment we detach ourselves from our mother's womb. [...]' (*ET* 177)

In the conclusion the various strands of the novel unite in a striking and unexpected way. The use of rooms as tropes for mental states is reversed as Krishna attempts to establish contact with Susila through the séances with the medium. 'She' has told him that in order to succeed in achieving communion with 'her', he needs to achieve a greater mental detachment and when he finally makes the break with Albert Mission School, he achieves a state of mind in which he has divested himself of the trappings that have previously hampered their contact. The trope of the room recurs, but now, instead of a physical room providing a metaphor for a mental state, his mind is referred to as a room: the various memories that have been coursing through his brain are 'overwhelmed and swept aside, till [his] mind became clean and bare and a mere chamber of fragrance' (*ET* 184). This mental condition makes his supposed visitation from 'Susila' possible and the novel's paranormal conclusion comes down on the side of the spiritual, leaving little room for ambiguity. Yet, since Krishna's regeneration is facilitated by Leela, whom he hardly thinks of at all in the early stages of the text, and her head-master, this conclusion has the effect of bringing the domestic, the political, the psychoanalytic and the spiritual together. The concluding episode privileges the spiritual, but like every-thing else in *The English Teacher*, it is a product of Krishna's consciousness: from first to last the novel is circumscribed by his first-person angle of focalization and it is about his state of mind. The transcendental conclusion is complemented by a domestic resolution, in which, denied conventional movement into the role of *grihastya*, Krishna has progressed towards becoming a caring and responsible father; and it is a secular movement that it is associated with ancient Hindu religious beliefs – the temple on the medium's lot has been founded by Sankara.

In short, these various levels intersect and overlap in a novel, which despite its paranormal conclusion operates on a range of levels. The implied cultural politics are, however, problematic in that, if one accepts Krishna as a reliable narrator and the tone and progress of his narration encourage such a reading, they promote an exclusivist social vision. Krishna's world is shattered by his transgressive encounter with polluted, non-brahmin space. The schoolmaster retreats from the responsibility of the *grihastya asrama* into a vision of fulfilment predicated on a sentimentalization of childhood and in so doing takes Krishna with him. Krishna's particular sense of loss is related to the primal sense of loss that the new-born infant suffers as it leaves the womb and an answer to these problems comes though a form of spiritualism, whose exponent is associated with a ruined ancient Hindu discourse: the temple dedicated to the primal *Vak Matha* figure, a theological equivalent of the rupture from the womb mentioned above. In its conclusion, then, the novel could be seen to desert the everyday realities of South Indian life for a mystical dialogue with the after-life, but the totality of its various strands makes it an altogether more complex work and ultimately these suggest the tensions and confusions in Tamil brahmin culture, which leave the protagonist pulled in different directions by the various possible choices of *dharma* that are open to him. The autobiographical origins of the work make it a highly personal text on one level, but such a perspective does not preclude the possibility of reading it as an allegory about Tamil brahmin society in the second quarter of the twentieth century. Nor does it invalidate the claim that it is the most assured of Narayan's early novels.

Middle-period novels: *Mr Sampath* to *Waiting for the Mahatma*

Beginning with *Mr Sampath: The Printer of Malgudi* (1949) and culminating with *The Painter of Signs* (1976), the novels of Narayan's middle period represent his finest achievement. The protagonists of these novels are usually small businessmen in the second *asrama* of life, whose occupations are contemporary versions of the scribal and priestly roles traditionally undertaken by Tamil brahmins. Sampath in *Mr Sampath* and Nataraj in *The Man-Eater of Malgudi* (1961) are printers and printers also figure elsewhere in these novels; Raman in *The Painter of Signs* pursues an occupation that is equally involved with representation and takes pride in his calligraphy, even though drawing sometimes has to take precedence over writing in his case; Srinivas in *Mr Sampath* is a publisher. Raju in *The Guide* (1958) finds himself transformed from a tourist guide into a supposed spiritual guide and Sriram in *Waiting for the Mahatma* (1955) follows an altruistic quasi-spiritual path in his devotion to the Gandhian ethic. Margayya in *The Financial Expert* (1952) and Jagan, the protagonist of *The Vendor of Sweets* (1967), seem to pursue more obviously mercantile lines of work, but their occupations engage them in activities in which Saraswathi, the goddess of learning end enlightenment, vies with Lakshmi, the goddess of prosperity. Margayya becomes involved in a publishing project; Jagan is a daily reader of the *Gita* and both men have scribal ambitions for their sons.

Though their particular subjects and angles of focalization vary, the recurrent concern of the middle-period novels is an exploration of the conflicts that occur when seemingly settled Hindu values, usually personified by the protagonist, are challenged by the incursion of alien forces. Subtly battle is joined and as the narrative unravels, it becomes clear that the pivot of the action lies inside the protagonist's head, as he strives to find an appropriate *dharma* for his contemporary situation. So, although the social dimension of the novels often appears crucial and *is* always important, the hero's struggle to come to terms with changing circumstances is primarily psychodrama rather than commentary on changing social mores. By the conclusion he has usually managed to resolve his dilemmas, arriving at a more mature version of the values he espoused at the outset, though the conclusions are never completely clear-cut. Moreover, the extent to which traditional Hindu values are reinstated varies and in the later middle-period novels, where the pace of omnipresent social change accelerates, the reaffirmation of such values proves more difficult to sustain.

Complementing these thematic conflicts, the shifts in tone that characterize Narayan's early fiction are replaced by a new dialectical complexity and the disjunctions that mar sections of the first four novels give way to a tonal ambivalence that is integral to the form and meaning of the texts. The middle-period novels demonstrate an investigative approach to the narrativization of Malgudi, implicitly asking what discursive modes are appropriate for this purpose and staging a debate on the relative merits of Western and Hindu storytelling traditions. There is, however, little sense of an adversarial response to the imported conventions of the novel genre, nor for that matter many elements that overtly foreground the dialectic involved. The varied influences and intertexts are generally used in an eclectic manner, as reference-points in the exploration of what may constitute an appropriate *dharma* for the South Indian *grihastya* in transitional late colonial and post-Independence Indian society.

Explicit political references are comparatively rare and only one novel, *Waiting for the Mahatma* introduces macro-politics in *any* kind of sustained way. Narayan frequently disclaimed any political intent in his novels[1] and many commentators on his work have taken this disclaimer at face value. Graham Greene, for example, refers to Malgudi as 'never ruffled by politics'.[2] Yet read from a certain vantage point, several of the novels of the middle period can be seen to be dramatizing the impact of late colonial, Gandhian and post-Independence policies on Narayan's South Indian microcosm. Conversely, read from another point of view, these novels, as numerous commentators have suggested,[3] repeatedly invoke classic Hindu narrative discourse, in which the secular and spiritual co-exist and in which the political and social are not exactly missing, but are viewed simply as another aspect of *maya*, the illusion of existence.

Comments on this subject by one of Narayan's most interesting and provocative critics, V.S. Naipaul, a writer who began life as a third-generation Trinidadian Hindu, are particularly illuminating, albeit ultimately wrong-headed. Like Graham Greene, the young Naipaul seems to have turned to Narayan for some kind of insight into quintessential Indianness and Narayan is a fairly obvious influence on his own early fiction, particularly *The Mystic Masseur* (1957).[4] However, unlike Greene, Naipaul is alert to the nuances of Narayan's social background. Coming from a diasporic brahmin family himself,[5] he is sensitive to the contemporary situation of Tamil brahmins, a group that has particularly engaged his attention in the three books he has written about India.[6]

According to Naipaul, who focuses on two novels from the middle period in *India: A Wounded Civilization* (1977), Narayan's fiction appears to deal with a conflict between social action and a quietistic renunciation that finds analogues in classic Hindu narrative, but in reality the possibility of active intervention is illusory and so the dice are irrevocably loaded towards fatalistic acceptance. Naipaul recounts how, re-reading Narayan after a period of years, he came to the realization that his novels were 'less the purely social comedies I had once taken them to be than religious books, at times religious fables'.[7] Talking about the protagonist of *Mr Sampath*, he writes:

> [...] For Srinivas nonviolence isn't a form of action, a quick-
> ener of social conscience. It is only a means of securing an
> undisturbed calm; it is nondoing, noninterference, social
> indifference. It merges with the idea of self-realization,
> truth to one's identity. These modern-sounding words
> [...] disguise an acceptance of *karma*, the Hindu killer, the
> Hindu calm, which tells us that we pay in this life for what
> we have done in past lives: so that everything we see is just
> and balanced, and the distress we see is to be relished as
> religious theatre, a reminder of our duty to ourselves, our
> future lives. [...]
>   The novel I had read as a novel was also a fable, a classic
> exposition of the Hindu equilibrium, surviving the shock
> of an alien culture, an alien literary form, an alien language,
> and making harmless even those new concepts it appeared
> to welcome. Identity became an aspect of *karma*, self-love
> was bolstered up by an ideal of nonviolence.[8]

This, then, suggests a significant conflict in both the theme of
the novel *and* the generic tension associated with it. However,
Naipaul's privileging of the fabulist over the social is inadequate
as an account of how the admixture of discursive elements in
Narayan's work functions. He constructs a binary opposition
between Western social comedy and Hindu fable, but the two
are not exclusive in Narayan; they operate together and there
is no real suggestion that the presence of the one need involve
the erasure of the other. This said, classical Hindu intertexts are
more prominent in the middle part of Narayan's career.[9]

Naipaul's account of *Mr Sampath* tells how Srinivas, a
'contemplative idler',[10] ventures into the active world by setting
up a weekly newspaper,[11] the first manifestation of the concern
with printing and related scribal activities that informs the
novels of the middle period. When he is forced to close the paper,
Srinivas becomes involved in the making of a film. Both these
worldly occupations are, however, supplanted by a vision of the
millennia of Indian history, in which he imagines episodes from
the *Ramayana*, the lives of the Buddha and Shankaracharya
and the colonial period. These convince him that there is an
unchanging archetypal order, underlying the apparent chaos of

his personal and professional life and he renounces the commercial world for what Naipaul sees as 'undisturbed calm', a retreat into 'nondoing, noninterference, social indifference' and a form of non-violence that is a travesty of Gandhianism. This is why, in his view, *Mr Sampath* deserts the real task of the novel form, which he describes elsewhere as 'a form of social inquiry, and as such outside the Indian tradition'.[12]

Mr Sampath's initial focus does seem to be on social comedy, in that it opens with an emphasis on the day-to-day struggles of Srinivas, a 'little man' protagonist in the tradition of characters such as George and Weedon Grossmith's Pooter, H.G. Wells's Mr Polly or Naipaul's own slightly later version of the type, Mr Biswas,[13] but gradually the comic, gently ironic portrayal of this put-upon Walter Mitty figure gives way to a mode that accords him a kind of seriousness as a modern-day equivalent of Rama.[14] Or, putting this another way, Narayan can be seen to be indebted both to the tradition of the English comic novel, as written by practitioners such as Dickens[15] and Wells,[16] *and* to the Sanskrit epics and the *puranas*; and the vision of the millennia of Indian history having inhabited the space that is now Market Road, the epicentre of Malgudi, goes further than Naipaul suggests in adumbrating a pluralistic view of the Indian past, since it encompasses several faiths and transcends the Hindu model he suggests. The episode which is initiated by an exorcism certainly suggests a transcendental solution, in much the same way as the séances in *The English Teacher* propel the novel into a paranormal plane of reality that provides a resolution to the existential crisis in which Chandran finds himself. However, the social and the spiritual have not been discrete earlier in *Mr Sampath* and, although this epiphany can, as Naipaul argues, be seen to provide an answer to the 'chaos' and 'complications' of Srinivas's life, it is not the novel's final conclusion. Both the social and the fabulist elements need to be seen in the larger context of Srinivas's quest for an appropriate *dharma*; and, important though the visionary episode may seem at the moment near the end when it occurs, the novel as a whole is more concerned with his day-to-day experiences. These are played out against the backdrop of a range of Malgudi locations, which are once again invested with symbolic associations, and in relation to a range of characters, among whom the eponymous Sampath is paramount.

The impulse for *Mr Sampath* seems to have come from Narayan's dealings with a real-life original of the title-character, who went by this name, and, while the transposition of this Mysore figure into the fictional world of Malgudi inevitably involves invention, knowledge of the original 'Sampath' illuminates the central Srinivas-Sampath relationship. Although Srinivas is the main protagonist and his first appearance is delayed, the novel is named after Sampath and, tellingly, it concludes with a memorable image of his vanishing presence:

> While turning down Anderson Lane [Srinivas] looked back for a second and saw far off the glow of a cigarette end in the square where he had left Sampath; it was like a ruby set in the night. He raised his hand, flourished a final farewell, and set his face homeward.[17]

The simile's metamorphosis of waste (the cigarette end) into precious stone (the ruby) suggests some kind of magical transformation of the enigmatic Sampath, a character who has kept Srinivas guessing to the last, and the novel's ending on this elegiac note lends weight to the view that it is the relationship between the two men, and in particular what Sampath represents to Srinivas, that is the main axis on which it has turned, even if this has not always been apparent. Like several subsequent Narayan novels, notably *The Man-Eater of Malgudi*, the pairing of two characters who are complementary opposites lies at the heart of *Mr Sampath*'s structure. As Ranga Rao, whose emphasis on this element neatly links Hindu typology with more general commentary on oppositional syzygies puts it: 'they are two psychological types, the introvert and the extrovert; [...] the satvic and the rajasic; two worlds of man: the idealistic world and the realistic'.[18]

So who was the real-life Sampath, what kind of dealings did Narayan have with him and how are these reworked in the novel? 'Sampath', as he was called, was M.S. Cheluviengar, the proprietor of the Mysore printing press which Narayan used for the production of his journal *Indian Thought* and several details in the novel and also in *The Man-Eater of Malgudi*, where the protagonist Nataraj is a printer, appear to have been taken over directly from the real-life Sampath's press.[19] For example the fictional Sampath's request that Srinivas supply the paper for his magazine, *The Banner*, parallels M.S. Cheluviengar's requiring Narayan to do this and Srinivas's exasperation over Sampath's failure to print on time is also a reflection of Narayan's own experience.[20] 'Sampath' was, however, far more than just a printer. Seven years Narayan's junior, he was also a popular local actor, who in an instance of art anticipating life went on to become a successful film director. In *My Days*, Narayan comments that he has gone on to 'become a very busy film personality, with a shooting schedule almost every day in studios in Mysore and Madras' (*MyD* 160). Most important of all, he seems to have been a charismatic man who fascinated the comparatively unworldly Narayan and as such he became the inspiration for traits in several subsequent Narayan characters, among them both Nataraj and Vasu in *The Man-Eater of Malgudi* and Dr Rann in *Talkative Man*.

Narayan's most interesting anecdote about him is told in the sketch, 'Sampath's Elephant', which appears in his collection, *Salt & Sawdust* (1993). Here he tells how he took his American publisher, Lyle Blair, Director of Michigan State University Press, to meet 'Sampath' at his press in Mysore and how Sampath 'overwhelmed the visitor with his courtly welcome', [21] finally asking him, '"is there anything else you would like?"' When Blair replied he would like to see an elephant, Sampath clapped his hands and, in what Narayan refers to as 'a coincidence in a million',[22] an elephant, complete with his mahout, appeared as if to order. For Blair this apparent conjuring became the stuff of storytelling, the kind of anecdote that he could dine out on for years afterwards. And, although Narayan's account emphasizes the coincidence, it is possible to see his response to the mercurial Sampath in a similar light. 'Sampath's Elephant' appears in

Salt & Sawdust in a selection of his '*Table Talk*' (my italics) and his earlier response in *Mr Sampath* can be seen as having been similarly fired by Sampath's charming persona.

Srinivas's fictional alter ego in *Mr Sampath* is quickly identified as a Hindi-speaking newcomer to Malgudi. He lives in the recently developed New Extension and is also associated with modernity through his involvement in a film project, which supersedes his work as a printer in the middle part of the novel. Like Sampath, the film and the 'jargon' associated with it seem to represent a threat to older Malgudi values, as embodied by conservative Kabir Lane:

> [...] No two persons met, nowadays, except in a conference. No talk was possible unless it were a discussion. There were story conferences and treatment discussions, and there were costume conferences and allied discussions. Lesser persons would probably call them by simpler names, but it seemed clear that in the world of films an esoteric idiom of its own was indispensable for its dignity and development. Kabir Lane now resounded with the new jargon. (*MrS* 93)

Interestingly, then, the film is associated with a different kind of discourse; the physical incursions into Malgudi space are accompanied by new idioms, suggestive of both the commercialization of art and the erosion of the Tamil brahmin monopoly of the word. In this respect Sampath's role is liminal. Srinivas first encounters him in 'the *Bombay* Anand Bhavan in Market Road, where he had gone for a cup of coffee' (*MrS* 65; my italics) and is fascinated by his voice:

> He was attracted to his future printer by his voice, a rich baritone, which hovered above the babble of the hall, like a drone. Srinivas understood little of what he had been saying, since he spoke in Hindi and could easily be mistaken for a North Indian, with his fur cap and his scarf flung around his neck. (*MrS* 65–6)

As a Hindi-speaker Sampath represents alterity, but he is not a North Indian and as a Market Road businessman, he has at the very least a firm toehold in the old town. Above all, though, he is Srinivas's complementary opposite, because he is a trans- gressive figure and a man of mystery. During the course of shooting the film he embarks on an affair with the 'Parvathi' he has recruited from Madras and when he re-emerges at the end to tell Srinivas, in a confessional scene that brings the two men closer together than ever before, that she has deserted him, Srinivas is left wondering whether or not he is telling the truth. Sampath has seemed to combine the attributes of a shaman and a con man and he remains elusive to the last. As he and Srinivas part and Srinivas looks back to his glowing cigarette in the final paragraph, the question of whether he is a magician or char- latan is left open, as it has been with the medium in Narayan's previous novel. Whatever particular interpretation one chooses to put on the scene, its positioning, *after* Srinivas's vision of the millennia of Indian history, has the effect of returning the reader to the world of secular reality, undermining Naipaul's view that a mythic quietism has supplanted the novel's apparent concern with social issues. The vision proves to have been a penultimate conclusion; the final chapter opens up fresh questions about the mysteries surrounding character and day-to-day life.

Should one, then, conclude that *Mr Sampath* is aimless and centrifugal in its form and content? Arguably not. Again the novel's various strands spiral around a quest for *dharma* and this also serves to bring the various generic elements together. In an article for his magazine, *The Banner*, written just before the outbreak of World War II, Srinivas has written:

> '*The Banner* has nothing special to note about any war, past or future. It is only concerned with the war that is always going on – between man's inside and outside. Till the forces are equalized the struggle will always go on.' (*MrS* 6)

He subsequently comes to see 'a touch of comicality in that bombast', viewing it as 'an odd mixture of the sublime and the ridiculous' (*MrS* 7), and yet what is foregrounded as comic is, as is so often the case in Narayan, also serious. Satirical irony is subsumed in a broader philosophical irony, an irony of the kind that has been labelled 'general irony'[23] and which accords with the traditional Hindu capacity for locating ephemeral events in a larger, cosmic scheme. Characteristically, though, Narayan shies away from such metaphysical terminology. And the same reluctance to engage with large abstractions is evident in a passage that debates the appropriateness of using the word 'cosmic', which comes after the epiphanic moment that Naipaul focuses on as the key to the book's meaning. Srinivas returns to his office and attempts to communicate his vision to the readers of the recently revived *Banner*:

> He jotted down the heading 'The Leaf on the Torrent'. He didn't like it. He noted down an alternative title 'The Cosmic Stage: the willy-nilly actor on the Cosmic Stage'. He thought it over. It didn't satisfy either. He didn't like to use the word 'cosmic' if he could help it. The intensity of the experience seemed to be disintegrating now in commonplace expression. (*MrS* 212)

At this point Sampath reappears and the problem of communicating the transcendental vision disappears, leaving it a significant moment in the novel's dénouement but not, after all, a life-changing experience for Srinivas. What links the various strands – social comedy, Hindu fable and psychodrama – is the quest for *dharma* and *dharma* in Narayan's novels is rooted in 'commonplace expression'. Its attainment has spiritual overtones, but ultimately it involves a secular quest, frequently though not always associated with the choice of a career.

It particularly expresses itself in terms of the problems facing the artist. Forced to give up *The Banner*, Srinivas finds his writing talents co-opted, by Sampath, into another form of scribal enterprise, when he becomes the script-writer for the commercial film. His initial story-line, which some readers will take with more than the proverbial grain of salt since it is prompted by an argument with his wife, involves a dramatization of the Gandhian ethic of *ahimsa* (non-violence). This is rejected by the film's producers and they are equally quick to reject mythological subjects, but reverse their opinion when they

see the romance possibilities of a plot based on the love-story of
Shiva and Parvathi. Narayan's treatment is overtly satirical and
the film becomes a metonym for the commercialization of South
Indian artistic traditions under the impact of what can be seen as
an early exemplification of American-led global capitalism: one
character opines that Malgudi "'will be called the Hollywood of
India"' (*MrS* 135), while Srinivas takes the view that '"They are
initiating a new religion, and that camera decked with flowers is
their new god, who must be propitiated"' (*MrS* 132–3). Subsequent Narayan novels include similar technological innovations,
which unlike the printing presses of an earlier generation, seem
to threaten the older brahmin scribal culture. These include the
novel-writing machine in *The Vendor of Sweets* and another film
in *A Tiger for Malgudi* (1983). In each case the main emphasis is
on the effect of new technologies on the protagonist's psyche.

In *Mr Sampath* the film is roundly satirized and when the
project collapses, Srinivas feels relieved to have escaped from the
'chaos of human relationships and activities' (*MrS* 196) through
his vision, which enables him to see it as part of a larger design.
But all of this remains inscribed within the mundane realities
of day-to-day living, the here-and-now contingency that characterizes the Western novel from its eighteenth-century infancy
onwards. Hindu fable is present, but Naipaul's view of this as an
all-important infrastructure distorts the emphasis. His reading
involves a narrowly prescriptive view of the novel genre, a reductive account of *karma* and a view of *Mr Sampath*, which even
though it still allows for the presence of social comedy – he says
his re-reading made him realize that *Mr Sampath* was *also* a religious fable – over-emphasizes the mythic elements. The central
dynamic of the novel relies on the syzygy, the psychological
opposition, between the two main characters. To repeat Ranga
Rao's words, the tension emerges from the interaction of 'two
psychological types, the introvert and the extrovert, the satvic
and the rajasic; two worlds of man: the idealistic world and the
realistic'.

The physical and mental geography of Narayan's next novel,
The Financial Expert is subtly different from anything to be

found in his earlier fiction. The novel opens with the eponymous protagonist Margayya, another character inspired by a real-life Mysore original,[24] conducting his business under a banyan tree outside Malgudi's Central Co-operative Land Mortgage Bank. The bank has colonial origins, having been founded by a famous Registrar of Co-operative Societies whose ghost is believed to haunt the building. Now, however, the values of the co-operative movement seem to have been taken over by Margayya, whose dealings under the banyan clearly constitute a rival set of financial practices. He even keeps a set of records which duplicates the details the bank holds of its clients' accounts. So from one point of view Margayya can be seen to be subverting the bank's dealings through an economy which shadows and appropriates the co-operative values on which it has been founded. However, given the age of the banyan tree under which he conducts his business in what he refers to as its 'god-given shade'[25] and the comparatively recent establishment of the colonial bank, in 1914 (FE 1), Margayya would seem to be the repository of an older economy. In this phase of his career, he mainly operates by attracting loans secured against the capital yielded by previous loans and sees money as a crucial part of what it is to be human: 'If money was absent men came near being beasts' (FE 27).[26] Later in the novel, having installed himself in a small shop in Market Road, he becomes the richest man in Malgudi,[27] enjoying financial success beyond his wildest dreams during the inflationary climate of World War II and flourishing through a black economy predicated on deposits rather than loans. However, when there is a run on his bank, he loses everything and the end of the novel finds him reinstalled under the banyan tree, a sadder and a wiser man.

This might suggest a moral fable of the kind that Naipaul finds in Mr Sampath, in that Margayya's life seems to be shaped around a settled routine, which is disrupted in the middle part of the novel and then reinstated as a kind of reaffirmation of an older social order at the end. However, his entrepreneurialism makes him an untypical Narayan protagonist in some ways and his character both embodies and challenges traditional values.

Although he is a Tamil brahmin in the second *asrama* of life, a man beset with the cares of householding, family and occupation, his ancestral origins are less securely established than those of most Narayan heroes. The first part of the novel shows him preoccupied with his image, a motif that suggests low self-esteem and there are repeated references to spectacles and other signifiers of sight, which foreground his sense that identity is constructed by perception, both self-perception and the views of others. Margayya's financial dealings seem to be as much motivated by an attempt to promote himself into a new, money-based aristocracy as by a desire to acquire wealth for its own sake; and a passage towards the end of the novel clarifies the sense of social inferiority he has felt:

> There was a family secret about his caste which stirred uneasily at the back of his mind. Though he and the rest were supposed to be of good caste now, if matters were pried into deeply enough they would find that his father's grandfather and his brothers maintained themselves as corpsebearers. (*FE* 183)

This is followed by a brief debate on how long it takes to escape from such a stigma and although the consensus is that it only requires two or three generations, the revelation of this secret helps to explain both his low self-esteem and the motives behind his desire for financial advancement.

So Margayya comes from a less respectable Malgudi background than most of Narayan's earlier protagonists; and he also lives in a more liminal situation – in Vinayak Mudali Street, close to the centre of Malgudi, but a far less prestigious address than Kabir Street, the bastion of conservative Malgudi values.[28] Situated on 'the very edge of the town' (*FE* 34), Vinayak Street is very obviously a borderline milieu, but although it is a world away from the Kabir Street aristocracy, it has a complex past of its own. Margayya's own house, No. 14 D, has already attained the status of 'a famous land-mark, for it was the earliest house to be built in that area' (*FE* 9) and his father has been seen as heroic for deciding to settle in such an insecure spot. This claim to fame is, however, mitigated by the insalubrious aspects of the street: it is close to a cremation ground and a wide, unsanitary gutter runs in front of its houses. Anything that falls into this gutter sinks 'deeper and deeper into a black mass' (FE 40) until it is irrevocably lost. Once again such physical geography seems to be associated with waste and pollution, suggesting that the street may be a similar site to the unsanitary New Extension house, where Susila contracts her fatal illness in *The English Teacher*.

Vinayak Mudali Street is, however, more complex than the trope of the gutter suggests. At one end of the street there is a small temple with a shrine to the god Hanuman, supposedly built on a spot which the monkey god's foot touched during his journey south to Lanka, where in *The Ramayana* he helped Rama destroy the demon king Ravana. So, seen from another angle, far from being associated with pollution, the street is on the edge of hallowed ground. One way of reading this might be in terms of a Foucault-like view of the past as archaeologically layered rather than a product of linear historiographical discourse. And, given that physical spaces invariably have cultural and psychic correlatives in Narayan's fiction, such a view of how places undergo transformations could be seen as the topographical equivalent of the belief that human identities are transformed in different incarnations. Certainly Vinayak Street, then and now, seem very different places and Narayan is clearly suggesting that the same physical space can assume different, even opposed, identities. This said, the archaeological model of place as a set of superimposed palimpsests is inadequate to account for the ambivalence of the street in the present, where it is on the edge of town, situated between New Extension and the residential and commercial centres of established Malgudi, Kabir Street and Market Road. Compared with Lawley Extension, which figures prominently in the novel, it seems to be *in* Malgudi and it has been built on ground, which like the shade under the banyan tree, can at least be claimed as sanctified, but viewed from another perspective it is a location that is close to being beyond the pale. It only receives any attention from the Municipal authorities when elections are looming and the gutter is the main metonym for its unsanitary, disease-ridden condition. Election times apart, 'the gutter continued its existence unhampered, providing the cloud of mosquitoes and the stench that characterized existence in Vinayak Mudali Street' (*FE* 41).[29] So the street resists unitary construction, offering different interpretative possibilities depending on the viewpoint and value-systems through which it is perceived. Most importantly, it is simultaneously both hallowed and polluted ground in the *present*. These two versions of its identity co-exist and so the archaeological model which suggests that one layer has been superimposed on another simplifies the text's complex representation of space. More than just this, Narayan's anti-palimpsestic view of place also suggests that the two elements overlap in an unstable conjunction, which generates varied formations at different points in the novel.

No. 14 D is equally ambivalent, since it has been partitioned down the middle during a dispute between Margayya and his brother after their father's death,[30] an episode which has also contributed to Margayya's low self-esteem, as it has left him feeling socially inferior to his brother. Now they inhabit separate halves of the house, which are self-contained apart from their having to share a well, while their wives continue to feud. So the house is both a haven for Margayya and an uncomfortable kind of 'home', since it is a split, contested site, in which the traditional values of the joint family have been negated. And, as in earlier Narayan novels such as *The Dark Room*, rooms also take on particular identities and are subject to transformations. Thus, when in the first part of the novel Margayya decides to devote himself to the goddess Lakshmi, in the hope that she will favour his business enterprises, he converts a small room in the house into a shrine where he can undertake a forty-day penance to enlist the goddess's help. Later, during his period of greater financial prosperity, this room is assigned another identity, when along with other parts of the house it becomes a storing-place for the vast deposits of cash he has accumulated.

These spatial dynamics underpin the central conflict in the novel, which centres on a debate about the relative merits of

Margayya's financial entrepreneurialism and the more conservative aspects of Tamil brahmin culture. Again, Margayya's physical situation mirrors his position in the society. He is an interstitial figure, whose business ethics distance him from the older scribal culture, personified in other novels of Narayan's middle period by protagonists such as Srinivas (*Mr Sampath*), Sriram (*Waiting for the Mahatma*) and Nataraj (*The Man-Eater of Malgudi*). Both his situation in Vinayak Street and his occupation as a 'specialist in money' (*FE* 134) are products of his having inherited very little from his father, who has had to pay dowries for his three sisters, and the situation of the partitioned house is also both a cause and an index of his comparative impoverishment. He prides himself on being a self-made man, professing egalitarian values and a disregard for 'status' (*FE* 181). So, to a much greater extent than a character like Srinivas, whose fundamentally traditional way of life is challenged by the advent of outside forces, Margayya is himself a figure who embodies the co-existence of ancient and modern values – here specifically in the context of brahmin attitudes to money. And just as *The Financial Expert*'s representations of place frustrate binary categorizations, so Margayya's attitudes towards money involve shifting perspectives that enable the novel to present its debate on finance and business ethics.

Margayya particularly eludes definition in terms of the opposition that Naipaul uses to discuss *Mr Sampath*, since his attitude to money challenges the notion of *karma*. In the latter stages of the novel, he tries to influence an astrologer's verdict on the compatibility of the horoscopes of his son, Balu, and his potential bride.

> [H]e was consulting the astrologer purely as a formality. These were not days when he had to wait anxiously on a verdict of the stars: he could afford to ask for his own set of conditions and get them. He no longer believed that man was a victim of circumstances or fate – but that man was a creature who could make his own present and future, provided he worked hard and remained watchful. (*FE* 185)

At this point, Margayya has reached the height of his financial success. He still remembers the need to propitiate Lakshmi, but now adheres to this in a more perfunctory way than hitherto. So, in short, Narayan is dramatizing the tension between a local South Indian version of capitalist modernity and more traditional Hindu attitudes to money but, although there are moments when Margayya's belief that he can be a self-made man is in the ascendant, these two value-systems are not presented as mutually exclusive. Instead Narayan demonstrates their interplay and the metamorphoses they undergo within a single character's consciousness. The effect is to make Margayya a tearing-point for the novel's debate about the relative merits of particular aspects of Indian modernity and tradition and render him one of Narayan's most psychologically complex characters.

The tension personified in Margayya is particularly evident when he considers the rival claims of Lakshmi and Saraswathi, the goddess of wisdom. His early devotion to Lakshmi is prompted by advice from the priest of the temple at the end of Vinayak Mudali Street. However, like many of the holy men who appear in Narayan's fiction, this priest is an enigmatic figure and when he subsequently disappears, supposedly having gone to Benares and the source of the Ganges (*FE* 78) as a *sanyasi*, Margayya is suspicious of him. Initially, though, he feels the priest lives 'in a sort of timelessness' (*FE* 30) and adopts him as a guru, who can guide him towards financial success, just as he himself has helped others, albeit in a more obviously secular way. At the outset readers are informed that Margayya's name means 'The Way' (*FE* 1), but although it is not generally known, he has originally been christened Krishna. As such he is a kind of lapsed Krishna figure, whose caste credentials are open to question, and who has made his way through the common-sense secular pragmatism embodied in the name Margayya. Now with colonial business interests, in the shape of the Co-operative Bank, stacked against him he turns to the priest for advice on financial success and is told he should follow Lakshmi. In one sense this is entirely predictable. In the words of Nirad Chaudhuri, 'every normal Hindu home' has 'a little sanctum [...] devoted to the goddess Lakshmi',[31] but the devotion expected of Margayya is more total than this and the priest tells him that he can afford to neglect everything else:

> '[...] A devotee of Goddess Lakshmi need care for nothing, not even the fact that he is in a temple where a certain decorum is to be observed. It's only a question of self-assurance. [...] It's only the protégé of Goddess Saraswathi [the deity presiding over knowledge and enlightenment[32]] who has to mind such things.' (FE 50)

The priest follows this with a disquisition on the rivalry between the two goddesses, first suggesting that '"when Saraswathi favours a man, the other Goddess withdraws her favours"' (FE 50), but then conceding that a few people are fortunate enough to be claimed by both goddesses. The implications are particularly interesting, not just because the two goddesses stand as personifications of the competing claims of financial entre-preneurialism and scholarly devotion, but also because their respective portfolios underpin the central debate within the novel, which has particular ramifications for twentieth-century brahmin culture.

The second and third of the novel's five parts seem to diverge from the focus on financial enterprise, which has seemed to be its main subject. However, Margayya's *dharma* is not simply circumscribed by his desire for economic success. In the second and third parts, Margayya becomes more directly involved with Saraswathi and the brahmin scribal culture, first through a publishing project, which offers a different possible road to success and then, in a shift of emphasis which moves the focus from his business dealings to his family life, through an obsession with his son Balu's education. The publishing project suggests the possibility of rapprochement between Lakshmi and Saraswathi, though not without some passages of broad comedy. Margayya's attempts to secure exam success for his son are also comic, but are more exclusively directed towards Saraswathi, even if his engagement with her is undertaken vicariously through Balu, a schoolboy who makes a reluctant scholar like Swami seem positively studious.

The publication that Margayya becomes involved with is a kind of contemporary *Kama-Sutra*.[33] It has been written by a Tamil journalist and self-styled sociologist, Dr Pal, whom Margayya encounters in the promising heterotopian setting of a lotus pond located beside a ruined temple beyond the River Sarayu. Margayya has been directed to go to this spot to obtain a lotus by the priest who is instructing him in the materials he needs for his devotions to Lakshmi. Discovered as he is in such an auspicious setting, Dr Pal seems as though he may be another guru for Margayya, a guide to financial success sent by providence to complete the work begun by the priest. What follows suggests otherwise. Narayan's irony characteristically stops short of overt condemnation, but if the priest is a *possible* charlatan, by the end of the novel it seems clear that Dr Pal, a type of bogus 'academic man' (*FE* 213),[34] is very definitely one. He is a character beside whom the financially shrewd Margayya seems an innocent.[35] Dr Pal's claims to be an author and scholar are of a kind that only someone as ingenuous in the ways of Saraswathi and the scribal culture as Margayya is could take seriously. Comedy ensues when Dr Pal reveals the pornographic nature of his one completed book to date, *Bed-Life or the Science of Marital Happiness* (later re-entitled *Domestic Harmony*), particularly when prudery and prurience commingle in Margayya's response to Pal's suggestions that the book could have illustrations (*FE* 68)!

Even if *Domestic Harmony* is not to be taken seriously (it is, of course, as the sub-title *Science of Marital Happiness* suggests, a contemporary equivalent of the *Kama-Sutra*,[36] and so just possibly could be!), it leads to Margayya's fortunes becoming entwined, not just with those of Dr Pal, but also with the printer Madan Lal, who introduces him to the mysteries of different book sizes, fonts and typefaces (*FE* 83–4).[37] The episode concludes when Margayya sells his share in *Domestic Harmony* to Dr Pal, relieved to make a profit and to be rid of a book that has embarrassed him every bit as much as his tainted caste background, but prior to this he spends some time pondering the financial possibilities of publishing and it takes him some time to reach the conclusion that '"Book business is no business at all"' (*FE* 118). This realization is again related to a split between Lakshmi and Saraswathi which is expressed through Margayya's growing awareness that they represent different spatial economies He is ill at ease in Madan Lal's Printery and eventually concludes: 'Money was *not in its right place* here, amidst all the roar of printing machinery, ugly streaming proof sheets, and the childish debits and credits that arose from book sales with booksellers and book buyers, who carried on endless correspondence over trivialities' (*FE* 117; my italics).

The other section of the novel in which the scribal culture is very obviously to the fore, the episodes in which Balu's education becomes Margayya's overriding obsession, are also given comic treatment, not least when, after Balu has comprehensively failed all his exams, securing his best mark, 12%, in hygiene, Margayya decides that perhaps he is destined to be a doctor! Unlike Swami, who is a reluctant scholar, Balu is an out-and-out educational failure and the conflict between father and son is played out in terms of their attitudes towards books and papers. The very first time he appears in the novel, Balu is seen burning a piece of paper in a lamp (*FE* 10) and this establishes a pattern for what follows. While Margayya's confusion over the relationship between Lakshmi and Saraswathi suggests a degree of ambivalence towards brahmin scribal culture, Balu's actions present him as an instinctive and dedicated enemy of learning and the written word. As part of his attempt to persuade Balu to apply himself to his studies, Margayya tells him that he must follow in his footsteps by dedicating himself to 'the Goddess' (*FE* 112). Balu, for once well informed, interrupts to accuse him of having followed a different goddess, Lakshmi not Saraswathi, and suggests that he has conveniently elided the difference between the two. Balu suffers from no such misconception and their conflict over his schooling comes to a head when he tears up the note-book in which his school marks are recorded and throws it in the Vinayak Mudali Street gutter, the text's central trope for waste, pollution and irretrievable loss. This incident comes close to repeating an earlier one when he has seized Margayya's account book and thrown *this* into the gutter, an episode which contributes to the end of the first phase of Margayya's career as a financial expert. It is also revealing in other ways, since it involves the text's most explicit contrast between the supposed purity of the scribal culture and pollution. When Margayya attempts to retrieve the account book from the gutter, a passing schoolmaster suggests he is acting outside his prescribed caste *dharma* and should be 'call[ing] a scavenger' (*FE* 43). In this respect, too, then Margayya appears as an interstitial protagonist, caught between different conceptions of caste identity at a particular moment in South Indian social history.

As Fakrul Alam points out,[38] critics have tended to underestimate the extent to which *The Financial Expert* depicts a transitional world. Taking commentators such as Naipaul, M.K. Naik and Meenakshi Mukherjee to task for their essentialized view of Malgudi as a 'harmonious', 'Hindu upper-caste pan-India [that is] resistant to change, eternal and immutable',[39] Alam argues that Narayan is 'more interested in recording a Malgudi that is caught in the throes of change than in affirming a conservative or reactionary position'.[40] Such a comment has general resonance for the contested representations of place that characterize Narayan's fiction and the specific subject with which Alam is concerned, the changes wrought by the end of the Raj. Additionally, it has particular force where *The Financial Expert* is concerned. As Alam points out, Margayya is a unique product of a particular moment in history. Although, in Graham Greene's phrase, his desire to propitiate Lakshmi blends 'age-old convention and the modern character',[41] initially his entrepreneurialism is a direct response to late colonial conditions.

There are numerous other elements in *The Financial Expert* which indicate the social transitions that Malgudi is undergoing in the late colonial period and which suggest that self-determination is, *pace* Naipaul, replacing quietism. When Balu is to be married and Margayya calls upon the astrologer to examine the prospective bridegroom and bride's horoscopes, he has little compunction about turning to a second astrologer when his first choice fails to match them. Similarly, Margayya and the printer

Madan Lal agree on the value of non-commitment in business, while bargaining over terms for publishing *Domestic Harmony*. More seriously, the partition of No. 14 D Vinayak Mudali Street suggests the breakdown of the traditional family structure. At the end though, after Margayya's economic collapse has been accompanied by his physical collapse, some kind of restitution of an older social order seems to occur. The novel concludes with Margayya saying he will return to doing business under the banyan tree. The division in the household may be about to end, since his brother has intervened to ensure that the house itself is exempted from the schedule that dispossesses Margayya of his assets; and there is also a partial reconciliation with Balu, who prior to this has gone to live in New Extension, where he has fallen under Dr Pal's influence, but now returns to the family fold. The ending of the novel also reaffirms the importance of family as Margayya asks for his grandson to be brought to him.

So one is left asking whether the pattern that Naipaul finds in *Mr Sampath* can be applied to *The Financial Expert*. Certainly the wheel has more or less come full circle at the end and some kind of reinstatement of an earlier world-view is taking place and Naipaul is by no means alone in seeing the novel in cyclic terms that are rooted in ancient Hindu culture. Lakshmi Holmstrom sees its structure as based on 'a very similar construction'[42] to *Mr Sampath*, viewing both as exemplifying the 'wheel of existence' explained in the *Gita*,[43] with its strictures on the dangers of worldly attachment. However the novel does not end with Margayya actually back under the banyan tree and this situation with its immersion in worldly concerns can hardly be seen as a metonym for Hindu quietism or non-attachment.[44] From the first Margayya's activities outside the bank have pointed up tensions between competing economies, as he shadows and subverts the colonial bank and this is hardly the stuff of Hindu fable. More significantly, his business life points towards tensions in modern Hinduism, which make *The Financial Expert* seem contemporary more than half a century after it was first published.

Published eight years after India attained Independence and seven years after Gandhi's assassination in 1948, *Waiting for the*

Mahatma has generally been regarded as Narayan's most political novel. In many ways it does deserve to be viewed as such, not
least because a credible version of the historical Gandhi appears
in the novel and many of the main tenets of his philosophy and
episodes from his career are sketched in. These include his 1930
Salt March to Dandi, his advocacy of *ahimsa* (non-violence)[45]
in the struggle for *swaraj* (home rule), his injunction to wear
khaddar (homespun) produced on one's own *charka* (spinning
wheel), the institution of the Quit India campaign in 1942, his
opposition to Partition, his fasting to try to combat the inter-
communal violence that followed Independence in East Bengal
and finally his assassination, the episode which brings the novel
to its abrupt ending. Yet, despite this, *Waiting for the Mahatma*
maintains a degree of distance from its political subject-matter.
It dramatizes the Gandhian ethic and the hero Sriram's involvement in the freedom struggle, but offers little direct commentary on nationalist politics and, as always in Narayan, places its
main emphasis on a Malgudi brahmin's encounter with forces
that disturb his way of life, which in this case are initiated by
the Mahatma's visit to Malgudi.

Sriram is another variation on the familiar Narayan type of
the 'little man', who has passing delusions of grandeur. When
he reaches the age of twenty and his grandmother gives him the
pass-book for an account in which she has saved his deceased
father's war pension, he dreams of breaking free from her and
fashioning an independent life of his own:

> He felt like a man with a high-powered talisman in his
> pocket, something that would enable him to fly or go
> anywhere he pleased. [...] Anyone was a big man. Himself
> not excluded. He had money, but people still seemed to
> think he was a little boy tied to the apron strings of his
> grandmother. His grandmother was very good, no doubt,
> but she ought to leave him alone. She did not treat him as
> a grown-up person. It was exasperating to be treated like
> a kid all the time.[46]

Sriram's financial independence and lack of family dependants
distinguish him from the other 'little man' heroes of Narayan's

middle-period novels. Unlike them, he has no occupation and he shows few signs of moving into the second *asrama* of the traditional Hindu life-cycle. However, although he has not yet assumed adult responsibilities, at the outset he seems to represent older Malgudi values to a greater extent than any of the other protagonists of the middle-period novels. After coming into his inheritance, he leads 'an unruffled, quiet existence' (*WM* 21) for four years and again the physical milieu he occupies is very obviously a correlative of his mental state. He lives in the bastion of conservative Malgudi values, Kabir Street, and Narayan's description of the street affords a fascinating contrast to that of Vinayak Mudali Street in *The Financial Expert*. It puts particular emphasis on the age of the street's houses and on the varying degrees to which they have been resistant to change. No. 14, where Sriram and his grandmother live, is especially associated with ancestral continuity:

> [...] All these houses were alike; you could see end to end the slender pillars and tiles sloping down as if all of them belonged to a single house. Many changes had occurred since they were built two centuries ago. [...] But there were still one or two houses which maintained a continuity, a link with the past. Number 14 was such a one. There the family lineage began centuries ago and continued still, though reduced to just two members – Sriram and his grandmother. (*WM* 10)

This physical and mental space is directly challenged by Gandhi's visit to Malgudi and when Sriram becomes a follower of the Mahatma, his arrested development, which has left him some way short of entering adulthood, quickly gives way to immersion in a completely different way of life. Yet it would be wrong to see him as entering into the second *asrama*, since the Gandhian social philosophy that he adopts contravenes orthodox Tamil brahmin beliefs.

Once again the spatial dynamics of the text, which are more varied than in any other Narayan novel, reflect the character's psychology and are central to the work's meaning. The enclosed world of Kabir Street and nearby Marker Road is contrasted with a number of other sites, which offer alternatives to its imagined security. Here, though, the canvas is broader and the reader who comes to *Waiting for the Mahatma* with a knowledge of the cause of the tragedy in *The English Teacher* or the pattern that Naipaul detects in *Mr Sampath* quickly comes to realise that the Gandhian challenge to caste exclusiveness is diametrically opposed to the brahminical psycho-social imperatives, which have dominated Narayan's earlier novels and which have demonized notions of polluted space. Naipaul's argument that Narayan's world is resistant to change is clearly likely to be problematic, when change is personified by India's most revered modern social thinker, and so it turns out. *Waiting for the Mahtama* is in no sense hagiography, but equally it is never critical of Gandhi and Sriram's involvement in the nationalist struggle foregrounds tensions in the fiction between a longing for conservative stability and a recognition, not just of the inevitability of change, but also of its more positive aspects.

Before Gandhi arrives in Malgudi, the local dignitaries who form the Reception Committee appointed to take care of the arrangements for his visit debate where he should be accommodated. One possibility is the town's Circuit House, a one-time East India Company building, where Clive is reputed to have stayed on his way to relieve the siege of Trichinopoly and subsequently the residence of colonial governors who have ensured that it has remained especially well appointed. Although Malgudi's citizens take pride in this building and distinguished visitors are usually housed there, the Committee quickly decides that its colonial provenance make it inappropriate for Gandhi. From the outset the Municipal Chairman has assumed that Gandhi will stay in 'the biggest and the best furnished house in Malgudi', Neel Bagh, his own 'palatial' (*WM* 38) residence in New Extension, and this alternative, a metonym for modern Malgudi luxury, eventually secures the Committee's approval. By the time Gandhi arrives, the Chairman has 'effected a few alterations [...] such as substituting Khaddar hangings for the gaudy chintz that had adorned his doorways and windows' (*WM* 44), replacing a picture of George V with those of figures such as Nehru, Sarojini Naidu and Annie Besant, along with one of Krishna instructing Arjuna in the *Gita*, and scattering a few *charkas* around the house. Narayan's satirical treatment of this cosmetic attempt to minister to the Mahatma's beliefs is underscored by a comment that makes its staged nature very explicit: 'No film decorator sought to create atmosphere with greater deliberation' (*WM* 45). The passage also involves dramatic irony, since it is narrated as a flashback from an account of the gatherings at which Gandhi has addressed vast crowds on the banks of the River Sarayu, as always the most spiritual site in the cultural geography of Malgudi, and how he has installed himself in a hut in the sweeper's colony beyond Sarayu, 'probably the worst area in the town' (*WM* 37). This is 'anything but a show-piece' (*WM* 51), though Gandhi, with *his* unerring sense of theatre, effectively makes it one when he decides to stay there. When he does visit Neel Bagh, he places a young urchin beside him on a divan, again very obviously transgressing the norms and exclusions of upper-caste Hindu society.

Earlier in Narayan's fiction such disruptive intrusions into the conservative establishment of Malgudi are generally seen as alien, but in a passage such as this, where Gandhi's behaviour exposes the Chairman's pretensions, sympathy clearly lies with the outsider rather than the Malgudi resident, perhaps because the Chairman represents the emergence of a new aristocracy. Be this as it may, neither the Chairman nor Gandhi is at the centre of the novel. Although there is more emphasis on external action and the geographical sweep is broader than in earlier Malgudi novels, the main drama is played out within Sriram's mind as he struggles to find his appropriate *dharma*. Within this psychodrama, the Chairman is no more than a bit-player, and although he is a catalyst who initiates Sriram into awareness that there is more to life than the values of Kabir Street and Market Road, Gandhi too remains a minor character, for the most part observed obliquely.

Drawn into the movement as much by his attraction to a young woman, Bharati, as by Gandhi's rhetoric, Sriram soon finds himself in a hut with the Congress workers and once again different attitudes to life are conveyed through a contrast between locations. Though Sriram is only a short distance from home, he is another Narayan protagonist[47] who finds a tiny movement away from his familiar environment initiates him into 'an entirely new world' (WM 72). Missing his room in Kabir Street, he nevertheless realizes that he is experiencing a complete reversal of values: 'There was a class of society where luxuries gave one a status, and now here was the opposite. [...] Here the currency was suffering and self-mortification' (WM 73). In a novel such as The English Teacher, the consequences of encountering the kind of polluted space that the sweepers' huts represent are disastrous and even the more worldly Margayya finds the gutter in Vinayak Mudali Street an omnipresent threat to his liminal existence. Here, though, respect for the Gandhian campaign against caste exclusiveness complicates the issue, again making it difficult to give much credence to the view that Narayan is representing an essentialist, unchanging India. Generally the regional specificity of his settings argues against this and virtually all the novels show their protagonists facing the changes brought about by modernity. However, Waiting for the Mahatma goes further in that Gandhi's advent quickly transforms Sriram from a 'contemplative idler'[48] into someone who actively espouses the new values that he introduces into Malgudi, as always a microcosm for South India. Orthodox values are personified by Sriram's grandmother who refuses to allow the scavenger who sweeps their Kabir Street backyard to come anywhere near her and prior to his politicization Sriram also baits the scavenger, but from the first time he hears Gandhi discourse on caste and untouchability, he is 'assailed by doubts of his own prowess and understanding' (WM 30). So, while his grandmother, who is suspicious of Gandhi, continues to stand for an older view of life, Sriram becomes an interstitial protagonist like Margayya.

His movement beyond the cloistered world of Kabir Street is paralleled by a similar shift of direction in the novel, which adopts a more open and inquisitive attitude to heterotopian spaces such as the hut than the earlier fiction and this is further extended in the second part, when Sriram becomes a social activist, taking the Mahatma's message into remote mountain villages. In this section the *novel* takes on a picaresque quality, travelling into rural locations which have little in common with Malgudi and effectively dramatizing the Gandhian creed that village India is the real India. The proximity of these villages – they are said to be 'within twenty miles of Malgudi and civilization' (*WM* 89) – forces Sriram to question his preconceptions and appreciate the limited parameters of his earlier physical and cognitive mappings of place. Previously he has had a pastoral vision of villages, founded on the stereotypical images provided by Tamil films (*WM* 87). Now he experiences a completely different spatial reality, which, as with the sweepers' huts in the first part of the novel, as well as being a physical eye-opener, engenders an epistemological sea change in his attitudes. And, although he sometimes has moments of doubt about the efficacy of his new vocation and longs to be back in 'the cosy isolation of Kabir Street' (*WM* 124) with his grandmother, the overall tenor of this section suggests the positive nature of the contribution he is making and further explodes the myth that Narayan's India is an essentialist conservative world.

In this part of the novel Sriram lives in another familiar Narayan heterotopian space, a ruined temple,[49] possibly suggesting that his involvement in social activism is underpinned by older spiritual codes and that there is continuity from the Hindu past. If so, this would not only be reconcilable with Gandhi's social philosophy, but also more generally the notion that progressive transformations need not necessarily involve a rupture with the past. Again, binary approaches to Narayan's work, such as Naipaul's construction of a generic opposition between 'social comedy' and 'Hindu fable', fail to allow for the co-existence and interplay between different social codes and discursive registers. Anticipating a theme that he would develop more fully in *The Guide*, where the reluctant Raja finds himself constructed by others as the modern-day equivalent of an ancient sage and comes to assume this persona, *Waiting for the Mahatma* is both a 'social inquiry'[50] into the changes being wrought in mid-twentieth-century South India and a study of the impact such changes have on the protagonist's choice of and adherence to an appropriate *dharma* for a brahmin in the second *asrama*.

Sriram has only a rudimentary knowledge of Gandhi's social philosophy and when he is joined in the temple by the photographer, Jagadish, a follower of Gandhi's rival Subhas Chandra Bose, who opposed his non-violent policies,[51] he is easily co-opted into more militant anti-British action, with the consequence that he becomes a wanted man. In addition to demonstrating his ignorance of competing views of Indian nationalism, an issue that the text also fails to explore, this section of the novel finds Sriram alternating between feelings of 'romantic importance', thinking he is 'a character out of an epic' whose actions will determine 'future history' (*WM* 168) and nostalgic longing for the tranquillity of his former Kabir Street life. The latter lead him to return to Malgudi in disguise. When he does so, he is shocked to be told that his grandmother has died, an event which would seem to signal the demise of the older Malgudi values of which she has been the main repository. However, during her cremation she comes back to life. Like most resurrections, this seems highly symbolic, but how exactly is one to read it? If Naipaul's view of the values that underpin Narayan's cosmos were correct, one might expect this to usher in some kind of reinstatement of the Hindu 'equilibrium',[52] but no such restitution takes place. Sriram's grandmother's brush with death at the polluted site of the cremation ground means that she has been irrevocably tainted and can never return to Kabir Street; a priest deems her a pariah whose re-entry into the insulated inner world of upper-caste Malgudi would threaten its very existence. So she departs for Benares, to live out her final days on the banks of the Ganges. In one sense this represents a happy ending for her, as it finds her following the path prescribed for older people in the *shastras*. From another point it is the complete opposite, since it signifies the end of the orthodox world she has personified *in Malgudi*. What she represents is lost to the liminal Sriram, the man caught up in the forces of social change, and he is subsequently shocked to discover that No. 14 Kabir Street has been rented out to a yarn merchant. Within the space of little more than a decade, the local impact of the nationalist struggle and the coming of Independence have brought about a radical change in the social and cultural landscape of Malgudi and this leaves Sriram, an orphan from the outset, dispossessed of both the last remaining member of his immediate family and his ancestral home. However, while this may suggest elegy, the overall mood of the novel is more complex, once again foregrounding the tensions and ambivalence generated by Gandhianism.

Tensions and ambivalence certainly inform Sriram's commitment to the nationalist struggle. His initiation into the movement by Bharati, who is more politically aware than he is, leads to a situation in which romance and political idealism are intertwined in his mind. At first his involvement in the cause seems to be inspired by motives that are far from political, but the dividing-line between the personal and the political in *Waiting for the Mahatma* is a porous one. Challenged by Bharati as to the meaning of her name, Sriram responds, '"Bharat is India, and Bharati is the daughter of India, I suppose"' (WM 59)[53] and the novel develops a set of analogies between its individual situations and public events, which lend themselves to interpretation as national allegory of a kind that is rare in Narayan. In this context the treatment of family, which dismantles the beliefs of orthodox Hinduism, is especially interesting. Like Sriram, Bharati is an orphan and when he proposes to her, she repeatedly avoids answering him, insisting they must *wait for the Mahatma*'s blessing. Close to the end of the novel, they finally receive this and Gandhi tells them they already have a family of thirty children who have been orphaned by the communal violence following in the wake of Partition. So the novel concludes with the possibility of the marriage of two orphans who, at the behest of a self-styled surrogate 'father' (WM 253) will raise an extended family of orphaned children. If one reads parentage as a trope for national genealogies and cultural transmission, a significance ascribed to it in many post-colonial texts,[54] then the novel would seem to be arguing for what Edward Said has termed 'affiliative identifications' as a replacement for 'filial' relationships.[55] Adoptive parentage is to replace biological bloodlines. Again this seems a far cry from the suggestion that Narayan's novels conclude with a reaffirmation of orthodox Hindu values.

Earlier Sriram's involvement in more militant anti-British action, such as derailing trains and exploding a crude bomb at an agricultural research station, leads to his being arrested and detained without trial. There is a symmetry about his finding himself in prison, since he has previously been told that the self-imposed Gandhian austerity of living in sweepers' huts is a preparation for jail, a fate which those involved in the struggle must expect. Despite this, prison, a 'heterotopia of deviation' in Foucault's taxonomy of 'other spaces',[56] is another location that throws the social codes on which Sriram has been raised into sharp relief. It is a space in which his brahmin desire to avoid any possibility of pollution expresses itself in resistance to communal ablutions; and his distaste for the food that he is given in prison leaves him nostalgic for his grandmother's cooking. Paradoxically, although it is a site of confinement, jail also proves to be an egalitarian space which renders brahmin exclusiveness impossible. The novel is part-*Bildungsroman* and Sriram's contact with lower-caste inmates blurs his sense of what constitutes humanness, as he becomes aware that he is 'running up against a new species of human being, speaking like monsters, but yet displaying sudden human qualities' (*WM* 193). Such transgression of categories destroys the 'well-defined boundaries [and] set activities' of his earlier world-view, in which everything has been 'calculable and capable of anticipation' (*WM* 223). The novel remains immersed in the viewpoint of the male brahmin protagonist, but far from reinforcing an orthodox world-view shows him, as a consequence of the independence struggle and the war, responding to other imperatives, many of which are rendered positively. William Walsh makes the point that, unlike the early work of his contemporary Mulk Raj Anand, Narayan's Gandhian novel stops some way short of protest.[57] This is undoubtedly true, but in its way *Waiting for the Mahatma* offers an equally probing interrogation of essentialist versions of 'India' by documenting the shift occurring within the consciousness of an upper-caste protagonist. While Anand imaginatively projects himself into the mind of a sweeper in his novel, *Untouchable* (1935), in which Gandhi also appears, Narayan's investigation of the struggle against conservative social values takes place within the mind of a South Indian brahmin, who might be expected to be more resistant to change.

Sriram's imprisonment is also highly significant in that he is in jail during the coming of Independence and so re-enters the outside world, which he finds alien, as a Rip van Winkle, a man who has been removed from the continuum of events leading up to and following Independence. Again Narayan emphasizes the adjacency of seemingly autonomous worlds: the jail turns out to be just outside Malgudi's town limits, but despite this physical proximity it is as if Sriram has been on another planet and where the novel is concerned, it means that the seismic political changes that have occurred are rendered even more obliquely. Narayan not only continues to keep macro-politics at a distance, but also suggests the extent to which nationalist discourse is manufactured, again doing so through understated commentary on how this has operated in Malgudi. This comes across vividly in a scene where, on his return to Malgudi, Sriram re-encounters Jagadish. The photographer shows him an album of pictures of Malgudi's Independence celebrations and Sriram is struck by the extent to which an image of the independent nation is being mediated; and when Jagadish speaks of himself as the 'chief architect of Independent India, the chief operator in ejecting the British' (*WM* 226), mirroring a fantasy that Sriram has entertained at an earlier point in the novel, the satire foregrounds the partisan nature of historiography.

At the end of the novel, in an episode reminiscent of a journey Margayya has made to Madras in *The Financial Expert*, Sriram travels by train to New Delhi to rejoin Gandhi and his entourage. And as in the earlier novel, although Malgudi's station provided the inspiration from which the whole of his fictional town grew,[58] the train proves an interstitial site, a space where different cultures come into contact. No single language unifies the various Indias travelling in its carriages and as Sriram journeys northwards, the lack of a shared language makes him increasingly aware of his South Indianness: 'He spoke Tamil and English, and they understood Hindi, Hindustani, Urdu or whatever it might be' (*WM* 234). Consequently, he feels 'more uncomfortable here than he had felt in the prison' (*WM* 235) and, as in the prison scenes, difference is also accentuated through another crucial marker of Indian regional identity, food. The train, the Grand Trunk Express, is as surely a trope for pan-Indian communication as Kipling's Great Trunk Road in *Kim*. It both functions as a space where identity is in transit and as a location that affords a microcosm of India, foregrounding differences between its communities, regions and classes.

Finally, in Delhi on the days immediately before Gandhi's assassination, Sriram is once again left *waiting* for the Mahatma, now in a colony of sweepers' huts. Initially, the most obvious significance of the novel's title is to the situation of the crowds of Malgudi residents who flock to the Mahatma's meetings on the banks of the Sarayu, but this is not its only resonance. The romantic plot also depends on *waiting* for the Mahatma and it is only several years after Sriram's first involvement with Gandhi and his followers that this waiting seems, in the conclusion of the novel, to be about to end. More than just this: although a version of the historical Gandhi is a presence in the novel and so waiting for the Mahatma is not an existential predicament like, say, waiting for Godot, a kind of representational deferral is also involved. Sriram becomes involved with Gandhi and the freedom struggle and yet the main events leading up to Indian Independence are reported obliquely at second- or third-hand. The dénouement appears to be moving towards a resolution of the romantic plot of the kind that concludes many Western novels of manners,[59] but when Gandhi who is to officiate as the priest at the wedding of Sriram and Bharati is assassinated, this pattern is frustrated and the novel concludes with an open ending which not only leaves the issue of whether the marriage will take place in abeyance, but also transgresses the conventions of both 'social comedy' and 'Hindu fable'.

Middle-period novels: *The Guide* to *The Painter of Signs*

Despite his involvement with Graham Greene and his tailoring aspects of his fiction to suit British tastes, Narayan did not travel outside India until the second half of his life. Then, after receiving a Rockefeller Foundation fellowship that took him to the United States in 1956, he paid a number of visits to American universities, among them the University of California at Berkeley and the University of Texas at Austin. Notable among these was a period as Visiting Professor at the University of Missouri in Kansas City[1] in the spring of 1969, a visit which he wrote about without identifying his hosts in one of his best-known essays, the title-piece of his collection, *Reluctant Guru* (1974). In this essay Narayan talks in characteristically witty vein about his difficulties in living up to the American belief that 'all Indians are spiritually preoccupied'[2] and expectations that he could provide 'the key to a mystic life' (*RG* 10). Claiming that the Indian contemporaries of Westerners of the hippie generation who were looking to India for spiritual illumination were more interested in learning how 'to organise a business or manufacture an atom bomb or an automobile than how to stand on one's head' (*RG* 14), Narayan wryly points up the ironies and misunderstandings inherent in such East-West encounters, focusing in particular on his own disinclination to play the part of spiritual sage:

> The belief in my spiritual adeptness was a factor that could not be easily shaken. I felt myself in the same situation as Raju, the hero of my *Guide* who was mistaken for a saint

and he began to wonder at some point himself if a sudden effulgence had begun to show in his face. (*RG* 15)

Nevertheless Narayan's experiences in the American academy *can* be related to a partial reinvention of his persona as a writer that had been taking place in the years after he first visited the country and, in writing a novel such as *The Guide* (1958), where Raju is taken to be a *sadhu*, Narayan had given explicit expression to elements that had been present, if latent, in his writing from the outset. Significantly *The Guide* was written during his visit to Berkeley,[3] suggesting that, consciously or unconsciously, he may in some way have responded to the West's fascination with Hindu mysticism, albeit before its enhanced interest in Indian spirituality in the 1960s accorded cult status to figures such as the Mahesh MaharishiYogi and Indian gurus, whether genuine or charlatans, became ten a penny. So, as in his early novels, which were partly shaped by the requirements of London publishers, Narayan once again appears to have been influenced by the demands of overseas markets. However, if one compares his acquiescence in his English make-over, with his later response to his type-casting as a spiritual guru when he became a Visiting Professor in America, the picture that emerges is that of a novelist who was willing, at least in part, to allow his identity to be trimmed to fit perceptions about the reading public in England in the 1930s, but more reluctant to allow himself to be subjected to a similar transformation in the America of the late 1950s and 1960s, even though he may seem to be sanctioning this in the novels he wrote after first travelling to the United States.

Influenced though he may have been by his sense of how India was constructed by Western eyes, it is reductive to see Narayan as having seriously compromised his writing to accommodate Western tastes. From the beginning of his career, his novels bring Western and Hindu – specifically Tamil brahmin – elements together in a variety of ways, to produce fiction that locates itself in a very specific discursive environment and is minutely attentive to the implications of place, but also succeeds in speaking to an international readership. Although he has often been misrepresented as an 'authentic' chronicler of a settled Indian world, Narayan's fiction fuses registers in an act of cultural brokerage that enables it to cross frontiers without losing a sense of Indian specifics, and demonstrates how fluid, fractured and fleeting these specifics can be. And, while his early English make-over resulted in a stifling of the Hindu elements in his fiction, his later American 'discovery' unleashed the possibility for according them centrality, thanks to the Orientalist vogue for Eastern spirituality that characterized Western, and particularly American, responses to India during this period. A shrewder businessman than many of the small-time entrepreneurs who are at the centre of most of his middle-period novels – he was, after all, the first Indian-English novelist to make a living from the profession of writing – Narayan saw the potential this vogue afforded for tapping the hitherto partly suppressed Hindu wellsprings of his narrative imagination. Turning the impetus to write for this new market to advantage led to the production of some of his finest novels and in this phase of his career the admixture of Western and Hindu elements that characterizes all his work resulted in narratives that fuse these two discursive strands in a range of unresolved and indeterminate relationships, while sometimes appearing to suggest that their infrastructure is Hindu. However, far from endorsing a mystical conception of India, this indeterminacy highlighted tensions in secular South Indian life in the third quarter of the twentieth century.

So, although Narayan had clearly become disillusioned with the cruder manifestations of stereotyping Indians as 'mystical' and 'spiritual', by the time he left the University of Missouri at the end of the 1960s, he seems, in the intervening years, to have enjoyed the license it offered him to write on subjects that had been an important part of his Tamil brahmin upbringing. During this period of his life, he embarked on a 'methodical study of the [mythic Hindu] tales [...]with the help of a scholar',[4] collected stories for the selection of retold myths that appeared as *Gods, Demons and Others* (1964)[5] and in the 1970s produced versions of *The Ramayana* (1972) and *The Mahabharata* (1978). Most significantly, in his new American incarnation the 'reluctant guru' found himself able to give freer expression to the Hindu layers of his imagination in his fiction and this led to the writing of two of his best novels: *The Guide*, which many consider to be his finest book,[6] and *The Man-Eater of Malgudi* (1961),which this study will argue is a superior work and his most consummately achieved piece of fiction.

The Guide may have been written in Berkeley, but like Narayan's two previous novels, *The Financial Expert* and *Waiting for the Mahatma*, its more immediate origins came from an actual Indian source and when asked in an interview about the possibility of elements in the novel having been 'transformed' by his American experiences, he referred to it as 'totally Indian'.[7] In *My Days*, he explains how the idea for 'a novel about someone suffering enforced sainthood' came to him from a Mysore source:

> A recent situation in Mysore offered a setting for such a story. A severe drought had dried up all the rivers and tanks; Krishnaraja Sagar, an enormous reservoir feeding channels that irrigated thousands of acres, had also become dry, and its bed, a hundred and fifty feet deep, was now exposed to the sky with fissures and cracks, revealing an ancient submerged temple, coconut stumps, and dehydrated crocodiles. As a desperate measure, the municipal council organized a prayer for rains. A group of Brahmins stood knee-deep in water (procured at great cost) on the dry bed of Kaveri, fasted, prayed, and chanted certain mantras continuously for eleven days. On the twelfth day it rained, and brought relief to the countryside. (*MyD* 167)

This potential for alternative interpretations afforded by this episode clearly made it ideal grist for Narayan's fictional mill. More than just this: the exposure of the ancient temple that had lain beneath the waters of the modern reservoir, an event which Narayan takes over in *The Guide*, served as a metonym for the notion of an archaeologically layered India, albeit one in which the different strata were coming to exist contiguously rather than in a temporal sequence, since an ancient infrastructure was now present on the surface.

Predictably the ambiguity over whether supranatural or normal meteorological forces were responsible for the coming of the rain to the area around the Krishnaraja Sagar reservoir is carried over into the novel, where, notwithstanding the views of some of Narayan's critics who have been eager to detect a causal relationship between Raju's fasting and the presumed end of the drought, the conclusion leaves the issue of whether spiritual intervention has occurred open. In *The Guide*, the group of brahmins is replaced by a single *sadhu*, the reluctant former tourist guide, Raju, who has resisted the burden of 'sainthood' imposed on him by the villagers among whom he finds himself and remains a suspect holy man to the very last. Weakened by hunger, he *says* he can feel rain coming from the hills and, although this may suggest the end of the drought is imminent, the open ending leaves this unresolved. Numerous critics seem to have missed this and the range of misreadings of the ending perpetrated by critics is a striking example of the extent to which books read people just as people read books.[8] The actual words of the closing sentences are as follows:

> It was difficult to hold Raju on his feet, as he had a tendency to flop down. They held him as if he were a baby. Raju opened his eyes, looked about, and said, 'Velan, it's raining in the hills. I can feel it coming up under my feet, up my legs – ' He sagged down.[9]

Various issues remain undecided. The text not only leaves the question of Raju's possible promotion to sainthood open, it also fails to offer any kind of definitive information on whether the rains are actually coming or what Raju's eventual fate will be. However, at least two eminent critics have said that he *dies* at the end of the novel[10] and others refer to his losing consciousness,[11] but 'sagg[ing] down' is hardly conclusive evidence of either. Similarly, although the people of the local village, Mangala (a name which denotes spiritual auspiciousness), convince themselves that Raju is a saint, particularly when he is seen to be fasting to break the drought, he initially deceives them by eating in secret and it remains a moot point as to whether or not he subsequently undergoes a transformation. It is equally uncertain whether the rains he anticipates will, as in the real-life inspiration for the story, arrive and, if so, whether they will have been sent by providence.

The crucial point is, of course, that Narayan chooses to end the novel here with all these issues unresolved. Commenting on *The Guide* on a later occasion, he said that he did not know what happened to Raju at the end;[12] and in an essay on the life of writing, he expressed exasperation at interviewers who asked him whether Raju 'dies at the end of the story and whether it rained, after all',[13] in this case demonstrating particular irritation at being asked the question by those who had only seen the film version of the novel, which he felt betrayed the spirit of his original.[14] In short, *The Guide* resists any form of closure. The ending raises the possibilities that some kind of spiritual transformation may be taking place within Raju *and* that this may be accompanied by divine intervention to end the drought, but the final scenes are narrated in a deadpan, documentary-like manner, leaving the possibilities that Raju remains a charlatan and that the drought will continue as reasonable alternative inferences.

Comparing the novel with V.S. Naipaul's *The Mystic Masseur* (1957), which also deals with the supposed metamorphosis of a rogue hero into a holy man,[15] M. K. Naik suggests that *The Guide* is finally very different from Naipaul's very slightly earlier novel, since in this case the hero *is* transformed 'from a picaro into a pilgrim'.[16] Certainly there is a difference: Naipaul's protagonist, Ganesh, fairly obviously remains a charlatan to the very end, though the ironic technique precludes this being said in as many words,[17] but Narayan's neutrality leaves the issue open. Raju's status as a *sadhu* is a product of the views of others and so it is as if Narayan is holding the phenomenon of the Hindu holy man up for inspection, while declining to offer any kind of definitive assessment himself. In the closing episodes, Raju's fast attracts a good deal of media attention and amid the crowd of reporters that flocks to Mangala to cover his story is an American documentary film-maker, Malone, who is eager to 'shoot' a documentary about the 'Swami' (*Guide* 216). Narayan simply reports, but one appealing way of viewing the figure of Malone is to see him as a surrogate for potential American readers of the novel. His response to Raju, which blends ingenuousness and disingenuousness, seems to mirror Narayan's later 'Reluctant Guru' comments on American interest in India and possibly also involves a metaliterary anticipation of how he feels the novel may be read in the United States. His comments on his identification with Raju, a secular man who finds himself the object of American interpretation and appropriation as a guru, certainly lend support to such a view, although in Raju's case 'enforced sainthood' is first imposed on him by the local villagers.

In its engagement with the possibility that classical Hindu discourse may provide an infrastructure for contemporary South Indian experience, *The Guide* is typical of Narayan's practice in this period of his fiction. The American-inspired legitimization of his interest in orthodox Hindu culture, based on classic Sanskrit and Tamil texts, encourages him into a greater engagement with his brahmin heritage and ancient myths and beliefs provide a possible bedrock of meaning for the novels of his middle period. Nevertheless, as with all his fiction, these novels are about contemporary secular Hindu society and the ways in which ordinary people react to everyday situations. So, while sometimes seeming to suggest that age-old archetypes and codes underpin modern behaviour, the novels are more concerned with demonstrating ways in which discourses on Indian society that may seem very remote from one another co-exist and intersect. Again, Naipaul's binary opposition between social comedy and Hindu fable distorts the complexity of tone to be found in Narayan's fiction of this period. Thus as a Hindu fable *The Guide* is inscrutably enigmatic, but it does allow for the possibility that paranormal forces, allied with ancient beliefs, *could* be efficacious in averting an ecological disaster; and it also works within the conventions of social realism.

The sections leading up to and dealing with Raju's fast are narrated by an omniscient third-person narrator. They are interspersed with Raju's confessional first-person account of his former life, as told to one of the villagers, Velan, and much of the novel's force emerges from the cross-cutting between its two actions and modes of focalization. Far from being a simple account of the way in which a picaro becomes a pilgrim, though one can argue that this progression is inherent in the juxtaposition of the two narratives, *The Guide* employs a complex contrapuntal structure. The movement between the story of how Raju becomes a putative *sadhu* in the present and his account of his past, which centres on his activities as a tourist guide and his affair with Rosie, a married temple dancer from Madras, involves a dialectical interplay between the two modes of narration as well as the two actions. The first-person narrative clearly enlists sympathy for a character whose transgressive behaviour might otherwise seem reprehensible, while the third-person 'camera eye'[18] view of him in his *sadhu* persona withholds judgement on the issue of whether the former tourist guide can now reasonably be viewed as a spiritual guide. Several critics have commented on this in their discussions of the novel's 'braided time-scheme',[19] for the most part arguing that the contrapuntal technique serves to emphasize the difference between Raju's earlier persona and the condition of enforced sainthood thrust upon him in the later action, though the effect of the dialectical interplay between first- and third-person narration has not gone completely unnoticed.[20] If, though, as most of its critics seem to assume, *The Guide*'s primary purpose is to demonstrate how a spiritual *dharma* is imposed on a hitherto worldly man, why, one wants to ask, does it devote far more space to his earlier picaroon phase? The answer may be that this is simply careless, unplanned writing,[21] but another possibility is that there are more extensive connections between the two narratives than have generally been noticed. If so, approaches which place most of their emphasis on Raju's possible transformation into a *sadhu* distort the overall thrust of the novel. Taken together, the details of his earlier life as a child, as a shop-keeper and as the tourist guide 'Railway Raju' and his account of his dealings with Rosie and her archaeologist husband Marco, his extra-marital affair with Rosie, his involvement with her in her career as a highly successful professional dancer and his imprisonment for forging her signature loom much larger.

One clear connection between the two narratives is that both suggest the performative nature of personality and although Raju's supposed transformation into a 'saint' suggests a fairly passive immersion in a new identity, it can be seen as a logical extension of everything that has preceded it, the final stage in his serial adoption of a range of personae. As William Walsh pus it, 'There is an unbroken connection between Raju, the guide who lived for others, whose character and activity were a reflection of otherness, and Raju (ex-jailbird, ex-lover of Rosie the dancer) the prophet surrounded by devout villagers waiting for a message or a miracle. In each case he is a projection of what people need.'[22] Perceptive though this is, it only partly explains the complex interrelationships between the two narratives that make up *The Guide*. Interaction between them also occurs in a number of other ways, most notably in parallels between the interests of the characters of Marco and Rosie and the issues that emerge in the third-person narrative of Raju's passage into 'sainthood'.

Rosie's dancing and Marco's archaeological work initially seem to be diametrically opposed. When Raju asks Rosie what interests her, she replies '"Anything except cold, old stone walls"' (*Guide* 72) and both her sexuality and her ambition to be a professional classical dancer in contemporary South India seem to be at odds with Marco's absorption in what Raju sees as a sterile past: 'Dead and decaying things seemed to unloosen his tongue and fire his imagination, rather than things that lived and moved and swung their limbs' (*Guide* 71). So they come across as an ill-matched couple who represent a contrast between stasis and kinesis, a dead past and a living present. Raju's narration tips the balance firmly in favour of the latter. Despite his familiarity with the ancient cave-paintings that Marco is examining, he is dismissive of the mythic past, seeing it as ossified and irrelevant to contemporary living:

> I was bored with his ruin-collecting activities. The
> wall painting represented episodes from the epics and

> mythology, and all kinds of patterns and motifs, with men,
> women, and kings and animals, in a curious perspective
> and proportion of their own, and ancient like the rocks. I
> had seen hundreds like them, and I saw no point in seeing
> more. I had no taste for them, just as he had no taste for
> other things. (*Guide* 71)

In contrast his fascination for Rosie not only leads him into his affair with her, but also into his becoming the agent who secures her rise to fame as a dancer.

Dance may seem to be a secondary concern of the novel, functioning mainly as a medium for developing Rosie's character, but it is a significant subject in its own right and the details of Rosie's training and career as a dancer afford Narayan with an opportunity to draw on his lifelong interest in Indian classical music, specifically the *karnatic* tradition of South India.[23] Rosie's success is as a practitioner of *Bharat Natyam*, generally considered to be the oldest and most traditional of the six major forms of Indian classical dance and still widely performed in Tamil Nadu,[24] and so, as she trains herself to become proficient in this ancient art, she is undergoing a possible transformation which is analogous to Raju's in the later action. Additionally, dance is a trope for performative identity more generally and Narayan seems to be tracing correspondences between ancient thinking on the nature and significance of *Bharat Natyam* and its manifestations in the present. Raju's possible metamorphosis takes place after the submerged ancient temple reappears; Rosie becomes a star performer of a classical art form that saw a 'resurgence'[25] at the beginning of the twentieth century and so the novel also deals with the relationship between ancient and modern thinking in the sections that focus on her career. Marco may be the professional archaeologist of the novel, but Raju and Rosie are also involved with excavations of the past.

Rosie is one of a number of Narayan's female characters who confound categories, partly but not exclusively, because of their caste backgrounds. She is, like Shanta Bai in *The Dark Room*, both educated (she has an M.A. in Economics) and a woman who feels she has a stigma attached to her because of her caste background. She comes from a '"family traditionally dedicated to the temples as dancers"' and, she explains to Raju, is consequently viewed as a '"public woman"'. His infatuation with her makes him dispute this categorization and he both tells her that she belongs to '"the noblest caste on earth"' (*Guide* 73) and asserts that caste discrimination is a thing of the past. Others, including his mother and his domineering uncle, who later appears on the scene in the role of protector of the family honour, take a different view of a *devadasi*. The novel, which sees her from Raju's unreliable viewpoint, remains ambivalent on the issue of her status, but exhibits little of the attempt to police caste boundaries that informs much of Narayan's early fiction and Rosie's character more generally is presented in a positive light. Unlike the siren figure of Shanta Bai, who serves as a foil to the more orthodox though equally complex Savitri in *The Dark Room*, she is represented as a woman who demonstrates both professional and personal integrity, behaving impeccably towards Raju after he has been dishonest towards her.

Rosie is defined by her dancing and when, with Raju's help, she embarks on her study of *Bharat Natyam*, her absorption in her art seems to distance her from the temple-dancer stereotype, with its lowly associations. In his next novel, *The Man-Eater of Malgudi*, Narayan would include a character, Rangi, who, though not unsympathetic, more straightforwardly embodies the traditional association between temple-dancers and prostitutes. Rosie's training to become a serious exponent of classical dance is, however, built around a study of Sanskrit texts, particularly the methods embodied in the classic work on the subject, Bharat's *Natya Shastra* (or *Science of Drama*), without which she feels it will be 'impossible to keep the purity of the classical forms' (*Guide* 107). Coupled with this, in a passage which reads as a fictional equivalent of Narayan's decision to enlist a scholar to help him with his own study of Sanskrit texts,[26] she asks Raju to find her a Sanskrit pundit, who can read episodes from the *Ramayana* and the *Mahabharata* to her. Narayan's study of ancient texts led to *retellings* of the epics and other mythic tales and fictional works in which they are transformed in contemporary situations. Rosie's study of the *Natya Shastra* may suggest an attempt to learn the conventions of an ancient form of dance, which if simply copied in a mimetic way would preclude creative *re*interpretation. In fact, though, she turn to classic writing on the subject as a source from which she 'can pick up so many ideas for *new* compositions' (*Guide* 108; my italics) and this is very much in keeping with the spirit of Bharat's treatise. The *Natya Shastra* outlines a theory of *rasas* or tastes, which, though developed primarily in relation to drama and dance, has implications for all artistic genres and stresses the relationship between artistic taste and food consumption.[27] As H.L. Seneviratne observes, the treatise sees the process of aesthetic creation as analogous to the consumption of food:

> Just as the *rasa* of food is an essence derived from cooking the gross material of the ingested food by the action of the digestive fires, the *rasa* of aesthetics is a fine emotion born of the transformation of gross and mundane experience by the multistaged extractive and distillative deliberation involving *anubhava* [extension of the stimulative process by suggestive behavior such as glances and body movement], *vibhava* [refers to external stimulus], and *vyabhicharibhava* [an instance of ancillary or transient emotion: the joy in love].[28]

Narayan would no doubt have baulked at seeing this kind of aesthetic theorizing applied to his work, but *The Guide* is centrally concerned with the performative aspects of identity and an awareness of this helps to pinpoint the particular quality of Rosie's dedication to performance arts. Though she is less of a chameleon than Raju, she too seems to undergo a transformation in her identity – in this case from denigrated 'public woman' to respected classical dancer – because of her devotion to older 'methods' *and* her capacity to restage these in new ways. Like Narayan's fiction, which transports ancient myths and beliefs into particular contemporary situations, Rosie's performances as a dancer open up the possibility of a re-enactment of classical modes, which transforms 'gross and mundane experiences'. Seen like this, then, her career as a dancer provides a loose parallel with Raju's perceived metamorphosis into a *sadhu*, which is the last in the series of roles that he occupies. But at this point the caveat that Narayan might baulk at such a reading should perhaps be remembered, since the episodes dealing with Rosie's rise to fame also contain satirical observations on the contemporary commercialization of *Bharat Natyam* as 'the greatest art business today' (*Guide* 143), a theme that Narayan also developed in his story, 'Musical Commerce'.[29]

The dance motif also has resonance in relation to the work of the third member of *The Guide*'s eternal triangle, Rosie's husband Marco. The couple seem to be on the edge of a reconciliation when he discovers a fresco of dance notations dating from around the fifth century.[30] At this point, Rosie's enthusiasm for Marco's find suggests a degree of convergence between their interests. However, Marco, resistant to any suggestion that the classical and the contemporary may be related, quickly rejects this, branding Rosie's dancing 'street-acrobatics' and 'not art' (*Guide* 130, 131). So he remains sceptical about her artistry, whereas the trickster Raju has the vision to see her dancing as 'pure abstraction' (*Guide* 110) and initially evinces a clear preference for her vitality over what he sees as Marco's sterility. Subsequently Raju's estimate of Marco's work is less dismissive. Having initially seen him as a copyist and, it would seem, having had little regard for this particular branch of palaeography, Raju later becomes more sympathetic to Marco's view that his discoveries will 'be responsible for the rewriting of history' (*Guide* 129). Marco's claim may be inflated, but it is partly endorsed when his work on the cave paintings appears in a beautifully produced monograph entitled *The Cultural History of South India* and is hailed in the press as '"An epoch-making discovery in Indian cultural history"' (*Guide* 176). As with Raju and Rosie, his excavation of an ancient Tamil mode opens up the possibility of transforming present-day experience through performative interaction with the classical past. It is no coincidence that the frescoes he finds contain what Raju calls 'abstract verse about some theories of an ancient musical system' (*Guide* 129), since this suggests an affinity between his project and Rosie's study of the *Natya Shastra*. Beyond this it is possible to read these passages as relating to Narayan's foray into ancient Sanskrit and Tamil lore, which becomes markedly more evident in this period of his career.

Despite this engagement with the classical past, *The Guide* does not delve very deeply into the realms of Hindu mythology, a field that had already provided a coda for *Mr Sampath* and a reference-point for several other elements in the earlier novels, such as the Savitri motif in *The Dark Room*. One critic has argued that the 'myth of Shiva and the Ganges, though not explicit, is the prototype underlying this story of a sinner-saint'[31] and developed this by seeing Rosie as playing the part of Parvathi to Raju's Shiva. Certainly, as always in Narayan, the Ganges is the archetypal river underlying the general reverence for river sites that pervades his fiction, particularly in his scenes set around the banks of Malgudi's Sarayu, and so this suggestion seems very plausible. Yet, assuming one accepts it, mythic correspondences are only latent in *The Guide*. In Narayan's next novel, *The Man-Eater of Malgudi* there is no such reticence about the use of ancient legend. The mythic infrastructure of the story is made explicit and yet the *Man-Eater* is every bit as ambivalent in its use of classical analogues. While it is more overtly mythical than *The Guide*, it is also a novel in which social comedy flourishes and although in one sense the co-existence of such comedy and Hindu fable legitimizes Naipaul's two readings of Narayan's fiction, the seamless way in which they overlap argues against seeing them as in any way opposed.

The Guide is a picaresque novel in both of the most commonly used senses of the term. Raju is, at least initially, a rogue hero and the novel employs a picaresque structure, particularly in the sections where it follows his excursions around Malgudi and the surrounding area as a tourist guide and his later travels as Rosie's manager all over south India, 'with Cape Cormorin at one end and the border of Bombay at the other, and from coast to coast (*Guide* 169). Familiar Narayan sites do reappear: his father's shop, where Raju works in his youth, is at the seminal Malgudi location of the railway station,[32] his period in jail is reminiscent of Sriram's imprisonment in *Waiting for the Mahatma* and the temple where he lives during his *sadhu* phase evokes the temples in the *The Dark Room* and *Waiting for the Mahatma* However, once he leaves his father's shop, Raju's travels into less enclosed spaces depart from the dominant pattern of the middle period novels, in which the orderly life of a small businessman is disturbed by the advent of outside forces. In some ways the broader geographical coordinates of *The Guide* make it similar to *Waiting for the Mahatma*, but the contrast between conservative Malgudi, as represented by Kabir Street in the earlier novel, and heterotopias which challenges caste orthodoxies is, despite the impugning of Rosie's background, less marked now. There is a brief return to Narayan's drawing of demarcation lines between the established centre of Malgudi and more modern areas of the town, when, during the period of Rosie's career as a dancer, the couple move into a 'stylish house at New Extension' (*Guide* 165), while Raju's mother is evicted from the family home. However, ancestral continuity plays a less significant role here and the place where 'Railway Raju' seems most at home, the station, is after all, as the main point of entry and exit for the town, a transitional site. So the physical and cultural geography of *The Guide* distinguishes it from the majority of Narayan's earlier novels, where the protagonists often feel that 'other' space begins just a few blocks away from their home.

The Man-Eater of Malgudi returns to more familiar Malgudi territory. Like Srinivas in *Mr Sampath*, Nataraj, the protagonist, is a printer with a shop in Market Road and his home is in long-established Kabir Street. His settled daily routine is disturbed when one day the man-eater of the title, Vasu, a bullying taxidermist, bursts into his premises. From the moment when he first appears, Vasu infringes the 'sacred traditions'[33] of Nataraj's press by going through a blue curtain that separates its inner sanctum – and with it Nataraj's sense of private space – from the little room at the front of his shop that he calls his 'parlour', a public space where he entertains his customers. In so doing, Vasu almost tears the curtain, an act of symbolic penetration which anticipates all his subsequent behaviour; and when he takes over Nataraj's attic, without Nataraj ever really agreeing to the arrangement, and uses it for his work as a taxidermist, the brahmin Nataraj is horrified to find that the room has been 'converted into a charnel house' by a 'murderer of innocent creatures (*M-E* 52). So Nataraj is faced with a crisis heterotopia within his protected inner space. Vasu's appropriation of the attic is clearly a psychic as well as a physical invasion, particularly since it violates Nataraj's belief in *ahimsa* ('the Hindu ethical idea advocating non-injury or kindness to other creatures'[34]). Characteristically, though, Narayan stops short of outright censure, instead presenting alternative possibilities that cluster around different interpretations of the word 'preservation', a central subject in the novel. When Nataraj expresses astonishment at Vasu's saying that he plans to launch a monograph about his work that he is writing at a conference on wild life preservation, Vasu brazenly claims that his profession makes him a preserver of life (*M-E* 98–9). Exactly what Vasu represents is open to debate. He claims to have a 'scientific outlook' (*M-E* 127) that is the opposite of Nataraj's sentimentalism and he clearly symbolizes the incursion of an outside force into the Malgudi cosmos. However, although he adopts an 'American style', which Nataraj feels he has picked up from 'crime books and films' (*M-E* 31), whether this force should be seen as epitomizing modernity generally or more specifically either Western encroachments or the intrusion of another part of India into the South remains a matter for speculation and by the end of the novel Narayan will have pointed readers in a completely different direction.

The consequences of Vasu's intrusion into Nataraj's world are, on one level, highly comic. However, the main story-line of the novel also involves a reworking of an archetypal Hindu pattern. From the moment when Vasu first appears, he is described in terms that suggest that he is a demonic force: 'a new head appeared [...] – a tanned face, large powerful eyes under thick eyebrows, a large forehead and a shock of unkempt hair, like a black halo' (*M-E* 15); and as the tale unravels, it becomes increasingly clear that he is being associated with the *rakshasas*, or

demons, of ancient legend. His taxidermy provides a direct challenge to Nataraj's belief in the sanctity of life and this is underscored by various mythological references. When Nataraj visits
the attic he is shocked to discover the carcasses of various animals
including a cat that has frequented his press, a tiger poached from
the forest and a stuffed crow. He is, however, most disturbed
to see Vasu working on a dead eagle and the full extent of his
repugnance emerges as he tries to convince Vasu that the bird is
a sacred *garuda*, 'the messenger of God Vishnu' (*M-E* 50).

This detail directs attention to a number of Krishna/Vishnu
analogies that permeate the text, possibly even informing the
choice of blue for the colour of the curtain that separates the inner
world of Nataraj's press from his parlour. Later, in what seems as
though it will be the climactic episode of the novel (though, in a
manner typical of Narayan's narrative technique, this turns out
to be a climax which is superseded by an anti-climax), Nataraj
feels that he may have to act, in direct opposition to Vasu's view
of preservation, as a Vishnu-like preserver of life. One of his
friends is a poet, who is writing an epic about the life of Krishna,
an incarnation of Vishnu, in monosyllabic verse, and during the
course of the action the poet arrives at the moment of the hero's
marriage to Radha. To celebrate this, it is agreed to hold an elabo-
rate ceremony, centred on an elephant, in conjunction with the
annual spring festival at the local Krishna temple. Worried that
Vasu, who has been quick to grasp the commercial possibilities of
a dead elephant, will try to kill it, Nataraj initially feels that he
must act as the elephant's protector, but then remembers a mythic
tale that suggests otherwise and this bolsters up his natural incli-
nation towards inaction. In the tale the elephant Gajendra is saved
from a crocodile's jaws through the intervention of Vishnu who
gives Gajendra the strength to save himself (*M-E* 132).[35] When
he remembers this, Nataraj is able to persuade himself that the
problem will solve itself without his having to lift a finger; and
when he falls prey to a seemingly psychosomatic illness, this is
exactly what happens.

Quite where comedy ends and what Naipaul sees as Hindu
quietism takes over is hard to pinpoint. Indeed, they seem to

be seamlessly co-existent, since the narrative seldom suggests any disjunction and even passages that offer themselves up for satirical reading are not unequivocally comic. The poet's mono-syllabic epic can be seen as farcical – it contains lines such as 'Girls with girls did dance in trance' (*M-E* 7); Nataraj's behaviour frequently smacks of self-interest; and his habitual response to crises is to surrender himself to 'a mood of complete resigna-tion' (*M-E* 57). Moreover, there is obvious irony when he uses Gandhian rhetoric to justify his inertia: 'Non-violence would be the safest policy with him [Vasu]. Mahatma Gandhi was right in asking people to carry on their fight with the weapon of non-violence; the chances of getting hurt were much less (*M-E* 155).[36] Ultimately, though, such comic passages remain poised somewhere between satire and a deeper philosophical irony and it is clear that the novel dramatizes an archetypal conflict, while seeing it through a Hindu lens. The two characters are very obviously foils to one another and at one point Nataraj calls Vasu 'a perfect enemy' (*M-E* 70). Vasu sets himself up as 'a rival to Nature' (*M-E* 50), while Nataraj champions 'the natural' and the balance is weighted in favour of the aspects of brahminical Hinduism that Nataraj represents, though not unequivocally or uncomplicatedly so.[37] Lest readers miss the mythic dimension, Nataraj's employee Sastri, whom he describes as 'an orthodox-minded Sanskrit semi-scholar', explains that Vasu 'shows all the definitions of a *rakshasa*' and goes on to characterize this figure as 'a demoniac creature, who possessed enormous strength, strange powers, and genius, but recognized no sort of restraints of man or God' (*M-E* 72). Sastri refers to the *Ramayana*[38] and various *puranas* to prove his point, particularly citing the story of Bhasmasura, a *rakshasa* who possesses the gift of scorching everything he touches, but eventually destroys himself when Vishnu, in the guise of the beautiful dancer, Mohini,[39] persuades him to imitate her gesture of placing her palms on her head (*M-E* 73).[40] Sastri points out that *rakshasas* always contain the seeds of their own destruction and when Vasu kills himself in the dénouement by striking his head violently in an attempt to kill two mosquitoes that have settled there, the Bhasmasura story has been acted out, albeit in a modern-day reworking that *could* be seen to involve comic deflation and, however one reads the tone, is clearly not a carbon copy of the *puranic* original. The dividing line between mock-epic and epic is a thin one[41] and again it is typical of the novel's practice that it collapses the distinction, providing a humorous twentieth-century equivalent of the ancient tale that is both consonant with the supposedly realistic mode of the novel genre *and* the mythic ethos of a *rakshasa* story.

The text is, then, restaging an ancient Hindu fable in the modern form of a novel, where there is at least the semblance of an appeal to social realism, and numerous critics have commented on its mythic underpinning.[42] The mythic dimension is consolidated at the end, where Sastri reminds Nataraj – and the novel's readers – of his earlier interpretation of events:

> '[...] Every demon appears in the world with a special boon of indestructibility. Yet the universe has survived all the *rakshasas* that were ever born. Every demon carries within him, unknown to himself, a tiny seed of self-destruction, and goes up in thin air at the most unexpected moment. Otherwise what is to happen to humanity?' He narrated again for my benefit the story of Bhasmasura the unconquerable, who scorched everything he touched, and finally reduced himself to ashes by placing the tips of his fingers on his own head. (*M-E* 173–4)

This provides a coda that could perhaps have served as the last statement of the novel, but having reiterated his explanation, Sastri is now ready to return to work. His pragmatic sense matches his capacity for philosophical punditry and he tells Nataraj, '"We must deliver K.J.'s [aerated drink] labels this week ..."'. Adhering to the comic reversal of employer and employee roles that has characterized their relationship throughout, Nataraj humbly replies '"Yes, Sastri, I am at your service"' (*M-E* 174). Having heard how the universe is ordered, he will knuckle down and follow Sastri's instructions to make sure that the bottle labels, which they have been working on since Chapter 2, will be completed on time. In short, philosophical speculation complete, normal everyday business can be resumed and the novel ends on a mundane secular note.

Naipaul does not discuss *The Man-Eater of Malgudi* in *India: A Wounded Civilization*, but since both comedy *and* mythic analogies loom large in the text, it is arguably the Narayan novel that most readily lends itself to discussion in terms of his contention that Hindu fable lies beneath the surface social comedy. Nataraj's inertia and the novel's apparent endorsement of it when the problems generated by Vasu are resolved without his having to take action, also provide a *prima facie* case for viewing *The Man-Eater of Malgudi* as a fictional manifesto for adherence to belief in *karma*, referred to by Naipaul as 'the Hindu killer, the Hindu calm, which tells us that we pay in this life for what we have done in past lives: so that everything we see is just and balanced'.[43] So both the fabulist elements and the philosophy of the *Man-Eater* provide evidence for viewing it as a contemporary reworking of not just ancient myth, but also of the metaphysical system it embodies. However, just as it is mistaken to read *The Guide* as a fable about how saints are made, it is inadequate simply to view the *Man-Eater* as a parable about how demons destroy themselves.

Although *The Man-Eater of Malgudi* readily lends itself to interpretation as mythic fable, particularly because Sastri, a mouthpiece for brahmin orthodoxy, is allowed to restate his viewpoint at the end, as a totality it resists enclosure in the strait-jacket of such a reading. This is especially so because of the extent and nature of its comedy, which make it particularly reductive to see Sastri's pontifical explanation, significant though it is, as expressive of the totality of the 'meaning' of the novel. As always, Narayan stops short of completely committing himself to any single ethical or stylistic imperative and the effect is to stage a complex debate on possible ways in which the events he has chosen to present may be interpreted. The 'Hindu fable' may appear to be given primacy at the end, but this does not erase the 'social comedy'. Whereas Naipaul's reading suggests that an *under*lying ancient level of meaning resurfaces, like the submerged temple of *The Guide*, to impose itself as a palimpsest that now *over*lays the everyday action, the novel as a whole suggests their interdependence.

In this, his most mythic novel, Narayan remains a commentator on the secular Hindu life and although the *Man-Eater* invokes the figure of the *rakshasa* to explain Vasu and much of its force emerges from the dialectical interplay between the two main characters, it devotes more attention to Nataraj's everyday life as a *grihastya*, going about his daily business and interacting with his friends, family and fellow-townsfolk. In the opening chapter he gives an account of his early morning routine, which takes the form of a walk to the river, where he performs both his ablutions and a *puja*, 'a prayer to the Sun, to illumine [his] mind' (*M-E* 9). This has the effect of establishing that he is an orthodox Hindu, but other details of his morning perambulation take the form of 'well-defined encounters' of a less spiritual kind. On the way to the river he encounters a milk-seller who magically extracts 'a milk-like product out of [a] miserable cow-like creature' (*M-E* 9), a gurgling asthmatic and a watchman; on the way back he speaks to the 'adjournment lawyer', who has been of little help to Raju in *The Guide* and will be similarly ineffective when he acts for Nataraj later in the novel and a septuagenarian, who also has a role to play in the action that follows. Simply put, Narayan is at pains to people the social world in which Nataraj lives and moves and to provide a broad panorama of the *comédie humaine* of Malgudi life. The amount of circumstantial detail offered in this opening chapter is at odds with a view of the *Man-Eater* as a novel grounded in 'mythic' archetypes. The welter of contingent detail here suggests an approach that refuses to interpret the complexities of lived experience through the grid of any particular closed system of values. By the end of the chapter other pieces of information have further fleshed out the contexts that have shaped Nataraj. Readers learn that he now lives in his family's ancestral home in Kabir Street with just his wife and son. A generation earlier his father and four uncles lived there in a traditional joint family situation, until his grandmother's death, resulted in a 'moment of partition' (*M-E* 11) that led to most of the family's possessions being cut up into five equal parts and the departure of Nataraj's uncles' nuclear families. The partition motif is reminiscent of the divided house that Margayya shares with his brother (in *The Financial Expert*), while the emptiness of Nataraj's large old house provides a variation on the situation of Sriram and his grandmother (in *Waiting for the Mahatma*). The precise composition of the present households in these novels varies, but in each case the collapse of the joint family seems to signal a broader erosion of older, communal values, for which the division or semi-emptiness of the house in Malgudi's most aristocratic street serves as a trope. Beyond this the use of the charged word 'partition' in a novel written less than fifteen years after Indian Independence opens up the possibility of a broader allegorical reading, even if the division here has little to do with the national schism that had more deadly consequences in the north of India than in the south.

The establishment of broader social contexts in this deceptively understated opening chapter is closely linked with its gently suggestive comedy, which is present from the opening paragraph and which also suggests a fictional approach that delights in individual specificities and oddities, even though it will go on to relate its narrative to broader mythic patterns. Nataraj tells readers that he is not mercenary, since although 'sordid and calculating people' (*M-E* 7) have considered him a fool for not taking the opportunity to rent his parlour out, he has preferred to keep it as a kind of communal space where passersby with aching feet can rest. The tone is delicately poised, but of a kind that suggests irony to many Western readers. While presenting himself as altruistic and comparatively unconcerned about money, Nataraj also mentions that he has a framed picture of Lakshmi, the goddess of prosperity, on his wall, saying that 'through her grace I did not do too badly' (*M-E* 7). This may seem to undermine his claim that he is not materialistic, but given the omnipresence of Lakshmi icons in Hindu homes, it could equally well be seen as commonplace.[44] It would, then, be wrong simply to see this as conclusive evidence of inconsistency, but ironic possibilities begin to multiply when Nataraj reveals that the personnel of his press is comprised of a single 'well-wisher (I dare not call him staff) Sastri' (*M-E* 8), a general factotum who does *all* the work, while Nataraj shouts instruction to the various staff-members that he supposedly has working for him behind the blue curtain. Meanwhile he takes pride in reporting how he attracts prospective clients by showing them the modern Heidelberg press of his next-door neighbour, a man who seems to get less business than Nataraj because he fails to offer prospective customers the hospitality that they find in Nataraj's parlour.

On one level, then, Nataraj can clearly be seen as a trickster. Yet simply to see his narration as involving 'irony of self-betrayal' or '*ingénu* irony', or even 'irony of simple incongruity',[45] is inadequate, since in Nirad Chaudhuri's words, written around the same time as *The Man-Eater of Malgudi*, Hindu 'religiosity covers every aspect of money-making. [...] Ever since the Rigvedic age we have had economic gods'.[46] The liminal site of the parlour is a metonym for the ambivalence surrounding Nataraj's business dealings. His benevolence in offering such a rest station to weary passers-by seems questionable when he mentions that those who stop there sometimes get ideas for printing work they need done, but he quickly tempers this by pointing out that 'many others came whose visits did not mean a paisa to me' (*M-E* 7) and his commercial dealings are generally conducted in a spirit of good-natured conviviality.

Subsequently the comedy often operates in a different way, as the put-upon little man figure of Nataraj becomes the victim of his compulsive tendency to take the line of least resistance. His passivity in allowing Vasu to move into his premises ushers in a series of situations in which he finds himself falling foul of the civic authorities and incurring the displeasure of his neighbours as a direct consequence of the anti-social activities of his uninvited guest. Nataraj is variously taken to task by the house rent controller, 'the most dreaded personality in the town' (*M-E* 57), when Vasu files a complaint against him as a landlord, even though he is not a tenant; the sanitary inspector, who accuses him of having infringed a bye-law that prohibits the tanning of

leather; and by a forestry official, who sees him as partly responsible for Vasu's violation of the game laws. As if this were not
enough, Vasu's intrusion into his life also leads to his incurring
the wrath of the septuagenarian of the opening chapter, whose
grandson's dog Vasu has killed; and his wife is shocked, when
Rangi, a temple dancer, who, unlike Rosie in *The Guide*, sees
herself as having remained true to the *dharma* of her profession
as 'a public woman' (*M-E* 115) and with whom he has become
involved as a consequence of Vasu's consorting with her, comes
to visit him at home. And when he turns to the adjournment
lawyer for help, he finds himself being manipulated by a man
who is as accomplished in the art of deferral as Narayan himself.
So despite his petty trickery, Nataraj emerges as a comparative
innocent in the ways of the world and far from being the butt of
satire he increasingly comes across as a character whose patho-
logical incapacity to act, which again is a world away from the
Gandhian credo of non-violence, seems to warrant Vasu's charge
that he typifies his 'spineless' countrymen, whose lack of spirit
has rendered them 'a prey to every invader who passed this way'
(*M-E* 97).

At first, then, it seems as though there may be satire of
Nataraj as a petty trickster. Subsequently, if there is satire at all,
it issues from the farcical situations into which his indecisive-
ness propels him. There is no sense of the stable irony that is
the dominant mode of one kind of classic English novel, such as
the works of Fielding and Austen, where irony operates to sati-
rize deviations from an assumed social norm. Written across two
traditions, Narayan's novels lack the monolithic conviction of
such fiction. Early in life, his uncle, T.N. Seshachalam's deathbed
advice that he should study Kamban's *Ramayana* had left him
feeling that he 'was a realistic fiction-writer in English and Tamil
language or literature was not my concern' (*MyD* 102). From
the outset, his writing had, of course, drawn on both 'realistic'
and Tamil traditions, while demonstrating more indebtedness
to the former. Now in mid-career, seemingly encouraged by
increasing American interest in the 'mystical' East, his earlier
repudiation of Tamil intertexts in favour of a Western 'realistic'

fictional practice gives way to writing that foregrounds its relationship to Tamil (and Sanskrit) classics. He did turn to Kamban's *Ramayana* and what he refers to as the 'perennial philosophy'[47] contained within it for inspiration; and, when he produced his own version of the epic, a book which he dedicated to his uncle, he referred to it as 'suggested'[48] by Kamban's eleventh-century Tamil retelling. Meanwhile in the years preceding this, he had gradually been shifting the emphasis of his fiction to incorporate mythic motifs and in the *Man-Eater* Sastri's catalogue of *rakshasas* includes Ravana, the abductor of Sita and Rama's adversary in the *Ramayana*. Since Sastri sees Vasu as a modern-day *rakshasa*, this opens up the possibility that Nataraj may be a contemporary Rama, albeit one who finally does nothing to defeat his Ravana!

In his Introduction to his own version of the epic, Narayan is adamant about the relevance of Ravana and Rama to contemporary life:

> The Ramayana [sic] has lessons in the presentation of motives, actions and reactions, applicable for all time and for all conditions of life. Not only in areas of military, political, or economic power do we see the Ravanas – the evil antagonists – of today; but also at less conspicuous levels and in varying degrees, even in the humblest social unit or family, we can detect a Rama striving to establish peace and justice in conflict with a Ravana.[49]

So, given the *Man-Eater*'s increased engagement with myth and Narayan's having arrived at a position where he feels ancient lore pervades everyday experience, is it reasonable to see the comedy of the novel as subordinate to its mythic theme? One possible answer lies in a re-reading of its comic mode which distances it from the kind of irony that satirizes deviations from social norms. Arguably Narayan's irony operates in a very different manner from such Western normative irony and although its origins may not be exclusively Hindu, it seems to embody a set of assumptions that transcend satire. The complexity of the tone, which opens up the possibility that the pathologically inactive Nataraj may nevertheless be some kind of a Krishna-like

preserver of social and spiritual balance or Rama-like cham-
pion of justice, certainly seems at odds with that kind of irony
which serves as the vehicle of satire by working to achieve 'the
amendment of vices by correction'.[50] An alternative is to see
it as a type of irony that has been termed 'general irony', in
which the object is not to 'expose hypocrisy, wilful ignorance,
pride, confident folly, rationalizing, or vanity',[51] but rather, in
Kierkegaard's words, to consider 'the totality of existence [...]
sub specie ironiae'.[52] The vindication of Sastri's view, when Vasu
kills himself, as all *rakshasas* must, could be seen as suggesting
that localized ironies have been subsumed in a larger pattern of
general, or philosophical, irony, but this, of course, is culturally
encoded (Sastri appeals to ancient legend), not simply a version
of the cosmic irony identified by Kierkegaard, who sees general
irony as directing itself 'against the whole given actuality of a
certain time and situation'.[53]

The identification of Vasu with a *rakshasa* may hark back to
ancient mythical beliefs, but insofar as it explains the action of
the novel it does so through the mediation of the contemporary
'Sanskrit semi-scholar', Sastri, who has no sooner provided his
final coda than he emphasizes the need to return to business as
usual. Arguably this reflects the co-extensiveness of the secular
and the spiritual in Hindu thought, but whether or not this is
the case, it certainly points towards the overlapping of genres
that enables *The Man-Eater of Malgudi* to succeed as a seamless fusion of social comedy and Hindu fable, without either
mode being privileged at the expense of the other and with the
relationship between them left indeterminate. As Harleen Singh
puts it in a discussion of *The Painter of Signs*, 'irony is mani-
fested in the ambivalent tonalities of Narayan's treatment of
Indian legends and myths, so that, even as one is aware of the
virtue of traditional wisdom, the absurdity of the application
of that very tradition is equally viable'.[54] The confirmation of
the mythic infrastructure at the end provides a limited form of
closure. Other questions remain unanswered and the fabulist
elements remain firmly entrenched within a text that is also
working within the conventions of comic social realism, because

Narayan's overriding concern is with secular life.

In *India: A Wounded Civilization*, V.S. Naipaul reports a remark that Narayan made to him during a conversation in London in 1961: '"India will go on"'.[55] For Naipaul this comment crystallizes what he views as Narayan's conservative belief in an 'old equilibrium',[56] a stable social order understood through a quietist philosophy with roots in orthodox Hinduism. However, again in Naipaul's view, Narayan's next novel, *The Vendor of Sweets* (1967), demonstrates the 'fragility' of this 'Hindu equilibrium' and the impossibility of insulating Malgudi from the encroachments of the 'larger, restless world'.[57] At first sight the situation of Jagan, the eponymous protagonist of *The Vendor of Sweets*, seems to be very similar to that of both Nataraj in *The Man-Eater of Malgudi*, the Narayan novel that appeared in the year that he was telling Naipaul that India would go on, and Srinivas in *Mr Sampath*, the other Narayan novel that Naipaul discusses at some length in *India: A Wounded Civilization*.[58] Like the heroes of these two novels, Jagan is a small businessman, living a secular brahmin life more or less in accordance with the second (*grihastya*) *asrama*. Like Srinivas and Nataraj, he is capable of petty deceptions – he regards any takings that come into his shop after six o'clock 'as free cash, whatever that might mean, a sort of immaculate conception, self-generated, arising out of itself and entitled to survive without reference to any tax.'[59] – and insofar as the novel is a social comedy he can be seen as the object of gentle satire. However, like all of Narayan's heroes, his character exemplifies a set of concerns that go beyond his social role to embody a view of identity that is only partly defined by his occupation, actions and standing in the community. These concerns have their roots in traditional brahminical thinking, but, as Tabish Khair points out, it is mistaken to see Narayan's characters as aspirants to '"spiritual maturity"; instead, they aspire to "existential maturity"'.[60] In Khair's view, 'a significant number of Narayan's protagonists are not very spiritual or religious. [...] They are primarily concerned with the secular problem of living, though (it must be stressed) they often mechanically observe religious customs'.[61]

The opening of *The Vendor of Sweets* locates Jagan very precisely in terms of one of the central discursive systems of both traditional and contemporary Hinduism: food tropology. Cooking, eating, dietary habits and food sites, such as kitchens and restaurants, are major markers of Indian identities; and, although the cliché 'You are what you eat' has resonance across cultures and periods, it has particular force on the subcontinent. In India, in addition to being a crucial aspect of everyday material existence, food is invested with social, spiritual and psychological associations, to a point where it becomes a crucial factor in the ascription of cultural and communal identities, as well as individual self-determination.[62] As soon as foods are inscribed within language, they become conduits for the transmission of culture; particular foods have specific properties associated with them, and again this is especially the case in India. According to Judit Katona-Apte, in Hinduism '[s]ome foods are believed to be symbolic, representing certain important concepts. For instance, rice is a symbol for abundance and fertility […]'.[63] Related to this is a belief that food flavours are analogous to aesthetic tastes. With reference to the classical dance text, the *Natya Shastra*, Lee Siegel explains:

> Playing upon the literal meaning of *rasa*, 'flavor' or 'taste'. [Bharata[64]] used the gastronomic metaphor to explain the dynamics of the aesthetic experiences [sic]. Just as the basic ingredient in a dish, when seasoned with secondary ingredients and spices, yields a particular flavor which the gourmet can savor with pleasure, so the basic emotion in a play, story, or poem, when seasoned with secondary emotions, rhetorical spices, verbal herbs, and tropological condiments, yields a sentiment which the connoisseur can appreciate in enjoyment. Love yields the amorous sentiment, courage the heroic mode.[65]

Narayan's use of gastronomical tropes is less concerned with the aesthetic emotions aroused by particular foods than this classical model, but nevertheless food and diet are major markers of social identity in *The Vendor of Sweets*. Jagan is both a maker and vendor of sweets and a man with very particular *rasas*, which serve to define his character. The novel opens with his saying, '"Conquer taste, and you will have conquered the self"' and his 'listener' asking, '"Why conquer the self?"', to which Jagan replies, '"I do not know, but all our sages advise us so"' (*VS* 5). He is a reader of the Sanskrit epics, from which he derives 'immense faith in the properties of margosa', which he calls '"Amrita" – the ambrosia which kept the gods alive' and '"Sanjeevini", the rare herb mentioned in the epics, which held at the nostrils could bring the dead to life' (*VS* 15). His reliance on classical food discourse is, however, complemented by his indebtedness to a more recent advocate of abstinence. In his earlier life, he has been a follower of Gandhi and, as a participant in the independence struggle, like Sriram in *Waiting for the Mahtama*, he has spent time in jail.

This period of his life informs his behaviour in the novel and Gandhian thinking particularly underpins his present-day quest for 'truth' and simplicity in the key areas of diet and dress. As he talks to his 'listener', an ever-present 'cousin' and hanger-on, in the opening chapter, he outlines a regime that has been shaped by his earlier involvement in the freedom struggle. Food has a central iconic role within this. Despite his occupation, he has progressively renounced a range of foods as part of a way of life that has both political and psychoanalytic associations. In line with Gandhi's boycott of imported salt, he has, on the morning when the novel begins, resolved to use only 'natural salt' (*VS* 6) and as the chapter progresses he explains how he has removed sugar and rice from his diet, replacing them with honey and 'a little stone-ground wheat' (*VS* 7). His dress is similarly influenced by Gandhian 'simplicity': he wears clothes made from material he has spun himself, during daily sessions at his *charka*; and his sandals are made from the leather of an animal that has died of old age.[66] Consequently it seems appropriate that his cousin, who has a convenient habit of arriving at times when he can taste Jagan's produce, compliments him on having '"perfected the art of living on nothing"' (*VS* 7), while noting the irony that his abstinence has not prevented him from continuing to work as a commercial sweet-maker. Later, when

Jagan once again expounds his belief in the Gandhian ethic of '"[s]imple living and high thinking"', the cousin puts this view more directly, saying, '"But what I don't understand is why you should run a trade, make money and accumulate it"' (*VS* 29).

It may, then, seem that *The Vendor of Sweets* is once again representing a world of compromises and accommodations, in which the 'little man' protagonist is satirized for the discrepancy between his actions and the high-sounding rhetoric of his avowed spiritual beliefs. The physical and human geography of Malgudi is certainly much the same as before: Jagan's world is as narrow as Krishna's in *The English Teacher* – at one point he thinks of his 'whole existence' as having been lived 'between the Lawley Statue and the frying shop' (*VS* 85) – and as he walks around the town he encounters such Malgudi stalwarts as the adjournment lawyer, Nataraj and Gaffur, the taxi-driver. However, Narayan's representation of Jagan hovers somewhere between mock-heroic and heroic, moving in and out of the mode of satire, in which it frequently seems to operate. Though Jagan's Gandhian rhetoric initially seems to be at odds with his inaction, it is not, as Naipaul suggests, a 'decayed' and 'self-cherishing' version of the Mahatma's philosophy,[67] but the product of an all-too-human confusion in the mind of a character, who acts pragmatically when he finds himself confronted with alterity. As the novel progresses, it becomes increasingly clear that his passivity is not of the same order as, say, Nataraj's near-pathological inertia in *The Man-Eater of Malgudi*. It is, though, once again a response to the challenge afforded to an insular Tamil brahmin world-view by external forces. Such forces not only represent alternative value-systems, but also contest the notion that cultures can remain hermetically sealed. Again Narayan constructs Malgudi as a site that can be seen as a social microcosm, in this case supplying more references than usual to support a reading of the text as national allegory. The town is now fairly obviously a metonym for India in flux, as older cultural codes and the forces of Western (or Westernized) modernity come into collision: the taxi-driver Gaffur relates the difficulties of acquiring a new car and the impossibility of importing a foreign car to 'the state of the nation' (*VS* 43); Jagan's son Mali believes that his plan to introduce a writing machine into Malgudi will solve 'the cultural shortcomings of the country', allowing it to 'take its place in the comity of nations' (*VS* 64). It is difficult to agree with commentators who see the Malgudi of Narayan's early novels as representing some kind of timeless, quintessential India;[68] it is impossible to do so when one comes to *The Vendor of Sweets*, where the impact of modernity is inescapable, both as a theme and in terms of its effect on the form and structure of the text. Social commentary may not finally be Narayan's main concern, but the novel responds to central tensions in South Indian society in the third quarter of the twentieth century, particularly ways in which changing value-systems give rise to inter-generational conflicts.

The main threat to Jagan's settled existence, which is built around reading ancient texts, nostalgic Gandhianism and his occupation as a sweet-vendor, comes from within his family and it represents a challenge to the *discursive* codes by which he lives his life, particularly his notions of purity. Mali returns from the United States with a 'wife', Grace, whose foreignness excludes her from caste identity. This is once again related to her eating habits: his cousin asks about his household's 'dietary arrangements', now that it includes a 'casteless girl' (*VS* 44); later his sister sees his acquisition of 'a beef-eating Christian' (*VS* 107) daughter-in-law as more shameful than his earlier involvement in the Gandhian campaign against caste. Given his background and upbringing, Jagan remains reasonably sympathetic towards Grace. However, when he learns that she and Mali are not married, he reverts to type in feeling that his private space has been polluted and he must do 'everything possible to insulate himself from the evil radiations of an unmarried couple living together' (*VS* 106). In Narayan's early novels, such as *The Dark Room* and *The English Teacher*, the divide between pure and polluted space is vast. Now it is not completely unbridgeable: it can be negotiated through the performance of purification rituals. So, as in *Waiting for the Mahatma* and *The Guide*, there is a movement beyond the stark pure/polluted binary of the early fiction. Grace's foreignness is not simply a *donnée*, but a problematic category, which taxes and ultimately defeats Jagan's cognitive mapping of the world, allowing the novel to maintain an interrogative stance with regard to identity. Shortly after she arrives in Malgudi, Jagan asks Grace about her birthplace and origins and she explains that, although she has been born in New Jersey, her ancestry is mixed. She is the daughter of a Korean mother and an American G.I. father. On an obvious level her ethnicity represents a challenge to 'pure' notions of culture and selfhood, but more significantly she refutes the very idea of originary conceptions of identity, telling Jagan '"Only the passport and income-tax people ask for details of where one was born and bred in other countries"' (*VS* 49).

So, irregardless of whether *Jagan* is able to transcend his conservative generation's beliefs about what constitutes identity, *the novel* posits an alternative possibility, opening up a dialogue on the subject, which is not present in Narayan's earlier fiction. Grace's foreignness, which excludes her from caste identity, is as much a challenge to the signifying systems through which Jagan has come to understand his world as a literal marker of alterity ands this is a pattern which is replicated elsewhere in the novel. Faced with the fact that she is almost certainly not Mali's wife, Jagan later struggles to find a signifier that will describe her adequately and thinks of her as his son's '"so-called – what do we call her, really? What name shall I give her?"' (*VS* 133) – a taxonomical conundrum that foregrounds the extent to which she exists outside the epistemes that have shaped his view of social relations. So Grace can be seen as the focal point for Jagan's struggle to understand anything beyond his familiar mental horizons, which are as limited as their physical correlative, the streets that he walks between the Lawley Statue and the frying shop. His older Tamil brahmin view of the world leaves him without the vocabulary necessary to understand the 'impurity' of modernity. When towards the end Mali rejects Grace, he tells Jagan that she needs to see a 'psychiatrist' (*VS* 110). Jagan does not know the meaning of the word, but the novel, which is more concerned with mental states than social commentary, *is* able to use the term knowingly. In short, even though the prime focus is on Jagan and even though he remains a sympathetic protagonist, he is a dramatized figure and the text brings other perspectives to bear on his situation. These make it clear that the Malgudi he represents is increasingly out of step with a world in which originary versions of identity are only required by officialdom.

The generational distance between Jagan and Mali is most clearly staged through their contrasting attitudes to narrative and, as suggested at the beginning of this book, *The Vendor of Sweets*, despite its immersion in social experience, can also be read as metafiction. Mali has gone to America hoping to become a writer and significantly, when Jagan first hears of his ambition from the cousin, he misunderstands what is involved. He thinks Mali intends to become a clerk, one of the legion of English-speaking intermediaries brought into existence by Macaulay's Minute of 1835: '"Writer" meant in Jagan's dictionary only one thing, a "clerk" – an Anglo-Indian, colonial term from the days when Macaulay had devised a system of education to provide a constant supply of clerical staff for the East India Company' (*VS* 21). Jagan's vocabulary is once again too limited to allow for any other meaning of the word and on one level Narayan's wry irony seems to be drawing attention to the supposed absence of creative writing in contemporary India, a position which reflects back on his own situation as a writer. Elsewhere Jagan's view of books is that they '"are a form of the goddess Saraswathi"' (*VS* 23), the tutelary deity not only of wisdom but also of libraries and his prototype for the writer is Kalidasa, whom he views as having been '"a village idiot"' until he was inspired by Saraswathi (*VS* 24); and he says Mali could learn more about storytelling from a '"village granny"' (*VS* 34) than study in America. He sees literature as synonymous with classical Hindu texts. He reads the *Gita* as part of his everyday routine and turns to it for guidance as to how he should act at key moments;[69] and at various points in the action he also refers to the *Panchatantra*,[70] the *shastras*[71] and the *puranas*,[72] regarding them as conduct books that assist the individual in making secular choices as to how to act as much as sources of divine wisdom. Mali, too, bemoans the lack of contemporary Indian writing, but as he outlines his scheme for remedying this state of affairs it becomes clear that his view of literature is diametrically opposed to Jagan's and there is little ambiguity as to where the text's sympathies lie. Narayan mocks Mali's project in a manner reminiscent of Swift's satire of the Royal Society's attempts to mechanize wisdom in his very similarly conceived detail of a writing machine in the third part of *Gulliver's Travels*.[73] The distance between the two writers' social milieus is considerable, but the parallel is close: both oppose ancient and modern attitudes to knowledge and resolve their battle of the books by coming down very firmly on the side of the former, though in Narayan's case the satire can be clumsy and the writing machine seems to be out of place in a primarily 'realistic' novel.

Once again, though, the novel demands to be read on another level. Plunged into crisis, Jagan starts discounting his produce, to the annoyance of other Malgudi food retailers, who send a deputation to him. Jagan takes the moral high ground, citing the *Gita* on the need for pure ingredients and appealing to it as an authority for selling more cheaply and at this point, like the fellow-retailers to whom he is speaking, readers are left unsure as to whether he has a hidden mercenary agenda. The earlier evidence that he is capable of petty trickery has raised this possibility, but the reality is more complicated. Like Margayya in *The Financial Expert* and Raju in *The Guide*, he is pondering entry into a different phase of existence, in which, despite ambiguities, worldly concerns are no longer paramount and this movement is accompanied by a partial shift in the mode of the novel. It continues to operate on the level of social comedy, but this mode is ambushed by a form of fictional discourse, in which psycho-spiritual issues loom larger.

Among the delegation that comes to see Jagan to try to persuade him to abandon his discounting policy is a mysterious bearded man. The other members of the group are familiar Malgudi residents, but the enigmatic bearded man has Jagan wondering whether he 'might not be a visitation from another planet' (*VS* 91). He explains to Jagan that he has been the disciple of a deceased master carver and invites him to visit the spot where his Master lived. The location in question lies on the far side of the river, as always in Narayan's cultural geography a trope for spiritual peace and tranquillity, and for Jagan it evokes memories of the days when Gandhi addressed mass audiences on the banks of the Sarayu.[74] Despite its proximity to Malgudi, the site, like the temples in *The Dark Room* and *The Financial Expert*, represents a heterotopian space that is a world away from the narrowly circumscribed environment in which Jagan's daily routine is lived and when he crosses the river with the bearded man, he feels that he is entering into an alternative reality:

> Watching [the bearded man] in this setting, it was difficult for Jagan, as he mutely followed him, to believe that he was in the twentieth century. Sweetmeat vending, money and his son's problems seemed remote and unrelated to him. The edge of reality itself was beginning to blur; this man from the previous millennium seemed to be the only object worth notice; he looked like one possessed. (*VS* 84)

The man is devoting the remainder of his life to carving an image of a goddess from stone and, when he asks Jagan to buy his garden and assist him in the completion of his task, both this occupation and the location offer an alternative *dharma* to Jagan. Hitherto it has seemed reasonable to assume that his success and failure will be determined in relation to his pursuit of his occupation and his behaviour towards Mali and Grace. At this point the novel, like so much of Narayan's fiction from *The Dark Room* and *The English Teacher* onwards, appears to change direction, suggesting that its concerns are existential rather than social.

One obvious way of explaining the apparent movement would be to see the shift in mode and focus as reflections of the protagonist's passage from the active second stage of the *varnashramadharma* to the meditative third,[75] and certainly a rite of passage is occurring in the second half of the novel. After his encounter with the bearded man, Jagan's mind is 'in a turmoil', but he also has 'a feeling that his identity [is] undergoing a change' and that an 'internal transformation had taken place' (VS 91). Although his cousin later warns him the man is a '"sorcerer [who] knows black magic and offers to transmute base metals into gold..."' (VS 140), as with many such other dubious other-worldly figures in Narayan, the issue of whether he is a charlatan is left undecided. The cousin's reference to him as an alchemist is, though, interesting, as he certainly offers the possibility of psychic transformation, which in the Jungian reading of alchemy was a part of the esoteric side of its practitioners' quest.[76] Again the distinction between the physical and the psycho-spiritual is porous. At the end of the novel Jagan, now sixty, resolves to renounce the world and his delinquent son and enter into a new janma, but he responds to the cousin's warning with hard-headed pragmatism:

> 'I don't care what he does. I am going to watch a goddess come out of a stone. If I don't like the place, I will go away somewhere else. I am a free man. I've never felt more determined in my life. [...] Everything can go with or without me. [...]' (VS 140)

Nevertheless his planned retreat does not signify a straightforward progression into the third asrama: after first meeting the bearded man, his actions continue to be bound up with work and family obligations. He continues with his daily routine, while segregating himself from the part of his house that Mail and Grace occupy, which he feels is tainted. In short, the novel suggests he is being initiated into a new way of perceiving existence, while still contending with the everyday realities of his secular life. Naipaul's view that the novel is 'a form of social inquiry, and as such outside the Indian tradition'[77] begins to seem very inadequate, since Narayan, again as so often in his fiction, is exploring the dialectical relationship, not only between two possible approaches to life, but also between two modes of fiction. The evidence suggests that the novel genre is being refashioned as a mode of existential inquiry,[78] in which the competing claims of social and psycho-spiritual life-styles are being assessed in relation to one another. The closing stages may seem to be moving towards spiritual renunciation, but although the novel ends with Jagan about to depart from Malgudi and some of the cares of active life, as Ranga Rao aptly puts it,[79] he does so carrying his cheque book with him. He leaves money to help Mali, who is about to stand trial for being found with alcohol in his car, another signifier of corrupting modernity. He tells the cousin that he is '"not flying away to another planet"' (VS 141) and that he will be available to meet any further expenses. Most interestingly of all, he also instructs the cousin to offer help to Grace, should he meet her. As at the end of *Waiting for the Mahatma*, the notion of family is broadened beyond its traditionally conceived limits. Grace may be a daughter-in-law *manqué* and a woman who transgresses the beliefs on which he has been raised, but he chooses to support her in a quasi-adoptive act of affiliative identification, which demonstrates the novel's engagement with social change as part of its larger project of psychodrama.

The Painter of Signs (1976) completes the sequence of novels that had begun with *Mr Sampath*, the first Narayan novel to be published after Indian independence. Again the subject is the impact of outside forces on Malgudi, although as in *Waiting for the Mahatma* and *The Guide*, the text travels beyond the narrowly circumscribed world inhabited by Narayan's more orthodox brahmin protagonists. In this case modernity takes the form of a zealous young family planner, Daisy, whom the protagonist Raman follows into village India, in much the same way as Sriram follows Bharati into mountain villages in *Waiting for the Mahatma* and, as in the earlier novel, national policies find their way into remote regions.

In a 1989 interview for the British *Sunday Times* Narayan linked *The Painter of Signs* and 'a time when thousands had been coerced into sometimes fatal sterilizing operations', saying:

> It takes time for contemporary Indian life to permeate the remote areas. [...] Political change won't be noticeable in a small place in the way you would notice it in Madras or Delhi. There is a gap, which I make use of, between the larger events and the individual lives of people. A man in

a village will be preoccupied with the rains, the monsoon, his neighbours and the cattle, though he will be aware of the important things from outside that affect his life, like chemical fertilisers.[80]

In *Waiting for the Mahatma*, the slow seepage of 'larger events' into the remoteness of village India takes the form of a backward look at the independence struggle, particularly as embodied by the Gandhian ethic. Here twenty years later, in a novel published during the period of Indira Gandhi's 'Emergency', the structure is similar, but the context very different: macro-politics take the form of the birth control policy that the Congress (I) government was vigorously pursuing at this time. Mrs Gandhi is only mentioned once, in an unfinished remark made by a friend of Raman's who is habitually incensed by government policies (*PS* 16), but she seems to be the moving spirit behind Daisy's crusade against procreation. Although it would be mistaken to see Daisy as a surrogate for Indira Gandhi, when Raman thinks of her as a potent female ruler, reflecting that, 'In her previous incarnation, she must have been Queen Victoria, or in a still earlier incarnation, Rani Jhansi, the warrior queen of Indian history' (*PS* 65),[81] there is a hint of such an identification. Earlier in what could be seen as a comic response to Mrs Gandhi's attempt to curb the population explosion through wholesale vasectomies,[82] he has thought that, 'If she were a despotic queen of ancient days, she would have ordered the sawing off of the organs of generation' (*PS* 47).

Remembering Narayan's interview comment that *The Painter of Signs* can be linked to the sterilization campaign of the mid 1970s, the suggestion that Mrs Gandhi's presence may lie behind the novel is hard to resist. If so, one is left wanting to ask why, when Daisy is for the most part presented sympathetically and there is no hint of the civil rights abuses that eventually led to the premier's downfall in 1977, is the correlation between the novel's events and what was happening on the national stage not developed in the way that it is in *Waiting for the Mahatma*? One obvious answer is that Narayan was writing about contemporary events and so anything approaching explicit political commentary, a genre into which he seldom ventures, might have involved him in uncharacteristic partisanship. Moreover the novel's comic playfulness, more marked here than in *Waiting for the Mahatma*, evades issues that would have been central in a more politically engaged novel. At one point Narayan has Raman alternating between thoughts of impregnating two women in each of the villages that he and Daisy are visiting in order to frustrate her planned decrease in the birth rate and on the other hand thinking that he may be impotent and hence a highly appropriate husband for Daisy (*PS* 52)! Ultimately, though, the crux of the action, as in all Narayan's post-Independence novels, takes place in the protagonist's psyche, not in the social world.

Nevertheless there *is* something more to be said where Indira Gandhi is concerned. Narayan had first met Mrs Gandhi in 1961, when he received the Sahitya Akademi Award for *The Guide* during the period of her father, Jawaharlal's Nehru's premiership. Subsequently he visited her regularly whenever he was in Delhi, finding her 'generally calm, gentle, and cheerful, and never display[ing] any sign of strain or irritation'[83] – in the novel Daisy comes across as more of a termagant, despite Raman's romantic attraction to her. In an essay on his relationship with Indira Gandhi, Narayan mentions her remarking during one of their meetings that his brother, the political cartoonist, R.K. Laxman, could be '"hard on us"',[84] but it seems that his own dealings with her remained immune from politics. He writes, 'I really had no definite purpose in seeing her, I had no requests, or comments to offer, or political interests'.[85] So it seems reasonable to conjecture that in *The Painter of Signs*, the Narayan novel which most obviously responds to one of Mrs Gandhi's social agendas, his characteristic reluctance to engage in macro-political debates was bolstered by his very real respect for this member of post-Independence India's most renowned family.

Again, though, the main focus of the novel is on the challenge that social change offers to the protagonist's *mental* equanimity and Raman's movement outside his cloistered world puts him in a liminal position, since he is more an observer of social change than a proactive agent in its service. He is also a liminal protagonist in another sense, since although the opening of the novel finds him totally absorbed in his occupation of sign-painter, he is ambivalent about the extent to which meaning can be fixed through scribal media and he oscillates between seeing himself as an arch-rationalist and impetuous flights of fancy which suggest a very different temperament. His name Raman, echoing that of the legendary epic hero, serves to point up ambiguities in both his character and the novel's tone, which again moves between high comedy and more reflective passages, flirting with mock heroic, but never fully committing itself to such a mode.

Raman's home is interestingly situated within the changing cultural geography of Malgudi. He lives in Ellaman Street, close to Market Road and Kabir Street, which he feels is 'choking' (PS 13). He finds the location of his own house equally uncongenial, viewing Ellaman Street as 'a wretched part of the town' (PS 115) and his own house, where he lives with his elderly aunt, an 'awful lonely home' (PS 26). The pace of change within Malgudi seems to have accelerated since The Vendor of Sweets and Raman, though no more than a thirty-something, seems happiest away from the bustle of contemporary life, now represented by the centre of Malgudi. He is most content when working in an untroubled way on his sign-boards in his backyard, where the seemingly unchanging constant of 'the river flow[s] softly' (PS 26). Again, then, location provides an index of a Narayan protagonist's state of mind. Within the semi-deserted ancestral house and looking towards the street, he is ill at ease; in his backyard, close to the tranquillity of the river he has a different perspective on his world, though urban sprawl and technological advances seem to have shrunk the space in which the protagonist can maintain a sense of mental equanimity. When, in the opening chapter, a traffic policeman blows his whistle to make him move on, he reflects:

> They won't leave one in peace. This is a jungle where other beasts are constantly on the prowl to attack and bite off a mouthful, if one is not careful. As if this were New York and I blocked the traffic on Broadway. He would not

recognize it, but Malgudi was changing in 1972. It was the base for a hydro-electric project somewhere on the Mempi Hills, and jeeps and lorries passed through the Market Road all day. The city had a new superintendent of police who was trying out new ideas. [...] (*PS* 13–14)

He is, however, attracted to modernity as personified by Daisy and when he embarks on an affair with her he contemplates escaping from the prying eyes of Ellaman Street by going to live in 'a more civilized locality like the New Extension' (*PS* 115) or leaving Malgudi altogether. This, however, is no more than a temporary idea and it is quickly supplanted by a reaffirmation of his sense of belonging in the locality where he has lived all his life: 'The more he thought of his home, the more he began to love it – there was no other spot in the whole town – such a coveted spot by the river with the breeze blowing' (*PS* 115). Earlier Narayan heroes such as Sriram have found themselves equally torn between a rooted past and a changing present, but in this instance the protagonist's interstitial predicament is exacerbated by a present which throws up ever more challenges to the 'conservative' Malgudi past.

Raman's work as a sign-painter, another twentieth-century brahminical occupation, also foregrounds this tension. On an obvious level the satisfaction and peace of mind that it affords him as he works on his boards in his backyard beside the river offer a degree of insulation from the intrusions of modernity; and passages describing his pride in his work – in the calligraphy, colours and materials he employs – locate him within the same scribal world as Narayan's printers, who evince a similar fascination with typefaces, fonts and page sizes. At the same time sign-painting represents something more to Raman: he sees it as a means of fixing identities through clearly designated labelling. In one of his many reveries in the novel, he muses about the possibility of designing a board for an arcade of new shops selling illicit goods which has sprung up in an alley off Market Road, but he quickly realizes the impossibility of assigning a clear identity to such a transitory locale:

Would it not be nice to write a sign-board to declare:
SMUGGLERS' ARCADE – STRICTLY IMPORTED
GOODS. [...] But the traders here were strangers constantly
disappearing and reappearing under new names, hence no
sign-board would be feasible. A sign-board pinned things
down to a sort of permanency – it gave things an air of
being established. (*PS* 35–6)

Here, then, Raman's quest for fixed signification suggests a
conservative desire for stability, which is thwarted by the fugitive nature of the 'strangers', who with their smuggled 'imported
goods' represent alterity in the form of a very different kind of
trade to his own. But it would be wrong simply to identify Raman
with the orthodox older faction in Malgudi. This is personified
by his aunt and in significant respects his behaviour is at odds
with traditional norms. Again the novel functions mainly as a
psychodrama, in which the protagonist is pulled in different
direction by conflicting forces. Despite his desire for the kind of
permanency and fixed signification represented by sign-boards,
Raman's favourite leisure haunt is an establishment on Ellaman
Street known as the Boardless Hotel, because of its proprietor's
refusal to put up a sign. He is well aware that he would lose
his livelihood 'if everyone adopted the boardless notion' (*PS* 14)
and jokes about this with the proprietor, but he continues to
enjoy the freedom that the hostelry offers him from his aunt's
company; and later, when he is with Daisy in a remote village,
he thinks longingly of the Boardless's afternoon coffee and the
male camaraderie he enjoys there. The Boardless, then, functions as a trope for resistance to labelling and this is particularly
associated with Raman's bachelor state, which has enabled him
to elude the domestic cares of the second *asrama*. Seen in this
way, the Boardless is an undefined physical space that parallels
a similarly uncommitted mental state and this exerts an appeal
to an aspect of Raman's psychology, which is the antithesis of
his desire for fixity.

Raman's relationship with Daisy dramatizes this mental
split from another angle. His work for her takes him into a world
where the scribal has little currency: she argues that they need

'"a pictorial medium rather than just words"' (*PS* 57) and the remote village terrain in which they are operating means that he has to inscribe her messages on walls, a departure from his habitual use of boards. So he comes to feel that she is luring him away from 'his legitimate normal activity' (*PS* 60) into a situation where his independence and self-respect are being compromised:

> He had always written his boards on the sands behind his house; after the present assignment, he must suggest some other device for wall messages. He'd write on wood or canvas and stick them up, but this kind of wall-writing, no, no. (*PS* 60–61)

In short, Daisy's project disturbs his customary mode of working and his attraction to her leaves him caught between what he considers 'legitimate' and 'normal' and the enticements of modernity.

Although the Boardless is the most obvious trope for the impossibility of assigning fixed signification, Daisy also frustrates encapsulation within the brahmin signifying codes that have shaped Raman's consciousness. As with Rosie in *The Guide* and Grace in *The Vendor of Sweets*, her Western name is an index of the challenge she offers to orthodox Tamil brahmin expectations concerning women's roles. Raman's aunt, the repository of older values, assumes she must be a Christian, but Daisy's choice of the name is a more radical departure from Hindu naming practices: she has chosen it for its 'non-denominational' (*PS* 121) quality. Raman's very first response to her focuses on her name and is perhaps the clearest indicator of the semantic disturbance it causes in his mind, since he instinctively realizes that it locates her outside the conventions in which names are indicators of caste, family and regional origins:

> She called herself just Daisy. She was a slender girl in a sari. No one could say who was her husband or father or brother, or where she came from – a sudden descent on Malgudi. Daisy! What a name for someone who looked so very Indian, traditional, and gentle! One would expect

a person on this job to be somewhat matronly, like the
Mother Superior in the convent – large, broad-faced,
towering over others, an executive type who could with
a flourish of her arms order people about. But this girl
looked like a minor dancer. He felt he ought to know more
about her. (*PS* 28)

The compounding of the Mother Superior and the dancer similes
in this passage suggest that Daisy erodes the distinction between
dichotomized female stereotypes, while her name, like that of
Grace in *The Vendor of Sweets*, negates the very idea of originary conceptions of identity. Raman's feeling that he 'ought to
know more about her' highlights his incapacity to place her in
terms of the gender discourses on which he has been raised and
when he later asks her whether she is a Communist, her reply –
'"What if I am or if I am not? Is there a label one should always
carry like a dog collar"' (*PS* 48) – demonstrates as much hostility
to unitary conceptions of identity as the Boardless proprietor's
resistance to onomastic fixity.

Daisy is, then, a very different modern woman from, say,
Savitri, the brahmin protagonist of Narayan's early 'feminist'
novel *The Dark Room*, who fails in her attempt to achieve a
degree of independence, although she is sympathetically drawn
from the inside. In *The Painter of Signs*, as with *Waiting for
the Mahatma* and *The Guide*, the angle of focalization remains
with the male hero, but the novel maintains a greater degree of
distance from him than is the case in Narayan's earlier variations
on the theme of the brahmin 'little man' in a changing world. The
above-quoted sentence, 'He would not recognize it, but Malgudi
was changing in 1972' (*PS* 13), suggests the distance between
Raman's character and an implied author who assesses him and
this is only the tip of an iceberg. Generally Narayan's narrative technique in the novels that employ a third-person narrator
closes down the distance between narrator and character. Here,
as Steve Carter has noted in a perceptive article on the novel's
use of defamiliarization, the technique operates 'to estrange the
reader from the act of narration itself',[86] particularly through
the use of internal embedded narratives. Narayan never ventures

into postmodern territory – indeed even to suggest this would involve viewing his work through an inappropriate Western lens – but his lifelong concern with the act of storytelling, ancient and modern, Tamil and European, comes out in a novel that both foregrounds its own practices with regard to point of view and on occasions introduces metafictive commentary on the genre that it inhabits.

The most overt instance of a passage that demonstrates a self-conscious use of point of view is a scene in which the novel completely departs from Raman's angle of vision and renders him, along with Daisy, an object of quasi-scopophiliac observation. Raman goes to visit Daisy at her home one evening and the novel suddenly introduces an otherwise undramatized character as the focalizer: 'If you had stood by the door and eavesdropped as did an urchin who had brought her dinner from a near-by restaurant, you would have heard his voice [...]' (PS 113). As the scene develops and the couple move towards consummating their relationship, the eavesdropping aspect in this narrative foreplay develops into an attempt at literal voyeurism:

> [...] And then one heard a scuffle and a struggle to reach the [light] switch, feet and hands reaching for the switch, and a click of the switch, off. The eavesdropper applying his eye to the keyhole at this point would see nothing. [...] And as the door bolt is heard drawn, the eavesdropper vanishes, leaving Daisy's food at the threshold. (PS 113–14)

The passage is reminiscent of *The Guide*, in which there is a similar admixture of narrative reticence and suggestiveness and a veil is drawn when Raju and Rosie are about to make love for the first time, but in the earlier novel there is no such defamiliarization: Raju, the first-person narrator, simply records that he 'locked the door on the world' (*Guide* 77).

Narayan often hovers between prurience and prudery in his attempts to write about 'romance' and the self-consciousness of the eavesdropping angle of focalization in this passage in *The Painter of Signs* suggests an uneasiness in dealing with such subject-matter. More knowingly, his metafictive references to romance conventions suggest their inappropriateness in his South Indian milieu. As early as *The English Teacher*, where Krishna teaches his students *Pride and Prejudice* but Jane Austen's world of court-ship and marital expectations seems to have little relevance to life as lived in Malgudi, Narayan had foregrounded the generic ambivalence of the Indian novel in English by drawing atten-tion to the irrelevance of Western romance conventions, whether drawn from the novel or Hollywood. Here Raman's bachelor status and comparative freedom from romantic entanglements, prior to meeting Daisy, have been built upon a rational repudia-tion of the discourse of love. Now he sees himself as succumbing to what he has hitherto viewed as a literary cliché:

> If Adam had possessed a firm mind, the entire course of creation would have taken a different turn. Mind condi-tioned by story-writers, poets, and dramatists from time immemorial, who had no other theme than love – easiest subject to deal with. This philosophy had been my armour and made me unique all these years. Now am I on the verge of defeat? […] This is true love-sickness, I suppose. I used to laugh at this condition whenever I came across it in stories. (*PS* 38–9)

Later he returns to the topic in conversation with Daisy, saying '"I don't believe in the romanticism created by the literary man"' (*PS* 99), while she goes further, attributing romantic discourse to 'novels and Hollywood films', adding that the words '""I love you""' sound '"mechanical and unconvincing. Perhaps credible in Western society, but […] silly in ours"' (*PS* 98). The reality of their relationship is that, for all Raman's avowed belief in ration-alism, his infatuation with Daisy implicates him in the very kind of romantic discourse that he rejects as a literary conven-tion, while Daisy's mental independence resists such Western conventions.[87] The consequence is a kind of textual impasse and although the dénouement has the couple entering into a union in the form of a Gandharva love marriage,[88] ultimately Daisy leaves Raman to continue the pursuit of a vocation which flies in the face of older ideals of Indian women's roles. There is the suggestion that they may live together in their next incarna-tion, but Raman is left to go back to 'The Boardless – that solid, real world of sublime souls who minded their own business' (*PS* 143). For Raman, then, 'reality' inheres in the world of male camaraderie not in the resolution of a Western-style happy marriage, which the modern Indian woman rejects.

Daisy has told him, '"You have your work, go on with it. You have your world, in which you have always existed happily, even before you knew me. It is always there, isn't it?' (*PS* 138). Raman goes back to the life he cherished prior to meeting her, but the collapse of their relationship does not, as in some earlier Narayan novels, return him to what Naipaul calls the 'old equilibrium' of orthodox Tamil brahmin life and in that sense his 'world' is not 'always there', as it does seem to be for the protagonists of Narayan's early fiction. It is, however, still personified by the aunt with whom he lives, a devotee of the temple at the end of Ellaman Street and a symbol of the unquestioning domestic role of the traditional South Indian woman. Prior to meeting Daisy, Raman's desired rationalism suggests distance from his aunt's receding world; after he meets her, the gap widens further, but he is still attracted to the permanence for which she is a metonym; 'Raman wished he had her stability of mind. She lived like clock-work, performing her duties at home without a question or doubt of any sort' (*PS* 86). Her religious and domestic devotion make her the complete antithesis of Daisy, but the novel is less concerned with illustrating this opposition than with dramatizing the conflict it engenders in Raman's mind. For all his desired rationalism, he occupies a midway position between the modernity represented by Daisy and the older Tamil codes of his aunt. Consequently when his aunt decides, like Sriram's grandmother in *Waiting for the Mahatma*, to fulfil her destiny by renouncing worldly concerns and going to Benares, the liminal Raman experiences a double sense of loss. Dispossessed of his older culture, he is equally unable to find a place in the modern world of work personified by Daisy. All that remains is a space that is resistant to any clear markers of identity, the Boardless.

The contrastive pairing of Daisy and Raman's devout temple-going aunt comes out particularly clearly in defining narratives of self and family-history, which they relate to Raman. The aunt's favourite monologue is a story of wifely devotion that Narayan subsequently returned to for the main plot of 'The Grandmother's Tale'. The monologue is only expressive of one side of her versatility with traditional forms of discourse – she also dispenses advice on domestic matters and herbal remedies, delivers homilies on the gods and reads horoscopes (PS 18) – but she repeatedly returns to it. It is the tale of how her grand-mother, deserted by her young husband, pursued him to Poona, reclaimed him from his 'concubine' and subsequently 'settled down in his original home [...] to a happy life', bearing him 'several sons and daughters' (PS 31–2).[89] It is a narrative that stands in stark contrast to the account that Daisy eventually gives of her origins. This tells of her discomfiture growing up in a joint family, her resistance to an orthodox arranged marriage and more generally her desire to escape from a world in which '[a]ll individuality was lost in this mass existence' (PS 102). However, the main tension of the novel emerges less from the obviously contrastive pairing of orthodox and modern women than from the liminal Raman's response to their competing narratives of self and his attempt to mediate between the various other discourses which vie for his attention.

As Steve Carter points out, the novel is full of 'self-contained act[s] of narration'.[90] As in other Narayan novels, the protago-nist is assaulted by the enigmatic utterances of guru figures – a character called the Town Hall Professor offers the gnomic advice, '"This will pass"' (PS 25; italics in original); later a village hermit prophesies that Raman and Daisy will have '"success, but trouble before and after"' (PS 63). Both pronouncements leave Raman, and the reader, pondering their possible applicability to the subsequent action, but in neither case does the potential psychic wisdom, which in any case is fairly platitudinous, result in a meaningful, sustained sequel. Arguably, like all the other voices that compete for Raman's attention, they are important only insofar as he sees them as such and in this novel of multiple mini-narratives, the debate between modernity and tradition is mainly conducted in terms of his response to his aunt and Daisy.

He proves to be a far more divided subject than may initially seem to be the case. Although he is obsessively 'determined to establish the Age of Reason in the world' (*PS* 8) and carries this mission into the minutiae of his work as a sign-painter, he is also an Indian Walter Mitty, a serial fantasist with an 'overactive' imagination (*PS* 85), whose musings, usually rendered as interior monologues, move between harmless daydreams and a disturbing part-Hollywood, part-novel-inspired fantasy[91] of raping Daisy, when they are left to spend the night alone together in a bullock cart in the mountains. Daisy's common sense pragmatism prevents this, but Raman thinks providential intervention has saved him from acting out this fantasy. Despite his longing for logic and reason, he exhibits many of the fatalistic traits of earlier Narayan heroes, among them a belief in reincarnation which seems to be associated with *karma*.

As his aunt prepares to depart for Benaras and her life of renunciation, he feels a deep sense of loss and, although at this point, he is expecting Daisy to move into their ancestral house, there is a definite sense of elegy for the passing away of what the aunt represents. Again the parallel with Sriram's situation in *Waiting for the Mahatma* is striking and the issue of house occupancy seems to relate to issues of cultural ownership more generally. Compared with Daisy, whose social activism stands in marked contrast to his tendency towards quietism and whose lecture on birth control to villagers at one point in the novel is explicitly contrasted with 'a *Ramayana* discourse' (*PS* 56), Raman seems to speak the language of tradition. She teases him over his ability to '"find a story for every occasion in the puranas"' (*PS* 133)[92] and one way of interpreting the textual impasse in which he and Daisy find themselves is to see them as responding to different discursive codes. Her remark that he is never at a loss for a puranic analogy is followed by a passage in which he refers to incidents in the *Mahabharata*, concerned with '"gods straying among mortals and producing demigods"'. He follows this up with the suggestion that he and Daisy could '"create a *story* on those lines"' (*PS* 133; my italics), while remaining unsure in his own mind 'as to whether the legendary gods were real or imagined' (*PS* 133) and telling Daisy, '"Anyway, my aunt has complete faith in the gods and possesses greater serenity than anyone else I have known"' (*PS* 133–4). So the issue of whether his aunt's orthodoxy or Daisy's modernity is to be preferred is left undecided, but while the novel's indeterminacy may balance their counter-claims, Raman is left with neither possibility open to him, as both his aunt and Daisy abandon him to pursue their particular goals in life. Different though these may be, both involve women seeking fulfilment through avenues that are not male-dependent and all that is left for the contemporary Rama figure is the male society of the unnamed Boardless. Malgudi in 1972 *is* changing and it seems a bleaker place for the brahmin 'little man'.

Late novels

The Painter of Signs is Narayan's last major novel. The fiction that he produced in his seventies and eighties is variable in quality, but generally demonstrates a falling-off in his talents. Nevertheless it develops interesting variations on several of the defining themes of his work, particularly the passage into the fourth stage of the *varnasramadharma*, the discursive constitution of space, oral mythologies and Hindu reverence for animal life and the natural world.

The last of these concerns is central to both the theme and the point of view of the novel that he has referred to as his favourite,[1] *A Tiger for Malgudi* (1983), in which the main angle of focalization is provided by the eponymous tiger, Raja,[2] a protagonist invested with a sensitivity lacking in most of the novel's human characters. It would be tempting simply to view Raja as an anthropomorphic creation, but unlike such figures in English animal stories (such as the white rabbit in *Alice in Wonderland* or Toad of Toad Hall in *The Wind in the Willows*), he is not so much an animal with human characteristics as a being that erodes the distinction between the animal and human. This liminal state of existence is implicit in his being the first-person narrator of the novel, though not its only focalizer. It also emerges from his variously being seen as a typical tiger, characterized by his elemental physical power, *and* as different from other tigers, because he has a spiritual side to his nature. And it is inherent in the suggestion that in a previous incarnation he may have been a human being, who is now reaping the consequences of his behaviour in this earlier life. Drawing on the doctrine of *karma*, the novel twice suggests roles that he may have fulfilled in previous existences.[3] Narayan's investigation of the nature of animal identity is, then, located within a Hindu framework, which challenges the construction of the human and the animal as binary opposites, but he also incorporates a range of other perspectives on animal identity into the novel.

In one sense *A Tiger for Malgudi* returns to issues explored in *The Man-Eater of Malgudi*. In the earlier novel, the occupation of the taxidermist Vasu challenges the sanctity of animal life and a tiger is among the animals that he kills and stuffs in the attic of the quietistic Nataraj, who finally emerges as a Vishnu-like preserver of life. Nataraj has been brought up in a household where the notion of *ahimsa* has prevailed and even the swatting of flies has had to be kept secret from his elders[4] and this early socialization informs his reverential attitude to animals, which stands in marked contrast to the 'man-eater' Vasu's behaviour. Fittingly, in Narayan's reworking of the Bhasmasura myth which has a central importance in the novel, Vasu destroys himself with a blow intended to kill two troubling mosquitoes that have landed on his forehead and the traditional Hindu attitude towards animal life is reaffirmed.[5] In *A Tiger for Malgudi*, making Raja the protagonist and allowing him to speak for himself reverses the pattern of *The Man-Eater* and in so doing stages a debate on the nature of tiger identity.

Animal tropes often speak volumes about the signifying systems that have produced them and representations of animals occupy a particular place in colonial discourse, particularly but not exclusively as a product of the nineteenth-century linking of ideas about evolution and 'race'. At its worst this predicated a parallel between the human-animal binary and the colonizer-colonized opposition. As Jopi Nyman puts it, in a discriminating study of animal tales that address issues of race, nation and gender, 'By its mere existence, the animal trope, as it is used in the colonial context, poses a threat to the maintenance of order and hierarchy, challenging conventional ideas of the primacy of masculinized reason and culture'.[6] However, all animals are not

equal and a writer such as Kipling reproduces colonial encounters through the characteristics he ascribes to particular animals
in *The Jungle Book*. Wolves, bears and mongooses operate within
rules that can be seen as a naturalized version of the authority
of colonial rule; snakes and monkeys threaten this code.[7] The
one animal which, it seems, resists socialization into the order
that Kipling's hero Mowgli represents is the tiger, Shere Khan.
Kipling's bestiary is far more complex than that of most of
his Anglo-Indian contemporaries and successors. Nevertheless
his construction of the tiger is in keeping with a more general
hostility to a creature, which in Sujit Mukherjee's words, 'represented some enduring spirit of India that the British felt they
had failed to subjugate'.[8]

However, readings of (post-)colonial animal fables which see
them as social allegories frequently display a tension between
locating individual animals in specific positions in a hierar-
chical social order and viewing animal identity as a condition
beyond cultural expression. To take examples from a writer who
has written particularly persuasively on the place occupied by
animals in national metanarratives, Margaret Atwood suggests
both the ways in which animal tales can be read as allegories about national identity *and* identifies the extent to which
animals become central tropes in a discourse of 'Nature', which
is postulated as an alternative to 'culture'. Commenting on such
classic American animal stories as *Moby Dick*, Hemingway's
'The Short Happy Life of Francis Macomber' and Faulkner's
'The Bear' in *Survival* (1972), Atwood suggests that in each case
the animals are 'Nature, mystery, challenge, otherness, what lies
beyond the Frontier' and sees the stories as 'a comment on the
general imperialism of the American cast of mind'.[9] In such a
reading animals are, then, both beyond the social order and the
quasi-colonized victims of such an order.

Comparing Canadian animal stories with British and American examples of the genre, Atwood continues:

> They are almost invariably failure stories ending with the
> death of the animal; but this death, far from being the
> accomplishment of a quest, to be greeted with rejoicing

> [as in the American stories], is seen as tragic or pathetic,
> *because the stories are told from the point of view of the*
> *animal.* That's the key: English animal stories are about
> 'social relations', American ones are about people killing
> animals; Canadian ones are about animals *being* killed, as
> felt emotionally from inside the fur and feathers. As you
> can see, *Moby Dick*, as told by the White Whale would
> be very different. ('Why is that strange man chasing me
> around with a harpoon?')[10]

Conversely, in seeing animals as synonymous with 'Nature',
Atwood suggests that they are resistant to such cultural interpretation and her early fiction promotes a similarly ambivalent
reading of animal identity. In *Surfacing* (1972), a novel which
was almost contemporary with *Survival*, animals function as
tropes for the appropriation of the Canadian natural world by
encroaching American imperialism. So the two positions are
not mutually exclusive. The animals of *Surfacing* function as
metonyms for a colonized culture, as well as 'Nature, mystery,
challenge, otherness'. They move between being representa-
tives of disempowerment and/or resistance *and* of a world that
is immune to cultural appropriation.

How does Narayan's tiger relate to such thinking? In
what ways, if at all, is Raja to be associated with Indianness
and possible colonial subjugation? As a way into this topic, it
is useful to consider some of the tropological associations with
which tigers have been invested in India. According to Sujit
Mukherjee, tigers do not figure prominently in ancient Hindu
texts and only emerge as significant literary presences during
the period of the Raj,[11] where there is particular emphasis on
their resistance to human control. Jim Corbett's various books
about his hunting exploits[12] depict tigers in just such a way,
while Kipling's allegorical animal fables isolate the tiger Shere
Khan as 'the only untrustworthy creature among all those that
befriended Mowgli in *The Jungle Book* (1899)'.[13] In both cases
the tiger is positioned at the point in the animal hierarchy that
is furthest away from the 'human'. For Corbett it is simply the
ultimate predator. Shere Khan is similarly dangerous, but more

of audible speech. Man assumes that he is all-important, that all else in creation exists only for his sport, amusement, comfort, or nourishment. (*Tiger* 7–8)

However, although A *Tiger for Malgudi* challenges human claims to primacy, it does not really bear scrutiny as, say, a forerunner of the work of an eco-conscious writer like J.M. Coetzee, whose later fiction investigates the ethical dilemmas surrounding responses to 'the lives of animals'.[23] Narayan's Introduction goes on to locate his sentiments about the sanctity of animal life in a classical Hindu context, citing a story told of Valmiki, author of the *Ramayana*, in which the sage expresses his empathy for a bird whose mate has been shot. The novel itself is similarly eclectic in its use of reference-points, but, without suggesting any sharp disjunctions between ancient and modern perspectives on animal life and the natural world, demonstrates a greater debt to classical wisdom. When a personification of contemporary conservationist thinking appears in the shape of the Chairman of the local chapter of the Ministry of Agriculture's 'Tiger Project' (*Tiger* 116), he is an obvious foil to Raja's Master, the *sadhu*, whose understanding of tigers and concern for their welfare emerges as superior in both pragmatic and spiritual terms. The *sadhu*'s appreciation of Raja's innate qualities and sensitivities, which immediately enables him both to control and empathize with him, is also favourably contrasted with the attitudes of the various other characters who in one way or another attempt to train or dominate Raja in the middle sections of the novel: the circus-ringmaster, a film-maker, a Malgudi school headmaster and a gunman. Much of this part of the novel is given over to not particularly well-handled satire of these characters' attempts to harness or destroy Raja's power, for example a Vasu-like *phaelwan* (strong man), who is supposed to dominate him in a film, runs away in terror and at times the progression of the plot seems to be subordinated to cheap comic effects – of the kind that Garfield would no doubt have approved of! What links these sections is the extent to which they offer variations on the theme of training and transforming animal nature, with Raja's Master demonstrating an immediate solution to the practical problem of understanding and handling a tiger and to some extent lifting the text from the self-indulgent comedy of its middle part.

Similarly, the novel's angle of focalization betrays uncertainties of direction. Initially Raja is the first-person narrator and *A Tiger for Malgudi* is at its best in passages such as the opening, where the situation and setting are defamiliarized by the use of his tiger's-eye view:

> I have no idea of the extent of this zoo. I know only my corner and whatever passes before me. On the day I was wheeled in, I only noticed two gates opening to admit me. When I stood up I caught a glimpse of some cages ahead and also heard the voice of a lion. The man who had transferred me from the forest stepped out of his jeep and said, after a glance in my direction, 'He is all right. Now run up and see if the end cage is ready […]'. (*Tiger* 11)

Subsequently, however, *A Tiger for Malgudi* moves between first- and third-person voices, occasionally allowing the two to overlap clumsily, and weakening its implicit thesis – that the tiger is a superior being – by deserting his perspective to pursue other themes, some of which appear incidental. A further problem is that Raja is variously seen in anthropomorphic terms as 'different from the tiger next door' because he possesses 'a soul' (*Tiger* 11) and as 'an unmitigated animal' (*Tiger* 22). This particular ambiguity is partly resolved through emphasis on the change that his Master effects in him, but it still remains problematic if one sees the interrogation of the boundary between the human and the animal as central to the novel's meaning. This idea is often explicit and it is bolstered by the references to the transformations of identity that creatures undergo in different incarnations, but it is not consistently maintained.

In short, like several of Narayan's novels, *A Tiger for Malgudi* seems to suffer from a loose, episodic structure and uncertainties in the handling of theme, tone and point of view, which can make its entire fictional edifice appear meandering and aimless. Usually, in such cases in Narayan's novels, an underlying pattern emerges towards the end. Here, again as in several of the earlier novels, the dénouement also operates on a philosophical level, but earlier the account of Raja's experiences at the hands of human society seems less philosophically charged; and at its worst their focus seems to be little more than an excuse for some fairly listless comedy. The appearance of Raja's Master two-thirds of the way through the novel moves it onto another plane, and the remainder is mainly concerned with outlining the renunciation of the two final *asramas*, initially through the figure of the Master, but also through the transformation in Raja, who is now in the final years of his life and about to enter the situation in which he has been found at the opening, Malgudi zoo. From his first appearance, the Master represents an epistemology that resists conventional categorizations of identity. Asked who he is, he replies, '"You are asking a profound question. I've no idea who I am!"' (*Tiger* 103) and the refusal to answer this question, which recurs several times in the closing pages of the novel (*Tiger* 131, 140, 147), is complemented by his insistence that Raja should not be called a '*beast* or *brute*' (*Tiger* 103; italics in original).[24] Names that confer individual identities are, it is suggested, insignificant in the larger scheme of things and once again a reference to the Boardless, where tiger identity is more openly debated than in the neighbouring Anand Bhavan (*Tiger* 130),[25] suggests the limitations of language. Details about the *sadhu*'s earlier life are revealed in the closing pages, but mainly for the purpose of suggesting how meaningless they are in relation to the ascetic identity he has now assumed; and when his wife comes to visit him the totality of his rejection of the life of the *grihastya* (householder and man of affairs) is underscored.

This progression has led Geoffrey Kain to argue, not unreasonably, that *A Tiger for Malgudi* is a novel that follows the same spiritual pattern as *Waiting for the Mahatma* and *The Guide*. In each case, Kain argues, 'the central character [...] is ultimately driven by appetite (self-absorption) to a transcendence of appetite, from an urge to have and control to a position of being claimed and controlled'.[26] On one level this is unexceptionable. *A Tiger for Malgudi* dramatizes just such a Gandhian ethic, in which the suppression of all but the most basic of appetites is the lynch-pin of a more general regimen of abstinence and self-control.[27] The difficulty here is that earlier sections of the novel move in an opposite direction, suggesting that such appetites are central to what it is to be a tiger. When, for example, Raja's circus-master Captain trains him to sit at a table and drink milk with a goat (*Tiger* 54–7), readers are given a strong sense that this is an *un*natural imposition of human will on animal instinct. In short, Raja's final induction into the last two stages of the *asramadharma* fulfils the pattern that Kain identifies, but it does so by moving in an opposite direction from the values that have earlier been dominant for most of the novel. The philosophical dimension has been present from the outset, but there is an unresolved contradiction: Raja is both a natural predator[28] and a creature who transgresses the divide between the animal and the human, displaying attributes that finally allow him to be initiated into the renunciation seen as appropriate to old age. The novel ends on this note, but without satisfactorily resolving its earlier more positive representations of untrammelled animality.

At least one strand of the narrative of Narayan's next novel, *Talkative Man* (1986), suggests a parallel with *A Tiger for Malgudi*. The narrator, TM (Talkative Man), tells the story of 'Dr Rann', a man who has assumed multiple aliases and who has been a serial womanizer and apparent bigamist. Rann's past, like that of Raja's Master, is mysterious, but some light is shed when, as in the earlier novel, a woman who says she is his wife comes to reclaim him as her spouse. There, though, any similarity ends. In *A Tiger for Malgudi*, the episode serves to confirm the *sadhu*'s renunciation of worldly concerns, which involves a repudiation of his earlier life as a family man. In *Talkative Man* there is no such spiritual progression underpinning the narrative. The arrival of Rann's wife, Commandant Sarasa, precipitates the dénouement, in which she abducts him and takes him off to Delhi, but this has little other significance, except with regard to issues of narrative transmission and reliability, which are increasingly prominent in Narayan's later fiction. Certainly there is no suggestion that Rann reforms, since despite the couple's temporarily settling down together again, true to form he subsequently elopes with yet another woman.[29]

Talkative Man is Narayan's shortest novel – at around 35,000 words, really no more than a novella – and in its postscript he describes how, although he originally envisaged it as a 'full-length novel', it refused to 'grow beyond 116 typewritten sheets' (*Talkative* 120). Ruminating on his early lack of success as a novelist and a comment from his agent that *Swami and Friends* had been a 'failure', because at 50,000 words it was 20,000 short of the 'minimum standard for fiction in those days' (*Talkative*121),[30] Narayan continues by speculating on how he might have lengthened *Talkative Man*. Basically, though, he suggests that this would have gone against his inclinations and that works of fiction determine their own length. In this context he remembers Graham Greene's early comments on the brevity of *Swami*, '"I hope you will get a subject next time which will run to a full-length book. Only if you see a choice of subjects and lengths ahead of you, do next time go for the longer"' (*Talkative* 121). In his later works Narayan seems to be struggling to find subjects that might lend themselves to narrative amplification and they contain passages that suggest padding, but in *Talkative Man* and the novella 'Grandmother's Tale' (1992), his last piece of fiction of any length, the brevity is consonant with the metafictive nature of the works, in which the storytelling mode assumes a central importance.

For Geoffrey Kain, apparent weaknesses in the construction of *Talkative Man* are resolved by a view which sees the novel as an instance of Narayan performing Narayan.[31] However, while this view of the novel is interesting to those familiar with the wider body of Narayan's fiction and draws attention to the extent to which it is self-consciously foregrounding its concern with narrative process, it fails to address what appear to be shortcomings in the narrative structure or to make a claim for *Talkative Man* as an autonomous work of fiction. Narayan's superficial aimlessness is once again to the fore, but in this instance the lack of obvious narrative focus and closure is not balanced by an alternative form of resolution. In novels as different from one another as *The English Teacher* and *The Vendor of Sweets*, apparent indeterminacy is negated by a redirection of focus which emphasizes tonal and thematic elements that have been implicit earlier on; in *Talkative Man* there is no such movement, simply a fairly perfunctory completion of a narrative which may leave readers wondering whether they have missed something.

Certainly they will be disappointed if they have anticipated the closure of a classic Western realist novel. Rann is suspected of being a rogue, whose succession of aliases is an index of his duplicity, particularly with regard to women. But even though the evidence that he is a 'lecherous demon' (*Talkative* 79) mounts to a point where the case against him seems overwhelming, Narayan stops just short of making it complete; and through his use of TM, who is partly fascinated by Rann, as the main focalizer of the novel, he interrogates the very notion that people are totally knowable.[32] The strengths of this comparatively slight novel have to do with the debate it stages on the nature of fictional authority and its exploration of the relationship between TM and Rann – and to a lesser extent Commandant Sarasa. *Talkative Man* is, as its title suggests, *about* 'talk', particularly oral story-telling, and since the central tension emerges from the TM/Rann relationship and TM is the main narrative voice, the crux of the tale emerges from the way in which a Malgudi narrator talks about the intrusion of the 'foreign' into the familiar milieu of the small town. It is as if the central conflict of *The Man-Eater of Malgudi* has been displaced onto the level of rumour. Rann is a character who has marked affinities with Vasu in the earlier novel, but he remains elusive to the end. At the same time the seemingly more knowable character of TM is rendered enigmatic, as a result of his relationship with Rann and more generally his place within a narrative in which focalization is central.[33] Like, say, Conrad's Marlow, as the main consciousness of the fiction TM is a figure who both enlists readers' sympathies and yet remains a dramatic construct of the text, whom readers may choose to identify with or to take sides against.

The comparison with Marlow may be useful, particularly for Western readers, as a way of suggesting the novel's emphasis on point of view and narrative instability, but an Indian reference-point provides a more obvious intertext. On the opening page, TM likens himself to Narada, the tale-telling sage of classical Hindu discourse, who is burdened with the dubious gift of gossip: 'I'd choke if I didn't talk, perhaps like Sage Narada of our epics, who for all his brilliance and accomplishments carried a curse on his back that unless he spread a gossip a day, his skull would burst' (*Talkative* 1). As such TM would seem to be like Narada, who even today in India is a byword for those who love to gossip and carry tales: such a person is often called a 'Narada Muni'.[34] In 'The World of the Storyteller' Narayan provides a slightly more serious provenance for Narada: he identifies the sage as a source for the story of *The Ramayana*, locating him in a long line of narrators of the epic, which dates back to Brahma and the 'Great God himself'[35] and forwards to the scribe Valmiki, to whom it is most commonly attributed. Narayan's comments here reveal an interest in tracing an *Ur*-narrative, an originary source for story, but place more emphasis on the transmission and reception of tales:

> [...] And so each tale goes back and further back to an ultimate narrator, who had, perhaps, been an eye-witness to the events. [...] The report travels, like ripples expanding concentrically, until it reaches the storyteller in the village, by whom it is passed to the children at home, so that ninety per cent of the stories are known and appreciated and understood by every mortal in every home, whether literate or illiterate (the question does not arise). (*Gods* 7)

This focus on the oral, dialogic aspects of storytelling helps, then, to reconcile the compulsive tittle-tattle qualities ascribed to 'Narada Muni' in the popular imagination and the more serious function ascribed to him in classical Hindu contexts. He is clearly a figure who fascinated Narayan, and increasingly so in his later work. The eponymous hero of Narayan's next novel, *The World of Nagaraj* (1990), plans to write on Narada, seeing his role as a newsmonger as responsible for temporary conflicts, but ultimately viewing it as an activity that promotes stability and the triumph of good over evil in the cosmic order:

> The sage floated along with ease from one world to another
> among the fourteen worlds above and below this earth,
> carrying news and gossip, often causing clashes between
> gods and demons, demons and demons, and gods and gods,
> and between creatures of the earth. Ultimately, of course,
> such clashes and destruction proved beneficial in a cosmic
> perspective. Evil destroyed itself.[36]

Again this is the kind of thinking that informs the destruction
of Vasu in *The Man-Eater of Malgudi*, but Rann is not finally
identified as a 'lecherous demon', or any other kind of *rakshasa*,
and the indeterminacy surrounding his character suggests the
extent to which notions of identity are the products of narrativization, existing at the level of rumour rather than verifiable
truth. In an illuminating discussion of this aspect of the novel,
entitled 'Will the Real Dr Rann Please Stand up?', Krishna Sen
argues that there are at least three Ranns in the novel: those
narrated by TM; by Commandant Sarasa in her inner narrative
of Rann's earlier life; and by Rann himself, through the version
he provides of himself through his conversation and journal
entries. A fourth possible Rann is indicated through the vignette
provided by Girija, a girl who hopes to run off with him in the
latter stages of the novel.[37]

As TM tells his story to Varma, the proprietor of the Boardless Hotel and a 'born listener' (*Talkative* 2) whose taciturn
nature complements TM's loquaciousness, the novel seems to be
wrestling with the problematics of providing reliable biographical information. Once again the Boardless is a site that resists
naming within a recognizable sign system and using it as the
setting in which TM tells his tale seems highly appropriate for
the kind of account he provides. Narayan's fiction, from *The
English Teacher* to 'The Grandmother's Tale', frequently blurs
the distinction between fact and fiction in the compositional
elements that have gone into its making and in a novel such
as *Talkative Man* this ambivalence translates into a tentative,
dialogic exploration of how versions of identity are constructed.
Rann's many names may suggest fraudulence, but from another
perspective they represent the difficulties inherent in arriving

at a definitive version of self, as surely as the Boardless resists conventional labelling. *Talkative Man* is, then, the Narayan novel is which his life-long obsession with the problematics of storytelling is expressed in its most metafictive form. TM's struggle to place the 'real Dr Rann' is a metonym for the text's concern with the problem of narrating identity; and viewed from this angle, far from being a garrulous gossip, TM can be seen as an author surrogate, a figure whose difficulty in constructing a satisfactory biography for Dr Rann reflects the novel's metafictive questionings.

Beyond this, Rann presents a particular challenge to TM, since, as so often in Narayan's fiction, he represents alterity. His name, TM learns, is a contraction of Rangan, which he has 'trimmed and tailored to sound foreign', so that '[o]ne would take him to be a German, Rumanian or Hungarian – anything but what he was, a pure Indian from a southernmost village named Maniyur' (*Talkative* 2) and a cultivated foreignness informs all the other markers of his assumed identity, particularly his 'outlandish' dress (*Talkative* 76), which includes such items as a blue three-piece suit, olive-green shorts, a solar topee and a Japanese kimono. The statement that he comes from a South Indian village may provide a seemingly authentic account of Rann's identity, but his erasure of this through the assumption of a foreign persona problematizes the notion that identity can be 'pure' and single. In this sense the challenge Rann offers to TM's conservative Malgudi standpoint – TM is specifically identified as another member of 'the Kabir Street aristocracy' (*Talkative* 26) – is not that of actual foreignness, but rather that of a view of identity which, like Grace's in *The Vendor of Sweets*, disputes the validity of originary conceptions of self; and his accounts of his travels to far-off places replace such conceptions with a nomadic view of subjectivity.[38]

The key signifier in this pattern is 'Timbuctoo'. When asked by TM where he comes from when they first meet, Rann immediately replies, '"Timbuctoo, let us say"' (*Talkative* 9). The 'let us say' suggests invention and, although it is followed by specific comments on the rapid modernization that the African town is undergoing, these erroneously locate it on the west *coast* of the continent, suggesting that it is as much a fantasy-place for Rann (and possibly Narayan?) as it is for TM. It functions as an image of exotic alterity, which is directly contrasted with the familiarity of Malgudi. Malgudi, in TM's view, is a great leveller, a locale that neutralizes the intrusions of alien oddities: 'Malgudi climate has something in it which irons out outlandish habits' (*Talkative* 27). 'Timbuctoo' in contrast is a signifier, which in TM's view connotes '"a fairy-tale or cock-and-bull setting"' (*Talkative* 29). So once again the novel's central theme is predicated on a spatial opposition: between the familiarity and supposed stability of Malgudi, which, though subject to change itself, still represents conservative Hindu thinking when personified by the contemporary Narada figure of TM, and an ill-defined complex of external forces, variously associated with technological advances, modernity more generally, the West, travel, changing social codes and other parts of India. After first taking up residence in the seminal Malgudi site of the station waiting-room,[39] a liminal location subsequently occupied by Commandant Sarasa, Rann literally invades TM's – and conservative Malgudi's – domestic space when he is admitted into his home, an even more personal form of violation than Vasu's appropriation of the attic above Nataraj's press. However, the most significant development in the exploration of this topos in *Talkative Man* is the clear indication that place – and especially foreignness – is a discursive construct, as much a product of narrative invention as the elusive Rann's identity.

Like Vasu in *The Man-Eater*, whose occupation as a taxidermist is anathema to the peaceful Nataraj's beliefs about the sanctity of animal life, Rann's views seem to suggest a particular, slanted aspect of modernity. When he gives a lecture to the Malgudi Lotus Club, it is on his specialist subject, 'Futurology', an apocalyptic discourse which predicts 'the collapse of this planet about A.D. 3000' (*Talkative* 105). It is an occasion that provides Narayan with ample opportunity to mock small-town pretentiousness, and this satire is particularly directed against the misuse of rhetoric. So once again *talk* is the main focus of attention. Rann is introduced by a Deputy Minister, said to be 'in charge of Town Planning, Cattle Welfare, Child Welfare, Family Planning, Cooperation and Environment, Ecology and other portfolios too numerous even for him to remember' (*Talkative* 100). The speech he gives is a travesty of dated nationalist rhetoric, interlaced with Gandhian and Nehruvian allusions, which finally amount to little more than name-dropping. When he is succeeded by Rann, talk assumes a complexion which, ostensibly at least, looks towards the future rather than the past. However, Rann's speech is a bizarre kind of ecological discourse, which revolves around two tropes from the natural world: a 'Cannibal Herb' (*Talkative* 105) and the threat of a plague of rats. The herb is one of Narayan's most powerful metaphors for the amorphous and ill-defined creeping forces that threaten Malgudi's insulated existence. In his address to the Malgudi Lotus Club, Rann describes it as follows:

> 'This is the future occupant of our planet [...]: This is a weed spreading under various aliases in every part of the earth – known in some places as Congress weed, don't know which congress is meant, Mirza Thorn, Chief's Tuft, Voodoo Bloom, the Blighter and so on. Whatever the name, it's an invader, may have originated out of the dust of some other planet left by a crashing meteor. I see it everywhere; it's a nearly indestructible pest. Its empire is insidiously growing [...].' (*Talkative* 75)

Although this description suggests a worldwide phenomenon, the references to 'Congress' and 'empire' also evoke meanings that have particular valency in an Indian context, while the 'various aliases' of the weed inevitably remind readers of Rann himself. So his apocalyptic discourse has an affinity with the characteristics that the novel ascribes to him: not just because of his multiple names, but also because of the difficulty of locating him in any single place. There is no suggestion that he is a critic of the phenomenon that he represents, but his exploits seem to be a personal equivalent of the spread of the weed 'in every part of the earth'. The weed comes to signify the complex of ill-defined forces that are supposedly eroding local identity in a harmful way,[40] as it renders everything with which it comes into contact a victim of its homogenizing, global tendencies.

It is one of the most powerful tropes of alien intrusion to be found anywhere in Narayan's fiction – not least because of the suggestion that it may have extra-terrestrial origins – but it is also an image founded on the paranoiac belief that 'pure' cultures are threatened by any form of external incursion. However, the ending of *Talkative Man* fails to offer reaffirmation of the older Malgudi *status quo*, which is at least partly reinstated in the conclusion of most of Narayan's earlier works, and throughout the novel the emphasis on talk makes for a particularly provisional and dialogic investigation of identity. In this respect *Talkative Man* develops and extends debates that inform many earlier Narayan novels. This said, its various narratives are not all accorded the same degree of authority and finally, the garrulous TM's point of view is privileged over the other accounts, not least because he is the main narrator of a text that pays passing homage to the place of the gossip Narada in Hindu discourse, ancient and modern.

In Narayan's next novel, *The World of Nagaraj* (1990), this passing homage is replaced by a full-blown consideration of the possible relevance of Narada for the contemporary Indian storyteller. Nagaraj is yet another member of the Kabir Street aristocracy and as such he numbers Talkative Man among his neighbours. Unlike the bachelor TM he is married, but he has escaped many of the responsibilities of the second *asrama* by virtue of being childless and, like Sriram in *Waiting for the Mahatma*, having independent means. So, although his daily routine bears some resemblance to the typical Narayan protagonist of the middle-period novels, in that he frequents Market Road and regularly encounters its small businessmen, as well as doing unpaid work for a sari centre, Nagaraj seems less burdened by either domestic or business cares than earlier Narayan heroes. As he walks down Market Road early on in the novel, his 'world' seems uncomplicatedly settled, and the apparently omniscient narrator comments, 'You could not find a more contented soul in Malgudi at that moment' (*WN* 16).

His peace of mind is, however, about to be disturbed in two ways. The opening sentence identifies him as 'a man with a mission' (*WN* 1) and his ambition, which he tries in vain to realise during the course of the novel, is to write a magnum opus on Narada, to tell the story of the archetypal storyteller. Meanwhile the tranquillity of his home life is upset by the arrival of his nephew, Tim, whom he takes into his home, after Tim has left his father. In another rehearsal of the theme of the partitioned family (previously employed in *The Financial Expert* and *The Man-Eater of Malgudi*) the novel describes Nagaraj's past separation from his older brother, Gopu, after their father's death and how the father's property was divided between them. Gopu has gone to live in a village, where he has espoused the political philosophy of modernization, while Nagaraj has stayed in the traditional Malgudi ambience of Kabir Street. Nagaraj has been especially fond of his nephew and 'heartbroken' (*WN* 34) when Gopu has refused his request to let him stay in Malgudi, after the partition deed. So in one sense the two brothers' rivalry over Tim makes him the tearing-point of the novel and his return to Malgudi in the present might seem to suggest the triumph of the values that Nagaraj represents over the sub-Gandhian village rhetoric of his brother.

However, the novel's spatial dynamics are more complicated than the simple contrast between town and village implied here suggests and seeing its view of place as structured around a binary opposition between Malgudi conservatism and village 'progress' is unsatisfactory. As in virtually all of Narayan's novels, though more markedly so in his later work, Malgudi itself is heterogeneous, a location that encompasses a range of very different spaces, particularly as a consequence of the impact of outside forces. Once again the small town contains areas that are unfamiliar to the protagonist; and at the beginning of the novel Nagaraj is blissfully unaware of parts of Malgudi that are only a comparatively short distance away from his customary haunts in its traditional centre. Like the space inhabited by several earlier Narayan protagonists – from Krishna in *The English Teacher* onwards – the *world* of Nagaraj, foregrounded in the title, is very narrowly circumscribed and places such as New Extension constitute an epistemological challenge to his view of life. After Tim returns to Malgudi, in episodes reminiscent of Balu's behaviour in *The Financial Expert*, he takes to frequenting Kismet, a club in New Extension which is, constructed in an oppositional relationship with the familiar Boardless. When Nagaraj discovers from Talkative Man that Tim has been seen at Kismet, he asks TM what Kismet is and is told, '"A sort of club and restaurant and bar – started by a North Indian – very popular and fashionable"' (*WN* 59). Again, then, extraneous modern influences are seen to be finding their way into Malgudi and threatening the supposed stability of the older, orthodox way of life; and it is these influences, not the declining world of Kabir Street,[41] that attract Tim. Tim is not particularly fully drawn, but he clearly represents the changing values of the younger generation. His Western name – 'his actual name at the naming ceremony was Krishnaji' (*WN* 10) – is, like those of Rosie in *The Guide*, Grace in *The Vendor of Sweets*, Daisy in *The Painter of Signs* and Rann in *Talkative Man*, an index of the extent to which he represents the encroachments of modernity into conservative Malgudi society, for which Kabir Street is again a metonym. Krishna has become Tim and when he marries and brings his harmonium-playing wife, Saroja, into Nagaraj's household, the mental peace that Nagaraj craves, in order to embark on his work on Narada, is shattered. So the invasion of the physical space of the house, which parallels changes in the town at large, once again operates as a trope for the disturbance of the protagonist's psychological equanimity. Again, Narayan dramatizes the conflict between apparently settled older Malgudi values and a complex of external forces which challenge its capacity to remain insulated from the intrusions of modernity.

'The world of Nagaraj' is, then, both a physical and a mental space, a site in which competing ideologies engage in battle, with the most interesting encounters taking place inside the hero's mind. Thus, when Gopu returns to Malgudi in search of Tim and demands that Nagaraj take him to New Extension to find his son, the movement into this alien space engenders a sense of paranoia in Nagaraj. Although it is only a short distance from the Malgudi world with which he is familiar, going to New Extension is a journey into the unknown for Nagaraj and, as in *The English Teacher* and *Waiting for the Mahatma*, this location, in which brahminical taboos about cleanliness appear to be unknown, seems threateningly polluted. When the two brothers find Tim, it is in a 'narrow lane, littered with rubbish in a colony of thatched huts' (*WN* 157). Gopu and Tim leave Nagaraj at this point and, sitting alone on a stone bench where there is no shade, he finds even the uncongenial *climate* of this part of the town outside his experience. He also ruminates on another intrusion into Malgudi space, which is changing its character: 'Quite a lot of junglees have invaded the town, attracted by the promise of work on the new railway line to Mempi' (*WN* 159). Just before this he has been distressed at the thought that his work on Narada is being threatened 'in this *jungle* of harmonium lovers' (*WN* 158; my italics) and the conflation of New Extension space, the never-reached North Indian-owned Kismet, rubbish, heat, 'junglees' and modern music in his mind induces a panic attack. Revealingly, as he sits alone on the bench, he feels paralysed and thinks: '"everyone is in a hurry and passing on. I am stationary like a milestone. The procession passes. Why can't I also pass instead of being a milestone? People take advantage of my milestone nature [...]"' (*WN* 160).[42] The distinction that emerges here is, then, less a contrast between New Extension and the older parts of Malgudi than between two dialectically opposed approaches to experience: a settled, sedentary mentality and a restive, nomadic sensibility, which frustrates the very notion of cultural fixity.[43] This is the central tension explored in the Tim plot of *The World of Nagaraj*. Tim, and Saroja, are comparatively shadowy characters but, along with the various other modern forces that are coming into Malgudi society, they represent a changing way of life that offers a direct challenge to the perceived stasis of Tamil brahmin orthodoxy.

However, readers who focus on the Tim plot are likely to be disappointed by the novel. As the main representative of a younger generation's modern values, Tim lacks the vitality of the other Narayan versions of this type, such as Mali in *The Vendor of Sweets;* and this element of the plot drifts to a lack-lustre conclusion which offers little in terms of narrative closure, nor any other kind of obvious resolution. In one sense the Narada plot is equally inconclusive, since Nagaraj never even begins his magnum opus, let alone completes it. However, abortive though his pursuit of Narada is, it is not satirised in the same way as, say, the poet Sen's Krishna epic is in *The Man-Eater of Malgudi. The World of Nagaraj* goes beyond the incipient metafiction of *Talkative Man*, to provide a more extensive and fundamentally serious investigation of the problematics of storytelling and this is more central to its agenda than the tensions generated by Tim and Saroja's intrusion into Nagaraj's world. Yet finally neither aspect of the plot is complete it itself: the force of the novel, as so often in Narayan, emerges from the tension generated by the interaction of these two seemingly divergent strands.

The first chapter of the novel finds Nagaraj asking a *sadhu* where he can get ochre cloth, so that he can perform his morning *puja* in robes akin to those of a *sanyasi*. However, although he ponders the changes in one's life-style that come with advancing years, there is no suggestion that he is actually contemplating moving into the fourth *asrama*. When the sadhu asks him if he wants to be come a *sanyasi*, he pleads family commitments as a reason for not embarking on the final stage of renuncia-tion and the more comic sections of the novel represent him as something of a hen-pecked husband, a mock-heroic figure who generally defers to his wife Sita, whom he compares with Lady Macbeth on numerous occasions in the novel.[44] Although he is married to a Sita, like Nataraj in the *Man-Eater* and Raman in *The Painter of Signs*, he is an unlikely Rama. Earlier in his life, his father has likened him to the epic protagonist's supportive younger brother, Lakshmana (*WN* 27) and, while this parallel stops short of the highest accolade, the very use of such a mythic analogy in relation to a Malgudi 'little man' raises the question of what constitutes heroism, suggesting a possible renegotiation of the terms in which it is commonly understood.

It is in this context that his obsession with Narada needs

to be seen and his desire for the partial detachment signified by wearing ochre while performing his daily *puja* seems to be related to this. Narada is important to him both as a subject of story – a mythic figure with whom he can identify – and as a purveyor of tales, a man responsible for narrating the stories of others. In order to tell the storyteller's story, Nagaraj has to achieve a degree of detachment from worldly concerns, but to become a *sanyasi* would, it seems, leave him too removed from everyday life to engage with the writer's task at all. Wearing ochre is, then, it appears, a crucial adjunct of his literary project. Read as an expression of the novelist's own concerns, the account of Nagaraj's agonizings over the problematics of storytelling seem to relate to Narayan's struggle with the problem of being an older novelist: how does a brahmin retain his purchase on social affairs at an age when the *varnasramadharma* prescribes a retreat from active life? And more generally, this raises issues relating to the ethics of the life of writing. As Rajini Srikanth puts it, 'In the context of the author or the artist [...] *dharma* takes on a dialectic twist. The author is in the strange position of having to be both in and out of this world at the same time.'[45] On this level *The World of Nagaraj* is a novel that investigates what *dharma* is appropriate for a writer; and in exploring this issue it is again a text that pursues metafictive questions.

Nagaraj's choice of Narada as the subject for his great work seems particularly apposite in this context, since the sage, despite being a byword for gossip-mongering in contemporary India, is one of the more elusive figures in Hindu mythology, as much a construction of rumour as a spreader of rumours himself. Nagaraj is partly motivated by the belief that Narada has not received sufficient attention, but various factors frustrate him in his attempts to tell the storyteller's life-story. His difficulties stem from both external causes, notably the presence of Tim and Saroja in his house, which necessitate his having to fulfil a not particularly demanding version of the duties of the second *asrama* and, more seriously, the intractability of Narada as a subject. There is, the novel makes clear, no definitive account of Narada and this is the central paradox that faces Nagaraj: he wants to write about Narada, because, at least according to one school of thought, the sage has not received his due, but his comparative neglect means that sources for writing his story are lacking.

Nagaraj finds three local repositories of potential information on Narada and they represent three possible modes of writing available to the South Indian novelist. The first is a Sanskrit pundit, Kavu, who lectures Nagaraj on the need to be able to read the '"Language of Gods"' (*WN* 96) in order to have access to ancient Hindu wisdom, but refuses to translate classical texts and generally alienates Nagaraj through his exclusivity. The second is Talkative Man, who represents local (presumably Tamil) orality. Disillusioned with Kavu pundit's closed attitude to knowledge, Nagaraj sits on the river steps, as always a spiritual location in Narayan, hoping that meditation may help him in his search for his elusive subject and at this point has the sense that Narada has 'responded and [is] manifesting himself' (*WN* 101). The object of this epiphany is in fact TM and, as in *Talkative Man*, he functions as a modern-day equivalent of the mythic gossip, but the only way in which he is able to assist Nagaraj is by taking him back to the pundit, albeit with the more pragmatic suggestion that he pay him for his assistance. The third is the stationer Bari, who comes from a part of North India, Aligarh, where Narada is supposed to be particularly revered and who possesses an ancient tome, *Narad Puran*, which purportedly contains the story of Narada and which, Bari says, is as highly valued as Valmiki's *Ramayana* in his part of the country. However, the sections from this volume that he reads to Nagaraj never reach a point where the sage appears. Nagaraj takes notes assiduously and subsequently studies what he has taken down in the hope that it will inspire him to start writing, but the material relates only to Creation and the primeval Flood, not Narada.

So Nagaraj finds himself caught in a seemingly infinite set of deferrals, no more able to get to the supposed real beginning of his story, the moment of the hero's birth, than the narrator-protagonist of Sterne's classic metafictive novel, *Tristram Shandy*. Like Tristram, Nagaraj is comically forced back to an *ab ovo* ('from the egg') starting-point – in Tristram's case an account of the moment of his conception – rather than the *in medias res* ('in the middle of the thing') beginning, for which Horace praised Homer's epics.[46] In Nagaraj's case, this assumes a literal dimension, when his quest for Narada leads him into trying to decipher the meaning of an obscure phrase, '"the Great Egg"' (*WN* 130), which he has taken down from Bari's readings. Try as he will, he finds himself unable to hatch this mysterious egg and begin telling the story of Narada:

> Thus it went on, day after day. [...] He could have no objective view of his own composition, but went on spinning his yarn, groping in the darkness with the tremendous Egg still intact, wafting in the ocean. When it burst Creation would begin, and surely Narada would be the first to emerge. (*WN* 131)

So the difficulty of reaching a moment of cosmic Creation, from which other narratives may follow, is comically rendered, but Nagaraj's angst is also a serious expression of the problems surrounding literary composition. Narayan's novel clearly overcomes these problems on the most basic level, since a story *does* get told, but this is first and foremost a self-reflexive account of the problems of writing rather than an attempt at describing an external social or, as in so many Narayan novels, an inner psycho-spiritual reality. Both of these characteristic Narayan elements are present, but in *The World of Nagaraj*, they are subordinate to the self-referential comedy.

Ultimately each of Nagaraj's three potential sources of information on Narada proves useless, but within the novel's metaliterary and metalinguistic scheme, they represent possible portals through which classical knowledge may be attained: Sanskrit scribal exclusiveness, Hindi-mediated hybridized transcription and everyday Tamil talk. The dramatization of these three possibilities clearly raises issues in relation to the ownership of classical Hindu knowledge; and Nagaraj's own choice of language, English, opens up a fourth possibility within this metalinguistic debate. This is a choice that relates directly to Narayan's own practice from the very beginning of his career, both in his fiction and his retelling of Hindu myths in his versions of *The Ramayana* and *The Mahabharata* and in *Gods, Demons and Others*, and the reasons given for Nagaraj's preference of English seem to endorse its perceived superiority as a mode of communication. Nagaraj chooses it because he sees it as a medium that resists narrow communal and other interests. However, hesitant about his choice, he asks TM's opinion, telling him: '"I thought it would be best in English, to reach the wide world. After all, I want Narada's personality to be understood universally, irrespective of caste, creed, nationality or religion"' and TM supports this by saying that English is less prescriptive grammatically: '"Excellent idea. For this purpose English is the right language – the only language free from the grammarian's tyranny"' (*WN* 125). The suggestion is that English is both an international language and a language that offers more flexibility.

The broader implications of this are, of course, controversial. As the language of the former colonizer and the new global superpower, English has traditionally been the language of the elite in India, though increasingly less so as the number of Indians speaking it has grown along with the expansion of the middle classes and the boom in the Indian economy that began around the time *The World of Nagaraj* was published. In Narayan's case, the use of English seems comparatively innocent,[47] though it is clearly a product of his education and upbringing and debates that he had been having with himself ever since his boyhood. The suggestion that using English enables the writer to transcend barriers of 'caste, creed, nationality or religion' may well reflect a typically South Indian preference for it, as opposed to Hindi, as a language to of pan-Indian communication as well as an international *lingua franca*, but the words put in the mouth of TM at this point suggest a more general reason for favouring it. English is preferred as a language of 'freedom' and in this sense Narayan's choice of it is markedly at odds with views of his work which suggest he is trying to preserve a fossilized brahminical view of experience. Stories told in English are, it seems, particularly malleable and prone to transformation. Like all his

fictions, *The World of Nagaraj* brings a hotch-potch of traditions
together, but it goes further than most of his novels in staging
this debate on a metaliterary and metalinguistic level.

Most interestingly of all, it seems to suggest that there are
no authoritative versions: stories are reinvented each time they
are told. The difficulties that Nagaraj encounters in his quest
to write about Narada extend beyond the problem of finding
a helpful mentor; they also stem from the fugitive nature of
Narada's reputation and the problem of arriving at a version
of his identity and his mythic role. Convinced that Narada is
a figure who 'created strife, no doubt, by passing disturbing
gossip from one quarter to another, [though] it always proved
beneficial in the long run, in an eternal perspective', Nagaraj
struggles to understand 'the *concept* of Narada' (*WN* 44; my
italics), a phrase which suggests that the sage's character may
have metaphysical as well as metaliterary significance. Suggestions of underlying cosmic harmony are introduced at the end
of several earlier Narayan novels, including *Mr Sampath*, *The
Guide* and *The Man-Eater of Malgudi* (without ever providing
definitive closure), but in *The World of Nagaraj* the metafictive
deferrals continue to the last and Narada's identity remains a
conundrum. So there is no comfortable resolution; the novel
retains the ambivalent attitude towards Narada's standing in
Indian myth that it has displayed throughout. Earlier in his life
Nagaraj has discussed the difficulties of writing about Narada
with the elderly librarian of the Town Hall Library, complaining
that '"There are no authentic references to Narada anywhere
and I feel handicapped"', which elicits the reply, '"Why don't
you *invent* something about the sage?"' (*WN* 19; my italics).
Paradoxically, Narada's story is seen as both common knowledge
('The story of Narada is known to everyone in our country, even
a child knows it', *WN* 117) and yet needing to be invented. The
old librarian also tells Nagaraj that it was through invention
that 'the Saint's biography grew and became authoritative literature over a range of a million years, each narrator inventing
and adding some stuff, the great sage himself inspiring every
story-teller in his own way' (*WN* 117). A similar ambivalence

concerning how much is known about Narada's biography can also be seen in a conversation at the end of the novel between Nagaraj and his wife Sita, who takes a fairly negative view of his writing project:

> 'Still I don't understand your preoccupation with Narada. Everyone knows that he was a great sage – that's all. No one has bothered to want to write his life story. Why should you alone bother?'
> He [Nagaraj] had no answer; he blinked unhappily. He could only say, 'But others have written. Kavu pundit has four volumes in Sanskrit on the subject, and Bari has a big tome, which is over a hundred years old.'
> 'So why should you take the trouble again over the same subject?'
> 'So that our people may also know.' (WN 179–80)

Whether the story has been told again and again or not remains unclear, especially since the anticipated access to it from Kavu pundit's knowledge and Bari's volume never materializes and their knowledge of the story is itself suspect. Yet Narayan's view that the great stories are told and retold, 'like ripples expanding concentrically' (Gods 7)[48] and come down to posterity as layered accretions, waiting to be told yet again by a new author, possibly for a different community, seems relevant to the view of inter-textuality implied in The World of Nagaraj insofar as several passages in the novel support the view that the storyteller's role involves reinventing the known. The difficulty with this is, of course, that Nagaraj does not get to tell Narada's story at all. So, although an attempt to write about an ancient figure is at the heart of the plot, The World of Nagaraj turns out to be more sceptical about the viability of reworking mythic subjects in contemporary contexts than any earlier Narayan novel.

The novel ends rather abruptly with Nagaraj feeling he has 'no hope of writing any more' (WN 184), because Tim, who has had an argument with the Secretary of Kismet, and Saroja, complete with a larger harmonium, return to the shelter of his roof. Finally, Nagaraj has to be seen as an aspiring writer rather than a successful novelist like Narayan. Forced to contend with

the conflicting demands of two kinds of *dharma*, family responsibilities and the contemplative withdrawal necessary to succeed
as an author, Nagaraj finally fails to achieve the degree of detachment necessary to realise his 'mission'. Narada's fugitive identity
may be a particular obstacle that frustrates him, but his social
situation is at least as important a factor. So, ultimately, although
the difficulties he experiences in even beginning his planned
story suggest a *Tristram Shandy*-like pattern of comic frustra-
tion, *The World of Nagaraj* is as much concerned with the practical problems that face the would-be writer who is also a family
man. Read in this way, the novel is another story of a secular
brahmin, struggling with aspects of the inherited scribal culture
in a contemporary situation. Its two plot strands complement one
another, as two sides of the same ethical dilemma; and Nagaraj's
psyche, not Tim, is the fulcrum on which the novel pivots.

Narayan's last extended work of fiction, the novella 'The
Grandmother's Tale' (1992),[49] which blends fact and fiction in
a manner reminiscent of *The English Teacher*, is ostensibly
an attempt at recording a chapter from his family history in a
neutral, unmediated way and as such altogether less metafictive
than *The World of Nagaraj*. It narrates the central event from
his great grandmother's life-story, as it was told to him as a boy
by his grandmother, framing this event with other details from
the family's history. However, the dividing-line between fact
and fiction proves porous, not least because calling it a 'novella'
suggests that the 'real-life' story is fiction.

Numerous details lend an air of factual authenticity to 'The
Grandmother's Tale' and with material in the novella echoing
information previously included in Narayan's autobiographical
memoir *My Days*, it would seem reasonable to assume that 'The
Grandmother's Tale' has more in common with life-writing than
fiction. Thus, the novella talks about the narrator's grandmother's role in the frame-narrator's early education in the following
terms:

> I had to repeat the multiplication table up to twenty but I
> always fumbled and stuttered after twelve and needed prod-
> ding and goading to attain the peak; I had to recite Sanskrit

verse and slokas in praise of Goddess Saraswathi and a
couple of other gods, and hymns in Tamil; identify six ragas
when granny hummed the tunes or, conversely, mention
the songs when she named the *ragas* [...] (*GT* 4)

My Days speaks of the instruction that Narayan received from
his grandmother in a very similar manner:

> She taught me multiplication; I had to recite the tables up
> to twelve every day and then all the thirty letters of Tamil
> alphabet [sic], followed by Avvaiyar's [[50]] sayings. She also
> made me repeat a few Sanskrit slokas praising Saraswathi,
> the Goddess of Learning. And then she quickly rendered a
> few classical melodies, whose Raga were [sic] to be quickly
> identified by me. If I fumbled she scolded me unreservedly,
> but rewarded me with a coin if I proved diligent. [...][51]

The lack of distance between the details of the supposedly
fictive grandmother's life and Narayan's own grandmother is
further confirmed by information included in Susan and N.
Ram's biography of Narayan's early years. For example, the
Rams mention Narayan's grandmother's love of gardening, her
'attentiveness to a range of domestic duties'[52] and her keeping
open house, even though she had been left in straitened circumstances by her 'husband's posthumous financial collapse'[53] – all
details that appear in the novella.[54] Most tellingly of all, at one
point in 'The Grandmother's Tale' Narayan temporarily deserts
past reminiscence and gives an account of a more recent episode
from what is fairly clearly his own life. The narrator records how
'two years ago' he went, along with his friend and biographer
Ram, to revisit Number One, Vellala Street in the Purasawalkam
district of Madras, the house in which he was born:

> It was totally demolished, cleared and converted into
> a vacant plot on which the idea was to build an air-
> conditioned multi-storeyed hotel. Among the debris we
> found the old massive main-door lying, with 'One' still
> etched on it. Ram made an offer on the spot and immedi-
> ately transported it to his house, where he has mounted it
> as a show-piece. (*GT* 56–7) [55]

The passage, it should be said, appears in brackets in the novella, but nevertheless the precise detail of the number of the house and the fairly obvious foray into the author's recent life seem to dispel any lingering sense that the story of 'The Grandmother's Tale' is simply fiction. And further proof of the (auto) biographical nature of the narrative, if any such proof be needed, is provided by a passage in Susan Ram's Introduction to the Rams' biography, which confirms how they found the 'solid teak door, studded with brass knobs' on the demolition site and how it subsequently 'became a much-visited showpiece in our house'.[56]

Yet the novella is not primarily concerned with the Narayan figure of the narrator. It is his *grandmother's tale of her mother* and as such a much more complex attempt to get to grips with the problematics of family historiography. Although Narayan's method appears to posit the possibility of direct access to the great grandmother's life-history through the agency of oral storytelling, the novella's interpellation of the figures of the storytelling grandmother and her grandson and interlocutor, the Narayan-like narrator, involves layers of indirection, which have the effect of suggesting that family history is Narada-like gossip. Beginning with *Swami and Friends*, where the protagonist's grandmother endeavours in vain to get him to listen to the story of the mythical king Harischandra,[57] the grandmother figure repeatedly functions as a repository of the oral tradition in Narayan's fiction;[58] and the Rams suggest that the particular 'Ammani' of 'The Grandmother's Tale' seems 'to speak to a larger experience of South Indian grandmothers', as well as evoking a particular genre of South Indian oral narrative.[59] Whether or not one takes this view, it is as if Narayan has come full circle to one of his earliest narrative sources and, while the schoolboy Swami is more interested in his classmates' exploits, the older writer now pays homage to the kind of ancestral storytelling of which grandmothers are the conduit by making her the narrator who carries the main burden of the tale. She is, however, a narrator who is framed by another narrator, a figure who functions in a rather different way to TM in *Talkative Man*, since although he, too, tells an oral tale *within* the larger scribal fiction that he narrates, he is not bounded by another dramatized narrator as she is. In 'The Grandmother's Tale' the storytelling situation is very explicitly foregrounded through the presence of the narrator, who prompts the grandmother to continue, supplement or be more precise at several points in the narrative.

The narrator describes the story as 'mainly a story-writer's version of a hearsay biography' (*GT* 8), which attempts to 'retain the flavour' (*GT* 7) of his grandmother's speech and the process of storytelling is accentuated throughout, with the effect that readers are made very aware of the narrativization of the life-story that is being told. And in this sense 'The Grandmother's Tale' follows on directly from *The World of Nagaraj* in that it addresses the difficulties facing the would-be storyteller. The tale is, however, altogether more personal – mythic reference-points are few, though at one point the grandmother does invoke one of his favourite archetypes, Savitri,[60] as an exemplum of the wifely devotion and strength displayed by his great grandmother – and among other things it serves to preserve an extraordinary episode in his family history that occurred almost a century and a half previously. Dates and places become vague in the grandmother's account of her mother's life, but the frame-narrator makes an assumption that locates the central events in the middle of the nineteenth century: 'My grandmother could not be specific about the time since she was unborn at the beginning of her mother's story. One has to assume an arbitrary period – that is the later period of the East India Company, before the Sepoy Mutiny' (*GT* 8). So, as the novella retells the story in the early 1990s, it has the effect of renewing the ancient mouth-to-mouth oral storytelling traditions of South India. Short-circuiting the usual generation-to-generation process of transmission, Narayan renders his grandmother's early twentieth-century version of his great grandmother's mid-nineteenth-century story, as told to her by the great grandmother herself, for a late twentieth-century readership and posterity. In so doing he operates in a Homeric or Valmiki-like manner, in that he gives written form to the 'oral' narrative of a Narada, and the act of storytelling provides the crux of the tale. Just as the central tension of various earlier Narayan fictions emerges from the interplay that occurs between two contrasted characters, here the main driving-force is the conversation between grandson and grandmother that frames the latter's tale. It is a conversation characterized by the grandson's repeated interruptions, which for the most part elicit an irritated response on the part of the grandmother, who is both incapable of furnishing him with the kind of detail that he desires, since she too is repeating a told tale, and, on occasions, deliberately obstructs him in his pursuit of a definitive narrative. The former response can be seen in remarks such as '"Why do you ask me? Am I a wizard to see the past? If you interrupt me like this, I'll never be able to complete the story"' (GT 25) and '"Why do you ask me? How do I know? [...] I can only tell the story as I heard it. I was not there as you know"' (GT 35). The latter response comes in a passage where the grandson tries to get her to tell him where his great grandmother and grandfather finally settled and he comes to realise that, although she deflects his questions by again pleading incomplete knowledge, she is well aware which town it is and has been teasing him (GT 51–2).

One critic, John Hawley, imagines 'Narayan in the role of the grandmother'[61] and if at first this seems to be a rather perverse reading of the novella, since the story-writer is much more obviously a Narayan figure, it is lent credence by the suggestion that the grandmother's exasperation at being questioned can be related to Narayan's resistance to 'those who wished to direct his writing in another direction, towards questions he chose not to address'.[62] On another level, though, this identification serves to suggest the extent to which the story is about narrative transmission and ownership, with its meaning gradually emerging from the interplay between its two main voices. Its ostensibly transparent account of the main event in the great grandmother's life and the history surrounding this becomes increasingly complex, as the text emphasizes the extent to which access to the past is hampered by 'hazy' memory, lack of information and gaps (GT 24), as well as the frame-narrator's difficulty in providing a verbatim transcription of his grandmother's or great grandmother's words. On one of the rare occasions when the great grandmother's words are rendered in direct speech, a brief foray into Tamil (GT 30) points up another level of mediation involved in the telling of the tale: the act of translation. The actual story told by the grandmother has, of course, also been narrated in Tamil and so its reconstruction in English involves a similar act of literal translation, while more generally the act of retelling stories, and particularly the rendering of oral tales in written form, inevitably involves a further level of transformation. The overall effect is to create a sense of the extent to which story is a process of layered accretion and this destroys any illusion of definitive narrative authority. The kernel of 'The Grandmother's Tale' is a compelling story about a nineteenth-century child bride who pursues and wins back the husband who deserts her and subsequently, once she has reclaimed her man, becomes a 'model wife in the orthodox sense' (GT 53). However, the storytelling context, which not only raises issues of ownership but also sees grandmother and grandson debating the ethics of the great grandmother's conduct, is altogether more central.

The grandmother provides a vivid account, but emphasizes her limitations as a narrator. Her grandson, the Narayan persona of the frame-narrator, may seem to speak with greater authority, but his angle of focalization is ambivalently handled and he comes across as something of a split subject. Although he is mainly presented as an authorial 'I', sometimes he is referred to in the third person and on at least two occasions the distance between first- and third-person narrative voices is completely collapsed: in one case the text refers to him as 'I (this writer)' (GT 45); later it speaks of 'My (this writer's) mother' (GT 66). On one level this elision seems to relate back to the text's conflation of fact and fiction and it may well be that it reflects a degree of uncertainty on Narayan's part about both this and the voice in which he is speaking: as family biographer or fictional 'story-writer' (the phrase he uses to characterize the grandson narrator)? Irregardless, the way in which the comparatively lean narrative of 'The Grandmother's Tale' is told throws up a range of questions about narration, making it another metaliterary text. It ends inconclusively with the words '...that's all we know' (*GT* 67) and these provide a fitting coda to the fictional career of a writer who, though sometimes associated with conservative Hindu thinking, is primarily concerned with dramatizing the dialectical interplay of opposites and whose narrative indeterminacy reflects a relativist habit of mind, which asks more questions than it answers.

Critical overview and conclusion

Graham Greene's shadow has hung over much of the critical response to Narayan's fiction, particularly reviews of his novels and, although Narayan was always grateful for Greene's patronage and editing, he was the originator of some of the delimiting stereotypes that have repeatedly been applied to Narayan's work. Greene's 1937 Introduction to *The Bachelor of Arts* paved the way for the surfeit of comparisons to Chekhov[1] that runs through Narayan criticism, being taken over as more or less *de rigueur* by early reviewers and recurring again and again in later responses. Similarly, Greene's frequently-quoted comment, 'Without him I could never have known what it is like to be Indian',[2] seems to have lent an air of legitimacy to views of Narayan's fiction which have seen it as offering some kind of guide to the essence of Indianness. Numerous reviewers followed these two clichés, often gleaning them from the cover blurbs and promotional material that Greene and Narayan's various publishers used to market his work, and both are also prominent in academic criticism of his fiction.

Greene's Chekhov analogy has been rehashed in varying ways by Western commentators who appear to have felt the need to genuflect towards it, perhaps as a way of making the initial unfamiliarity of Narayan's world more familiar through the use of a comparison with the supposedly known. For Greene himself the most significant Chekhovian quality in Narayan's writing seems to have been its tonal complexity, which he partly attributes to his response to the loss of Rajam, but on reflection also finds in the novels written prior to this:

Something had permanently changed in Narayan after *The Bachelor of Arts*, the writer's personal tragedy has been our gain. Sadness and humour in the later books go hand in hand like twins, inseparable, as they do in the stories of Chekhov. Perhaps if we had read more closely we should have seen that the shadow had been there from the beginning. A writer in some strange way knows his own future – his end is in his beginning [...].[3]

In the hands of other critics the Chekhov parallel has been used to refer to Narayan's prose style, his supposed pathos, his expression of 'a whole national condition',[4] his capacity to give voice to the languor of provincial life and his artistry in rendering the mundane. Meanwhile, Greene's view of Narayan as a mediator of essential Indianness for his Western sensibility recurs in the remarks of various later Western commentators, particularly prior to the advent of the post-Rushdie generation of fiction-writers.

Other Western responses, from before the last two decades, move in different directions. The most widely read book-length treatment of Narayan's work, William Walsh's 1982 monograph, mentions his supposed Indian authenticity, but pays comparatively little attention to the cultural specifics of his writing, preferring to locate him in relation to canonical English reference-points, which has the effect of appropriating him into a Western-conceived version of universalism. The very first page of Walsh's study manages to mention Chaucer, Shakespeare, Donne, Pope, Wordsworth, Lawrence and Eliot;[5] his final paragraph, which paraphrases another of Greene's comments on Narayan's tone without acknowledgement,[6] typifies the emphasis on the 'human' that characterizes his approach. Talking about Narayan's art's lack of 'precedent in English', Walsh writes:

> [...] It fascinates by reason of the authenticity and attractiveness of its Indian setting, and engages because of the substantial *human nature* which it implies and embodies. It carries along with it at every point a kind of humour strange in English writing which mixes the melancholy and the amusing. Perhaps it is in this humour that there

> [sic] lies its deepest wisdom, which communicates a sense,
> crisp and unrebellious, of *human* limitation, and an appre-
> ciation, positively amiable but quite without illusion, of
> *human* achievement. (my italics)[7]

Perhaps there is no contradiction in saying that humour varies
across cultures, but human values transcend this. However, such
commentary seems to elide cultural specifics, while wanting to
appeal to an undefined notion of 'difference', along with Indian
authenticity.

The view that Narayan's work depicts essential Indianness
has also been adopted by Indian critics such as C.D. Narasimhaiah
and K.R. Srinivasa Iyengar,[8] particularly commentators from
the South, for rather different ends. A cynical reading might
suggest that *their* erasure of Indian difference promotes upper-
caste Hindu exclusivism (in an altogether more innocent, but
not radically different manner from that of more recent Hindu
fundamentalists); a more generous reading of their emphasis
on Narayan's Indian authenticity might see this elision as an
attempt to extend their pride in the local into the national.
Lakshmi Holmstrom's 1973 study[9] also displays a tendency to
collapse the distance between Indianness and Hinduism, but
offers a more probing and lucid account of the Hindu background to his fiction. Her book serves as an excellent contextual
introduction to most of Narayan's work, though its discussion
of particular novels is uneven.

Numerous other critics have considered aspects of Narayan's
Hinduism, with the more perceptive commentators stressing
the secular nature of his vision. Mary Beatina's 1994 book[10]
puts the accent on the interaction between the mundane and
the spiritual in Indian thought, but still focuses on the movement towards transcendence in a novel such as *The Guide*. Two
more recent commentators go further in discussing the secular
nature of the Hindu ethic about which Narayan writes in
illuminating ways. Tabish Khair argues that Narayan's primary
focus is on 'existential' not 'spiritual maturity'[11] and that his
protagonists are primarily concerned with the secular problem
of living, though [...] they often mechanically observe religious

customs'.[12] Ranga Rao suggests that Narayan operates within the tradition of *gunas* comedy and that his heroes belong to two of the three main *gunas* (or personality types): the *satvic* (gentle-tempered) or *rajasic* (domineering, haughty and arrogant).[13] He contends that the *satvic* temperament is predominant in the pre-Independence novels and that the *rajasic* assumes central importance subsequently. Hindu myth receives considerable attention in many responses to Narayan's work, with the criticism of *The Man-Eater of Malgudi* affording numerous instances of this.[14] In a study which compares Narayan's use of classical myth with that of Raja Rao, Chitra Sankaran extends discussion of Narayan's deployment of mythology to include discussion of *Mr Sampath* and *The Guide*. Other discussions of the use of myth in Narayan include K. Chellappan's investigation of its interaction with irony.[15]

Narayan's narrative technique has received less attention than most aspects of his work, but several critics have appreciated the extent to which his early absorption in listening to and telling stories informs his work. Susan Ram and N. Ram's essential biography provides details of aspects of his early upbringing that furnished him with storytelling materials that he would return to again and again throughout his career, coming full circle back to his earliest experience of story in 'The Grandmother's Tale'.[16] Discussions of the later fiction particularly emphasize its metafictive aspects. P.S. Chauhan takes issue with the clichés of Narayan criticism in a lively discussion of Malgudi discourse focused on the figure of Talkative Man.[17] Steve Carter provides a narratological analysis of *The Painter of Signs*,[18] Rajini Srikanth explores metafictive aspects of *The World of Nagaraj*[19] and Sura P. Rath discusses the dialogic nature of *The Guide*'s narrative method.[20] Naipaul's characteristically provocative comments on the genre of Narayan's work,[21] which have been cited several times in this study's discussion of the middle-period novels, may finally be wrong-headed – but his emphasis on the extent to which Hindu fable underpins their social comedy does help to foreground two of the distinctive elements that feed into their construction, interacting in a manner that ultimately privileges neither mode, though Naipaul suggests that the fabu-list elements, which in his view lie beneath the surface comedy, have primacy.

For biographical information, Narayan's memoir *My Days* (1964) is the most important single source, while his encounters with American life are detailed in *My Dateless Diary* (1964), most memorable for an account of an interview with Greta Garbo, a particularly extraordinary East-West encounter. Several of the critical studies of Narayan's work provide details of his life and background, but they contain pitfalls for the unwary. There are frequent discrepancies in the factual information they offer, perhaps reflective of their subject's own reticence when it came to engaging with details such as dates. By far the most reliable account of Narayan's life to 1945 is Susan Ram and N. Ram's meticulously researched *R.K. Narayan: The Early Years: 1906–1945*, a work which benefits from its authors' friendship and close contact with Narayan in his later years.

There has been a fairly general consensus that Narayan is a comic writer, but comparatively few attempts to locate the specific qualities of his humour. Comedy has played its part in accounts of Narayan's tonal ambivalence in some critics' redeployment of the Chekhov cliché. Other commentary has attempted to iden-tify the particular characteristics of Narayan's irony, which has generally been seen to transcend satire. M.K. Naik's *The Ironic Vision*[22] is the fullest study of this aspect of Narayan's writing. My own discussion of this issue[23] (part of which is incorporated into *The Man-Eater of Malgudi* section of this book) considers the culturally encoded nature of irony in an attempt to demon-strate the particular mode of irony to be found in his fiction.[24] Ranga Rao's identification of Narayan's work as *gunas* comedy establishes a particular Indian comic genealogy.[25]

Narayan's treatment of gender has received attention from critics who have mainly been concerned to examine his repre-sentation of the role of women in twentieth-century South Indian life. Feminist and woman-centred readings include Usha Bande's[26] and Shantha Krishnaswamy's[27] readings of *The Painter of Signs*, while Britta Olinder discusses 'the power of women' in Narayan's novels more generally.[28] His treatment of masculinity has not received the same degree of attention, though his habitual focus on the four-fold division of the life of the twice-born Hindu, as outlined in the *Manusmriti*, is predicated on a male model. Consequently, bearing in mind that women were proscribed from reading Sanskrit, one could argue that this exclusivism means that any discussion of his work that focuses on such codes is implicitly male-inscribed. Of the novels, only *The Dark Room*[29] has a female protagonist, though developed studies of modern women appear in the characters of Bharati in *Waiting for the Mahatma*, Rosie in *The Guide*, Grace in *The Vendor of Sweets* and Daisy in *The Painter of Signs*.

Narayan's novels have also been read in numerous other ways. He has been seen as a commentator on Gandhianism,[30] colonialism[31] and cricket,[32] amid many other things. Finally, though, Narayan has always been seen as the chronicler of Malgudi: the inventor, populator and developer of perhaps the best-known fictional space in Indian fiction in English. Malgudi remains poised between the conurbations that are increasingly dominating the Indian scene in the age of globalization and the village India that Gandhi insisted contained the soul of the country. When Narayan died, several of the obituary tributes focused on Malgudi, some acknowledging that it had changed considerably over the years, others evoking it as a trope for an older India to be remembered nostalgically. One of the more fanciful, in which the writer engages in a reverie that transports him back to the beginnings of Malgudi and Swami's identification with the English fast bowler, Maurice Tate, directly addresses the issue of whether Malgudi is remote from the present, a metaphor for an older, supposedly less communally divided India admirably:

> I am wandering through Mempi forest in the twilight, eager, lost and frightened, heart pounding at with [sic] every snapping twig and twittering bird. The forest is my refuge from a perplexing, heartless world and a place where I dream to grow. In my dream I am Tate of the MCC, spinning my team to victory with a web of hat tricks.

[…] Outside, time and history move on, linear and provin-cial and vicious. In the name of history, members of 'one community' plot and execute murder against members of 'another community' and harmless short round men in tucked up dhotis hurry to catch the train but die bloodily in back alleys, and Attila whimpers piteously over the corpses.

I wish I could dream on, worshipfully watching you sculpt chipped perfection while I practice my off-breaks. But time runs out, processes dies [sic], and dreams end […]

Oh, historians will probably say that your tales were of an earlier era and more innocent world, and I needed to wake up anyway. To hell with them, I say, what do they know, they are useless mischief-makers who deserve to be slaughtered anyway. For myself, I know that, thanks to your company, I haven't wandered and practiced in vain, that somewhere there are unplayed unlost cricket dreams where I would be Tate.

Thank you, Talkative Man.[33]

There was more than a hint of nostalgia in many of these trib-utes, but those that saw Malgudi as representative of a stable, older India arguably said more about their authors than the world that Narayan had created. It was these authors' longing for an enduring, unchanging India that found expression in their comments. The reality of the novels themselves, as this study has argued, is that Malgudi is always a transitional site. The changes being wrought in the town seem to speak to the tension between tradition and modernity in the late colonial period (even Gandhi represents change in *Waiting for the Mahatma*) and later in the era of globalization. None of Narayan's work addresses the forces that have been transforming India into an economic super-power over the last two decades and yet in some ways, for example in his representation of Dr Rann's philosophy of 'Futurology' in *Talkative Man*, he anticipates the seismic changes that have been occurring on the subcontinent.

As argued throughout this study, his novels frequently introduce heterotopias. Sometimes these are locations that serve to define the supposed stability of Malgudi through contra-distinction. However, the ultimate heterotopia of his texts is Malgudi itself: an invented space where fantasies can be played out in the imagination in a manner reflected by the man who dreams of Malgudi offering him release into a world where he can be Maurice Tate. This fantasy is specific and remembering that Narayan's projected title for his first novel, *Swami the Tate*, was flatly rejected by his English patron and publisher, perhaps it was always the kind of fantasy that could only find favour with a particular colonial readership at a particular moment in time. The detail is, though, unimportant. Narayan's capacity to construct a desired fictional world has drawn many of his readers into situations where they can imagine themselves inhabiting such a world. How one characterizes this kind of fiction is debat-able. Is it to be seen as utopian, mythic or romantic? These three modes have at least one thing in common: they invite readers to live within an alternative space for the time it takes them to read the book in question. One of the staples of romantic fiction is that it is supposed to offer its readers escape from humdrum quotidian reality, irrespective of whether such escape is seen as providing genuine release or simply escap*ism* in the negative sense of the word. And one might say the same of mythopoeic fiction and utopian fantasy.

Ostensibly Narayan moves in a different direction, offering the kind of grounded and circumstantial vision of place and people that commonly has the label 'realistic' attached to it. Yet many of his readers, both Western and Indian, have in varying ways found Malgudi a heterotopian portal into an alternative world of the imagination, a world which is both comfortingly familiar and slyly disorienting. And perhaps this is what litera-ture about precisely demarcated milieus does when it invites us into the contingent reality of its local worlds. Assuredly the act of trying to transcribe the physicality of lives lived in particular locations always involves an element of fantasy, if only because of the slippage that occurs between signified and signifier. More-over, our notions of other nations are often said to be caught in the amber of the tourist gaze: Switzerland is a country of cuckoo clocks; Italy is variously the home of Machiavelli and the Renaissance; and India …? Well, India has always been many things to many people, but for some Westerners it has been a land of exotic alterity. Narayan's India moves away from this. Hence his reluctance to assume the mantle of a guru. Nevertheless Malgudi remains a landscape of the imagination, frequently sustained by its own internal dynamics as novel succeeds novel and familiar characters reappear with reassuring regularity. *Perhaps* Narayan's greatest achievement lies in his capacity to sustain interest in Malgudi over six decades, but if so this is because he remains sensitive to the dynamic, transformative nature of place, not because he constructs a static, conservative world locked in a time-warp. In one sense Greene's words, 'A writer in some strange way knows his own future – his end is in his beginning' are unerringly true of Narayan. His oeuvre is all of a piece, but the world he represents is a site of conflict from the Monday morning beginning of *Swami*, where the young protagonist is 'reluctant to open his eyes',[34] to the closing words of 'Grandmother's Tale': '… that's all we know'.[35] Without this his tone would be certain, his endings would be closed and his characters' quests for *dharma* would be neatly resolved. None of these is the case. Malgudi is a trope for uncertainty, openness and ongoing secular struggle.

Notes

Chapter 1

1 R.K. Narayan, 'Self-Obituary No. 5', *Illustrated Weekly of India,*
23 July 1950. Copy in Special Collections, Mugar Memorial
Library, Boston University, No. 737, Box 8, folder 39. Subsequent
references to this collection in this chapter cite MML.

2 *Ibid.*

3 Graham Greene, Introduction to R.K. Narayan, *The Bachelor of
Arts,* 1978; Chicago: University of Chicago Press, 1980, v. Subsequent references in this chapter cite *BA.*

4 C.D. Narasimhaiah, *The Swan and the Eagle: Essays on Indian
English Literature,* Simla: Indian Institute of Advanced Study,
1968, 136.

5 D.A. Shankar, 'Caste in the Fiction of R.K. Narayan', in *R.K.
Narayan: Critical Perspectives,* ed. A.L. McLeod, New Delhi:
Sterling, 1994, 137. Shankar does, however, demur from the
assessment of Narayan quoted here in one crucial respect. He
argues that Narayan's broad-brush approach to caste means that
he is 'forced to leave out all the little local details that go with an
individual's actual living that is co-extensive with his sub-caste
and class status' and sees this as characteristic of 'Indian fictionists
writing in English', who lack the 'density of meaning' to be found
in Indian regional writing, which displays 'direct, living touch
with the sub-castes' (144). This is not, however, always the case in
Narayan. In *The Bachelor of Arts,* e.g., Chandran's marriage prospects are specifically associated with the Iyer sub-caste to which,
like Narayan, he belongs, *BA* 114 and 253.

6 K.R. Srinivasa Iyengar, *Indian Writing in English,* Bombay: Asia
Publishing House, revised 2nd. edn., 1973, 359. The passage appears
to echo Raja Rao's oft-quoted comments on the use of English as
a medium for Indian literature in his Foreword to *Kanthapura*

(1938). See below and Note 10.

7   See Narayan's Introduction to his short story collection, *Malgudi Days*, 1982; Harmondsworth: Penguin, 1984, 8, and the discussion at the end of this chapter.

8   'Self-Obituary No. 5', MML, Box 8, folder 39.

9   See Chapter 4 for a fuller discussion of this aspect of *The Vendor of Sweets*.

10 Raja Rao, *Kanthapura*, 1938; New Delhi: Orient Paperbacks, 1992, 5.

11 *My Days: A Memoir*, New York: Viking, 1974, 102. Subsequent references in this chapter cite *MyD*. For further information on Seshachalam's commitment to Tamil writing, see Susan and N. Ram, *R.K. Narayan: The Early Years: 1906–1945*, New Delhi: Viking, 1996, particularly Chapter 4.

12 In an interview for the British *South Bank Show* broadcast in 1983, Narayan has a different recollection. Here he speaks of his attraction to Dickens and dislike of Scott, London Weekend Television, 1983. First televised ITV, 12 March 1983.

13 See the more detailed discussion of Narayan's adaptation of the genre of schoolboy fiction in *Swami* in Chapter 2.

14 R.K. Narayan, 'What Kind of Literature Do Our Students Need', Talk on All India Radio, Bangalore, broadcast on 16 June 1978.

15 *Ibid.*

16 See Nissim Ezekiel, *Collected Poems*, New Delhi: Oxford University Press, 2nd. edn., 2005, 237–40.

17 V.S. Naipaul, *India: A Wounded Civilization*, London: André Deutsch, 1977, 37.

18 Susan and N. Ram, *R.K. Narayan: The Early Years*, New Delhi: Viking, 1996, 344.

19 R.K. Narayan, 'Gods, Demons and Modern Times', *Barnard Alumnae*, Winter 1973, 4.

20 A work which included Narayan's versions of stories from *The Mahabharata*, *The Ramayana*, *The Yoga-Vasishta* of 'Devi', *The Shiva Purana* and the Tamil epic *Silapadikharam*, *Gods, Demons and Others*, London: Vintage, 2001, [v].

21 Lakshmi Holmstrom, *The Novels of R.K. Narayan*, Calcutta: Writers Workshop, 1973, 103.

22 Supposedly deriving from the sage Manu, the *Manusmriti* is one of the eighteen *Dharmasastras*. It outlines codes of conduct for

both personal and public life and is believed to have been transcribed into a written text around 200 C.E.

23   *Ibid.*, 104.

24   See the opening paragraph of this chapter.

25   'Explanation', *Grandmother's Tale*, Mysore: Indian Thought, 1992,
[ix]. This 'Explanation' is not included in the UK edition of the text,
used elsewhere in this study.

26   E.g. by H.R. Sharada Prasad in his obituary tribute, 'The Magician from Malgudi', Outlookindia.com, 17 May 2001: <http://
outlookindia.com/full.asp?sid=1&fodname=20010517&frame=sh
arda> (Accessed 23 May 2001). Also A. Hariprasanna, *The World
of Malgudi*, New Delhi: Prestige, 1994 in the passage quoted in
Note 40 below.

27   'Space, Knowledge, and Power', Foucault interviewed by Paul
Rabinow, trans. Christian Hubert, *The Foucault Reader*, ed. Paul
Rabinow, Harmondsworth: Penguin, 1991, 252.

28   'Of Other Spaces', *Diacritics*, 16, 1 (1986), 22–7, trans. Jay
Miskowiec from the journal 'Des Espaces Autres', a version of
Foucault's 1967 talk published by *Architecture /Mouvement/
Continuité* in October, 1984; <http://foucault.info/documents/
heteroTopia/foucault.heteroTopia.en.html> (Accessed 21 Septem-
ber 2006).

29   Michel Foucault, *Power, Knowledge: Selected Interviews and Other
Writings*, Brighton: Harvester, 1980, 7; qtd. in Edward Soja, *Post-
modern Geographies: The Reassertion of Space in Critical Social
Theory*, London: Verso, 1989, 10.

30   Doreen Massey, *Space, Place and Gender*, Cambridge: Polity Press,
1994, 2, 5.

31   *Ibid.*, 5.

32   'Of Other Spaces' < http://foucault.info/documents/heteroTopia/
foucault.heteroTopia.en.html> (Accessed 21 September 2006).

33   *Ibid.*

34   *Ibid.*

35   *Ibid.*

36   E.g. in Melvyn Bragg's opening remarks to *The South Bank Show*
profile of Narayan , London Weekend Television, 1983. First televised ITV, 12 March 1983.

37   See Susan and N. Ram, *R.K. Narayan: The Early Years*, 106.

38 Narayan in 1985, quoted in Susan and N. Ram, *R.K. Narayan: The Early Years,* 106.

39 Introduction, *Malgudi Days,* 1982; Harmondsworth: Penguin, 1984, 8.

40 Cf. A. Haripasanna, *The World of Malgudi,* New Delhi: Prestige, 1994: 'Various critics have attempted to identify the original of this mythical town. Iyengar speculates that it might be Lalgudi on the River Cauvery or Yadavagiri in Mydore [sic]. Others [are] of the opinion that Narayan's Malgudi is Coimbatore which has many of the landmarks – a river on one side, forests on the other, the Mission School and College, and , all the extensions mentioned in the novels. However, one is not likely to arrive at any definite answer as to its geographical locations, even if one shifts all the references to the town in the novels, such specific allusions as that "Malgudi is almost a day's journey from Madras". The simple reason is that Narayan has not drawn any map of framework for his Malgudi as Faulkner for example, did for his Yoknapatawpha or Hardy had in mind for his Wessex novels. ... But all efforts to identify Malgudi have remained futile, for it [is] a pure country of the mind.' Quoted < http://www.iit.edu/~jainank/reading/db/ narayan/malgudi.html>.

41 E.g. Rushdie, *Imaginary Homelands,* London: Granta and New York: Viking, 1991, 67: 'One of the most absurd aspects of this quest for national authenticity is that – as far as India is concerned, anyway – it is completely fallacious to suppose that there is such a thing as a pure, unalloyed tradition from which to draw'.

42 'After the Raj', *A Story-Teller's World,* Harmondsworth: Penguin, 1990, 31–2.

Chapter 2

1 The passage goes on to refer to the endings of *Mr Sampath* and his short stories, 'An Astrologer's Day' and 'Cyclone', both printed in various Narayan collections.

2 R.K. Narayan, 'Self-Obituary No. 5', *Illustrated Weekly of India,* 23 July 1950. Copy in Special Collections, Mugar Memorial Library, Boston University, No. 737, Box 8, folder 39. Subsequent references to this collection in this chapter cite MML.

3 They have been republished together as *A Malgudi Omnibus,* London: Minerva, 1994; and in an extended omnibus volume, *R.K.*

Narayan Omnibus, Vol. 1, which adds *The Dark Room*, London: Everyman's Library , 2006. The three novels have also been republished simultaneously in separate volumes, e.g. by the University of Chicago Press in 1980.

4   See Susan and N. Ram, *R.K. Narayan: The Early Years: 1906–1945*, New Delhi: Viking, 1996, 143–58; and the Narayan-Greene correspondence cited below. Also Narayan's remarks in *My Days: A Memoir*, New York: Viking, 1974, 115–16. Subsequent references in this chapter cite *MyD*.

5   In his very first letter to Greene, 11 August [1935], Narayan said, 'I have absolutely no objection to have [sic] my English corrected by you; on the contrary I shall feel honoured by it' (Graham Greene Papers, John J. Burns Library, Boston College, MS 95–3, D7, Folder I). Subsequent references in this chapter cite JJBBC. On 26 December 1935, Narayan wrote to Greene, 'Your corrections have very elegantly removed certain flabby patches in the original [of *Swami and Friends*]', JJBBC, Folder I.

6   See a letter from Greene to Narayan, dated 15 March 1966, in which he explains that he is too busy working on the film-script of *The Comedians* to edit *The Vendor of Sweets* 'with any rapidity'; and a similar letter to Narayan's literary agent, David Higham, dated 7 March 1966, in which Greene says that the novel 'needs more than the usual amount of editing' and explains that he does not have time to undertake this. Narayan had earlier promised to edit the manuscript of the *Vendor* 'ruthlessly' before sending it to Greene, letter dated 21 March 1966. All three letters are in JJBBC, Folder D. Greene did edit Narayan's previous novel, *The Man-Eater of Malgudi*. In a letter to [A.S] 'Frere' of Heinemann, dated 5 December 1960, he wrote, 'It took me about ten days to go through and I have done it rather too quickly I expect' and expressed the hope that he might be able to do further editing at proof-stage (JJBBC, Folder F) À propos of the same novel, he had previously written, 'Unfortunately, as I think you know, Narayan needs a good deal of editing to make his English smooth enough without destroying the Indian quality but I always do this myself' (Letter to Frere, 12 October 1960, *ibid.*)

7   Letter from Hamish Hamilton to Narayan, 10 August 1935, Special Collections, MML, Box 15, quoted by Susan and N. Ram, *R.K. Narayan: The Early Years*, 154; and a letter from Greene dated 23 August 1935, quoted by Susan and N. Ram, 155.

8   Cf. his brother, the famous cartoonist, R.K. Laxman.

9   Hamilton's letter of 10 August 1935 proposed the use of the

'pen-name of Narayan' to avoid the repetition of 'Swami', saying *'Swami and Friends* by Narayan Swami might be misleading', MML, Box 15. Narayan agreed to the shorter form, saying 'The name "R.K. Narayan" is quite correct', in a letter to Greene of 12 September [1935], JJBBC, Folder I.

10 Greene's letter, 23 August 1935, asks 'Have you any objection to the Swami being left out and your being styled R.K. Narayan? It's a silly thing to have to say, but in this country a name which is difficult for the old ladies in libraries to remember materially affects a book's sales', quoted by Susan and N. Ram, *R.K. Narayan: The Early Years*, 155.

11 Hamish Hamilton, in a letter to Narayan of 10 August 1935, rather tactlessly suggested that 'the title [which] you had given the book, *Swami, the Tate*, is quite impossible for this country', MML, Box 15, thus demonstrating less belief in an English readership's identification with a national cricketing celebrity than his 'colonial' author. In his first letter to Greene, 11 August [1935], which must have crossed with Hamilton's in the post, Narayan had written, 'I leave you free to give it any title you see fit', JJBBC, Folder I.

12 For a detailed consideration of the political implications of cricket in Narayan's fiction, see Feroza Jussawalla, 'Cricket and Colonialism: From *Swami and Friends* to *Lagaan*', *South Asian Review*, 23, 1 (2002), 112–28.

13 Edward Said's term, derived from Vico and used in contrast to *affiliative* identifications, for cultural relationships that use influence in a manner analogous to biological parentage, Said, *The World, The Text and the Critic*, London: Faber and Faber, 1984, *passim*, particularly 174 ff.

14 Hamilton's letter to Narayan of 10 August 1935 went on to point out that the proposed alternative, *Swami and Friends*, would also have 'some resemblance to Kipling's Stalky & Co [sic], with which I am comparing the book on the dust cover', MML, Box 15. Several contemporary reviewers responded to the invitation to make the comparison with *Stalky* that the dust cover blurb encouraged, but were divided as to whether there were significant similarities. Cp. an unidentified review, copy held in MML, Box 9: 'The book has been compared to Kipling's "Stalky and Co." But there is no real similarity'; and a review that appeared in *The Globe*, 4 January 1936: 'This is a book built apparently on the model of the famous "Stalky". It is a similar story of the life of a Hindu boy of the same age and position in society as Stalky: he is attending school and has much the same troubles as Stalky allowing for differences of race and longitude.'

15   K.M. MacLeod, *Derry and Co.*, 1934; London: Pickering and Inglis, 1952, 16.

16   For a discussion of *Stalky & Co.*, which argues that it goes further than earlier classic school novels that suggest parallels between public school life and life in the Empire, see Don Randall, 'Kipling's *Stalky & Co.*: Resituating the Empire and the "Empire Boy"', *Victorian Review*, 24, 2 (1998), 163–74. Randall argues that Kipling moves beyond other writers in the genre, breaking down supposed divisions between imperial centre and colonial periphery by representing the 'empire boy' as a hybrid figure.

17   See *ibid.*

18   See *MyD* 50. The school had a university entrance class and Narayan subsequently entered the Maharaja's College (a part of Mysore University). C.D. Narasimhaiah, who was Principal of the College much later, points out that Narayan insisted on viewing himself as 'a product of Maharaja's College' rather than Mysore University, *"N for Nobody": Autobiography of an English Teacher*, Delhi: B.R. Publishing Corporation, 1991, 22 and 205.

19   *MyD* 63; Susan and N. Ram, *R.K. Narayan: The Early Years*, 69.

20   Often regarded as the founder of the boarding school story, Reed was associated with the *Boy's Own Paper* from its inception and was its first assistant editor. Starting in 1880, several of his earlier novels had been serialized in the *B.O.P.* before subsequently being published in book-form. His cover-story for the first issue was 'My First Football Match by an Old Boy', though he had never attended boarding school himself.

21   H. Moore Williams describes the novel as 'a gentle more charming South Indian version of the British Richmal Crompton's "William" books', 'English Writing in Free India, 1946–1964', *Twentieth Century Literature*, 16, 1 (1970), 1–12; quoted by Cynthia vanden Driesen, *Centering the Margins: Perspectives on Literatures in English*, New Delhi: Prestige, 1995, 9.

22   R.K. Narayan, *Swami and Friends*, 1935; Chicago: University of Chicago Press, 1980, 4. Subsequent references in this chapter cite *Swami*.

23   James Joyce, *A Portrait of the Artist as a Young Man*, 1916; Harmondsworth: Penguin, 1960, 15–16.

24   See the discussion of Narayan's intertexts in Chapter 1.

25   R.K. Narayan, *Reluctant Guru*, 1974; New Delhi: Orient paperbacks, n.d., 13.

26   R.K. Narayan, *Gods, Demons and Others*, 1964; London: Vintage,

2001, 217–28. Subsequent references in this chapter cite *Gods*.

27   In the *Swami* version the spelling Harichandra is used.

28   Graham Greene, Introduction to R.K. Narayan, *The Bachelor of Arts*, 1978; Chicago: University of Chicago Press, 1980, v. Subsequent references in this chapter cite *BA*. Ian Almond offers a more particular explanation for Greene's identification with Narayan: 'There is a line from Graham Greene's novel, *The Heart of the Matter*: "He felt the loyalty that we all feel to unhappiness – the sense that that is where we really belong". [...] This unhappiness, quite possibly, was the "second home" Greene finally found in Narayan's work, something so close to his own fiction, so far from his land', 'Darker Shades of Malgudi: Solitary Figures of Modernity in the Stories of R.K. Narayan', *Journal of Commonwealth Literature*, 36, 2 (2001), 116.

29   Gobinda Prasad Sarma, *Nationalism in Indo-Anglian Fiction*, New Delhi: Sterling, 1978, 220.

30   See his various references to the novel in his letters in the Greene collection, JJBBC, Folder I.

31   Letter to Graham Greene, 21 January 1937, JJBBC, Folder I.

32   Ram and Ram, conversation with Narayan in Madras on 6 July 1993, *R.K. Narayan: The Early Years*, 182.

33   Edward Fitzgerald, *Rubaiyat of Omar Khayyam*, 29, line 115. In *The Dark Room* Shanta Bai is a devotee of *The Rubaiyat* and quotes the phrase, 'I am as wind along the waste', saying, 'In this world Khayyam is the only person who would have understood the secret of my soul', *The Dark Room*, 1938; London: Heinemann, 1978, 151. Subsequent references in this chapter cite *DR*.

34   'How to Write an Indian Novel', *Punch*, 27 September 1933, 341. Cf. a very similar article satirizing the use of formulaic elements in writing about India, 'How to Write on India', *Merry Magazine*, 1 June 1935, 44.

35   Greene, Introduction, *BA*, vi.

36   *Ibid.*

37   E.g. by Susan and N. Ram, *R.K. Narayan: The Early Years*, 187

38   E.g. William Walsh who sees it as 'belonging to a substantial human nature', *R.K. Narayan*, London: Heinemann, 1982, 36.

39   *Pace* D.A. Shankar, 'Caste in the Fiction of R.K. Narayan' in *R.K. Narayan: Critical Perspectives*, ed. A.L. McLeod, New Delhi: Sterling, 1994, 137–46, who takes the view that the importance of sub-caste is neglected in Narayan. In *The Bachelor of Arts*, Chandran's

marital prospects are determined not just by his being a brahmin, but also by his being, like Narayan, an Iyer. Also cp. Pankaj Mishra, 'R.K. Narayan', in Arvind Krishna Mehrotra, ed., *A History of Indian Literature in English*, London: Hurst, 2003, discussed below.

40 They are prominent in his later work, beginning with *The Painter of Signs* (1976). See the discussion of this novel in Chapter 4 and of Narayan's later work in Chapter 5.

41 See, e.g., Part 3 of *The Financial Expert*, where Margayya's son, Balu, runs away to the city.

42 See the passage chosen by Greene to illustrate the distinctive Indian 'twang' in Narayan's English, quoted above.

43 Michel Foucualt, 'Of Other Spaces', <http://foucault.info/documents/heteroTopia/foucault.heteroTopia.en.html> (Accessed 21 September 2006).

44 See my discussion in *The Web of Tradition: Uses of Allusion in V.S. Naipaul's Fiction*, Aarhus: Dangaroo and London: Hansib, 1987, 135–8.

45 Shirley Chew, 'A Proper Detachment: The Novels of R.K. Narayan', in William Walsh, ed., *Readings in Commonwealth Literature*, Oxford: Clarendon Press, 1973, 60.

46 See M.K. Naik's discussion of *The Guide* and Naipaul's *The Mystic Masseur* (1957), in which he distinguishes between the two novels, saying that in Narayan's case the hero is transformed 'from a picaro into a pilgrim', 'Two Uses of Irony: V.S. Naipaul's *The Mystic Masseur* and R.K. Narayan's *The Guide*', *World Literature Written in English*, 17, 2 (1978), 650. See also my discussion of *The Guide* in Chapter 4 below.

47 Pankaj Mishra, 'R.K. Narayan', in Arvind Krishna Mehrotra, ed., *A History of Indian Literature in English*, London: Hurst, 2003, 198–9.

48 E.g. in his 1978 Introduction to *BA*, v. Greene first used it in his 1937 Introduction to the novel, Ram and Ram, *R.K. Narayan: The Early Years*, 188. Also see Ram and Ram, 188–92, for quotes from several contemporary reviews which seized upon this piece of promotional hype in their efforts to categorize the novel.

49 Pankaj Mishra, 'R.K. Narayan', in Arvind Krishna Mehrotra, ed., *A History of Indian Literature in English*, London: Hurst, 2003, 199.

50 *Ibid.*

51 See *BA* 114 and 253ff.

52 This would appear to underlie much of V.S. Naipaul's fascination with Narayan. In his third non-fiction work about India, *India: A Million Mutinies Now*, London: Heinemann, 1990, Naipaul discusses a broad range of 'mutinies' (a term which he equates with communal protest), but the predicament of Tamil brahmins receives particular attention.

53 He is apparently based on Professor J.C. Rollo, the Principal of Maharaja's College, while the History teacher, Ragavachar is allegedly based on Professor Venkateswara Iyer and Professor M.H. Krishna Iyengar. See *MyD* 71–2; and Ram and Ram, *R.K. Narayan: The Early Years*, 83–7. Years later Narayan wrote a glowing obituary of Rollo, who died in 1977, in which he said he owed his 'love of English language and literature entirely to Professor Rollo's influence', 'Remembering Professor J.C. Rollo', *Literary Criterion*, 2 (1978), 5–6.

54 Entitled *Lightguns of Lauro*, it appears to be an invention of Narayan's own making. Cp. *The Dark Room*, where the cinematic references are to actual films and actors.

55 V.S. Naipaul, *India: A Wounded Civilization*, London: André Deutsch, 1977, 27. Naipaul goes on to disagree with this view. See below Chapter 3.

56 See Note 3 above.

57 Ram and Ram, who provide details from several of the reviews of *The Dark Room*, note that most of the early Indian reviewers were disparaging about this aspect of the novel, *R.K. Narayan: The Early Years*, 206–11.

58 William Walsh, *R.K. Narayan: A Critical Appreciation*, London: Heinemann, 1982, 43.

59 Usha Bande, 'Validating the Self: The Female Hero in R.K. Narayan's *The Painter of Signs*', in *Women in Indo-Anglian Fiction: Tradition and Modernity*, ed. Naresh K. Jain, New Delhi: Manohar, 1998, 103.

60 Nilufer E. Bharucha, 'Colonial Enclosures and Autonomous Spaces: R.K. Narayan's Malgudi', *South Asian Review*, 23, 1 (2002), 129–53, 137.

61 Usha Bande sees her as a forerunner of later 'emancipated' Narayan heroines, viz. Daisy in *The Guide* and Rosie in *The Painter of Signs*, 'Validating the Self: The Female Hero in R.K. Narayan's *The Painter of Signs*', in *Women in Indo-Anglian Fiction: Tradition and Modernity*, ed. Naresh K. Jain, New Delhi: Manohar, 1998,

103–4.

62   *Gods* 182–9. Savitri is also cited as an exemplar of wifely devotion in *The Guide*, Harmondsworth: Penguin, 1980, 136.

63   Cf. the following passage on the pilgrimage site of Dharmasthala in Narayan's travel book, *The Emerald Route*, 1977; New Delhi: Penguin, 1999, 37: '[…] Dharma has a wide connotation, applicable to many other aspects beside charity. It also means truthful adherence to a code or discipline, and everyone here performs his duty without any compulsion other than the inner one, and things always go right.'

64   Sandra M. Gilbert and Susan Gubar, *The Madwoman in the Attic*, 1979; New Haven: Yale UP, 1984.

65   K.R. Srinivasa Iyengar *Indian Writing in English*, Bombay: Asia Publishing House, revised 2nd edn., 1973, 371, comments: '"The dark room used to be as indispensable a part of an Indian house as a kitchen, and was a place for "safe deposits", both a sanctuary – and a retreat; but modern houses are apt to dispense with the "dark room". […] Narayan has thus done well to preserve – like the mummified curiosities of ancient Egypt – the "dark room" in the pages of his novel.'

66   Ramani also takes his children to see a Laurel and Hardy film, with which they become 'completely absorbed' (*DR* 150).

67   A Telugu film released in 1935, the year of Malgudi's fictional cinema's opening: <http://12.144.36.179/tool/post/princefans_board/vpost?id=1020602&trail=49#19> (Accessed 28 August 2006). The same website records: 'Out of the 46 films [produced in 1935], 35 were mythological, 3 social and 8 semi-mythological'.

68   One of a number of expressions used at this point in the novel, which seem more suited to English schoolboy fiction than the reworking of an epic episode. Others are 'classroom' and 'monitor' (*DR* 28). The disjunction suggests Narayan's continuing use of the conventions of such fiction as a way of mediating between his subject-matter and his English readership.

69   Narayan, Letter to Greene, 20 June 1939, JJBBC, Folder I. Part quoted by Susan and N. Ram, *R.K. Narayan: The Early Years*, 258. Ram and Ram also quote part of Greene's reply, in which he tells Narayan he will write again, though perhaps not 'for months' (259).

70   See Susan and N. Ram, *R.K. Narayan: The Early Years*, 254.

71   See *MyD* 148–50; and Susan and N. Ram, *R.K. Narayan: The Early Years*, 262–98 and 325–9.

72 Tamil editions of *Swami and Friends* and *The Dark Room* appeared in 1940, after having previously been serialized in the 'mass circulation' weekly, *Ananda Vikatan*, Ram and Ram, *R.K. Narayan: The Early Years*, 317–8.

73 Susan and N. Ram, *R.K. Narayan: The Early Years*, 259, note that a Narayan story appeared in *The Hindu* just five days after Rajam's death. This appears to have been written just before her death, but Narayan's fortnightly submissions continued without interruption.

74 *MyD* 151–60 provides a lively account of the magazine's genesis and demise, which is particularly interesting for its account of his relationship with the printer, Sampath, who became the original for the protagonist of Narayan's 1949 novel, *Mr Sampath*. (*MyD* 154). See Ram and Ram, *R.K. Narayan: The Early Years*, 330–54. A selection of work from the magazine has been published as *Indian Thought: A Miscellany*, ed. R.K. Narayan, New Delhi: Penguin, 1997. This includes Narayan's most substantive contribution to the magazine, his 'playlet', *The Watchman of the Lake*, and his short stories, 'Garden' and 'A Parrot Story'.

75 See Susan and N. Ram, *R.K. Narayan: The Early Years*, 249–52.

76 *MyD*, 135.

77 *The English Teacher*, 1945; Chicago: University of Chicago Press, 1980, 19. Subsequent references in this chapter cite *ET*.

78 *The Times*, 8 October 1945. Copies of this and the reviews cited in notes 79 and 80 are in MML, Box 9.

79 *Glasgow Evening News*, 29 October 1945.

80 Ruby Miller, *New English Review*, October 1945.

81 K.R. Srinivasa Iyengar, *Indian Writing in English*, Bombay: Asia Publishing House, revised 2nd. edn., 1973, 369–70.

82 Lakshmi Holmstrom, *The Novels of R.K. Narayan*, Calcutta: Writers Workshop, 1973, 47.

83 This phrase was used as the title of the American edition of the novel, East Lansing, MI: Michigan State College Press, 1953.

84 *King Lear*, Arden edn., London: Methuen, 1963, III iv 103–12.

85 V.S. Naipaul, *A House for Mr Biswas*, London: André Deutsch, 1977, 13. Naipaul may possibly have been influenced by Narayan in the use of this trope. He had read Narayan by 1952: see Chapter 3, Note 4. Cf. Naipaul's use of 'unaccommodated' in *India: A Wounded Civilization*, London: André Deutsch, 1977, 71.

86 For a discussion of the importance of jasmine in the novel, see

Gideon Nteere M' Marete, 'Krishnan's Jasmine-Scented Quest' in *R.K. Narayan: Contemporary Critical Essays*, ed. Geoffrey Kain, East Lansing, MI: Michigan State University Press, 1993, 37–47.

87   *Pace* C.D. Narasimhaiah, who takes the view that Narayan 'turns to the occult rather than the profoundly spiritual which his own heritage could have offered in abundance', *The Swan and the Eagle*, Simla: Indian Institute of Advanced Study, 1979, 146. Narayan characteristically blurs the issue and emphasizes the medium's secular involvements, but the site of his house and lot locate him in relation to ancient Hindu spiritual codes, however ruined these may be in contemporary South India.

88   The Minute introduced English as a language of pan-Indian communication designed to service the needs of the colonial administration.

89   See the account of *Swami and Friends* above for a discussion of the relationship between education, colonialism and the sporting ethic.

90   Named after Sir Frederick Lawley, whose statue is seen as a symbol of colonialism in the story, 'Lawley Road', which satirizes post-Independence attempts to eradicate traces of the Raj. Malgudi's Municipal Council plans to pull the statue down, until historical societies from all over India send telegrams to tell them that they are mistaken in their belief that Sir Frederick Lawley 'must have been the worst tyrant imaginable', 'a combination of Attila, the Scourge of Europe, and Nadir Shah, with the craftiness of a Machiavelli', *Malgudi Days*, Harmondsworth: Penguin, 1984, 113. Such a history, the Council is told, relates to another Lawley. Their Sir Frederick was a Military Governor, who played a major part in bringing Malgudi into being: 'He cleared the jungles and almost built the town of Malgudi. He established here the first cooperative society for the whole of India, and the first canal system by which thousands of acres of land were irrigated from the Sarayu, which had been dissipating itself till then. He established this, he established that, and he died in the great Sarayu floods while attempting to save the lives of villagers living on its banks. He was the first Englishman to advise the British Parliament to involve more and more Indians in all Indian affairs. In one of his despatches he was said to have declared, "Britain must quit India some day for her own good"'(*Ibid.*, 115).

Chapter 3

1   E.g. his 1986 comment that politics are 'the least interesting aspect of life in my view', Interview with Andrew Robinson, *The Independent*, 24 October 1986, 14. In the same interview, talking about his friendship with Indira Gandhi, he says, 'We never talked politics at any time' (*ibid.*). At the time of his death his former contemporary in the Rajya Sabha, Dr Y Shivaji said 'The litterateur eschewed politics', while a less sympathetic commentator, C.V. N. Dhan attacked him for not having participated in the freedom struggle, 'Tributes Paid to R K Narayan', *Times of India*, 17 May 2001, <http://www.timesofindia.com/170501/17mhdy2.htm> (Accessed 23 May 2001).

2   *The Financial Expert*, London: Methuen, 1952, v.

3   See, e.g., Chitra Sankaran, *The Myth Connection: The Use of Hindu Mythology in Some Novels of Raja Rao and R.K, Narayan*, Ahmedabad: Allied Publishers, 1993; and the numerous critics of *The Man-Eater of Malgudi*, listed in Chapter 4, Note 42, who have discussed the novel's mythic underpinning:

4   In his Foreword to his father, Seepersad Naipaul's *The Adventures of Gurudeva and Other Stories*, London André Deutsch, 1976, Naipaul refers to his having sent Seepersad 'some books' (10) by Narayan in 1952 and so appears to have been familiar with his work some time before the publication of *The Mystic Masseur*. He particularly discusses Narayan, focusing on *Mr Sampath* and *The Vendor of Sweets*, in *India: A Wounded Civilization*, London: Andre Deutsch, 1977, 18–27 and 37–43. See the discussions of these novels below.

5   Not, however, from South India. Naipaul's ancestors came from Uttar Pradesh. See his account of his Trinidadian upbringing in *An Area of Darkness*, 1964; Harmondsworth: Penguin, 1968, 27–43, 29.

6   *An Area of Darkness* (1964), *India: A Wounded Civilization* (1977) and *India: A Million Mutinies Now* (1990). *India: A Million Mutinies Now* is the most interesting of the three in this respect, since while it presents itself as a pan-Indian account of the various forms of sectarian dissent that were challenging the status quo in the late 1980s, it particularly focuses on the contemporary situation of Tamil brahmins.

7   V.S. Naipaul, *India: A Wounded Civilization*, London: André Deutsch, 1977, 25–7.

8   *Ibid.*, 21.

9   See the beginning of Chapter 4 for a fuller discussion and suggested explanation of this.

10   *India: A Wounded Civilization*, London: André Deutsch, 1977, 22.

11   Narayan drew on his experience as the editor of his war-time journal *Indian Thought*. See Susan and N. Ram, *R.K. Narayan: The Early Years*, New Delhi: Viking, 1996, Chapter 32, particularly 332–4.

12   *India: A Wounded Civilization*, London: André Deutsch, 1977, 18–19. Cf. *An Area of Darkness*, 1964; Harmondsworth: Penguin, 1968, 214, where he offers a similarly reductive proposition, in referring to the novel's '*Western* concern with the condition of men, a response to the here and now' (my italics).

13   Respectively in *The Diary of a Nobody* (1892), *The History of Mr Polly* (1910), and *A House for Mr Biswas* (1961). Narayan admired *Mr Biswas*, referring to it as 'a very charming novel' and 'almost like Malgudi', in an interview with Andrew Robinson, *The Independent*, 24 October 1986, 14.

14   A Western equivalent – and the suggestion that there could be any kind of precise analogue is probably an oxymoron – might be Leopold Bloom, who is both a comic version of Odysseus *and* a twentieth-century Ulysses.

15   Narayan frequently commented on his early admiration for Dickens. See, e.g., *My Days: A Memoir*, New York: Viking, 1974, 61: 'I picked up a whole row of Dickens and loved his London and the queer personalities therein'; and remarks on his preference for Dickens over Scott, *The South Bank Show*, London Weekend Television, 1983, first televised ITV, 12 March 1983. Subsequent references to *My Days* in this chapter cite *MyD*.

16   See *MyD*, 62–3, on Narayan's boyhood reading of Wells. In *The Bachelor of Arts*, Chandran reads Wells's *Tono-Bungay*, *Bachelor of Arts*, Chicago: Chicago University Press, 1980, 97. Subsequently Chandran is referred to as hating 'Dickens's laborious humour' (115),

17   *Mr Sampath – The Printer of Malgudi*, 1949; London: Heinemann 1979, 219. Subsequent references in this chapter cite *MrS*.

18   Ranga Rao, *R.K. Narayan*, New Delhi: Sahitya Akademi, 2004, 73.

19   See Susan and N. Ram, *R. K. Narayan: The Early Years*, 332–6.

20   Partly because of wartime paper shortages, Susan and N. Ram, *R.K. Narayan: The Early Years*, 350; and *MyD* 159–60.

21 R.K. Narayan, *Salt & Sawdust: Stories and Table-Talk*, New Delhi: Penguin, 1993, 191.

22 *Ibid.*, 192.

23 See D.C. Muecke's classifications of types or irony in *Irony*, London: Methuen, 1970, particularly 66; and the discussion of the irony of *The Man-Eater of Malgudi* in Chapter 4 below.

24 See Notes 27 and 33 below.

25 *The Financial Expert*, London: Methuen, 1952, 26. Subsequent references in this chapter cite *FE*.

26 Cf. several subsequent passages which refer to his feeling that his expertise with money makes him a financial mystic (viz. *FE* 94, 103 and 149).

27 Narayan's later Introduction to *The Financial Expert*, originally published in 1956 and reprinted in *A Story-Teller's World*, New Delhi: Penguin, 1989, 10–13, explains how the character of Margayya was inspired by a peon, dismissed from the government office in which his own brother worked. Nicknamed '*Dhur Margayya* – "One Who Shows the Way to Evil"' (10), because his shady financial dealings undermined the office's cooperative endeavours to offer assistance to its employees, this Margayya subsequently continued to conduct business on the office veranda, then by its gate and eventually under 'a large spreading tree across the road' (12). Narayan speaks of this original as the product of a particular moment in Indian history – the late colonial period – and emphasizes that he only provided a departure-point for his fictional character, who significantly has the *Dhur* element dropped from his name and is seen in much more morally ambivalent terms. Narayan also explains how another real-life original was conflated with the original peon, when, 'To mop up the post-war glut of money in various hands, a financial wizard [who] promised fantastic, dizzying scales of interest and dividends', appeared. 'So', he summarizes, 'Margayya is actually a combination of two personalities' (12).

28 The choice of name represents a probable allusion to the fifteenth-century mystic and philosopher, Kabir, a bhakti saint, who is revered as one of medieval India's most important poets. Nilufer E. Bharucha, 'Colonial Enclosures and Autonomous Spaces: R.K. Narayan's Malgudi', *South Asian Review*, 23, 1 (2002), 133, notes that Kabir 'was a symbol of Hindu-Muslim unity'.

29 Although it is mistaken to identify Malgudi with Mysore, Narayan's comments on sanitation and slum clearance in the city of

Mysore in his officially commissioned 1939 travel book on the state provide interesting background to this. After several pages lauding Mysore as 'India's most beautiful city' and detailing the civic improvements undertaken by the Municipality that have contributed to its high standards of cleanliness, he finally comes to speak of 'its dark spots, of the congested and slummy quarters that still disfigure its loveliness like so many ugly blotches, of the unsewered drains that run like tears down its beautiful face', *Mysore*, Mysore: Government Branch Press, 1939, 113. Narayan also talks of the continuing prevalence of malaria and the need for 'a great and wholehearted drive against the mosquito [...]' (*ibid.*, 114).

30   Cf. *The Man-Eater of Malgudi* (1961), where the protagonist Nataraj experiences a similar form of family partition, *Man-Eater of Malgudi*, Harmondsworth: Penguin, 1983, 10–12. Inevitably the signifier 'partition' used in novels published in the 1950s and 1960s invites interpretation as some form of national allegory, but Narayan makes no reference to the national Partition. Such a reading is rather more sustainable for *The Man-Eater*, which is set in the post-Independence era than for *The Financial Expert*, which is set in the early 1940s.

31   *A Passage to England*, New Delhi, Orient Paperbacks, n.d., 114.

32   Narayan's footnote.

33   In his later introduction to the novel, Narayan writes: 'Many years after finishing *The Financial Expert*, I finally set eyes on the original Margayya, pointed out to me by my brother. He was somewhat ragged now, as he sat on the bazaar pavement selling books. Apparently he sold prayer books, and calendar pictures depicting the gods, but to the favoured ones he produced from under cover a different category of books: nude picture albums and the *Kama Sutra* in simple language. [...] Here seemed to be an instance where actual life followed the pattern of fiction, and it rather confounded one's notions about fact and fiction and which arose first. One thing I may assure my readers of: since the original Margayya could not speak English, there was no chance that he could have copied his career from my book' (*A Story-Teller's World*, New Delhi: Penguin, 1989, 13).

34   Cf. the character of Dr Rann in *Talkative Man* (1986).

35   Cf. Graham Greene: 'how innocent is all his crookedness' (Introduction, *FE* v).

36   Sub-titled *The Science of Love*.

37 Cf. very similar passages in Naipaul's *The Mystic Masseur* (1957), in which the protagonist Ganesh evinces a similar fascination with the physical aspects of print culture, suggesting that Naipaul may have been influenced by Narayan in this respect, *The Mystic Masseur*, Harmondsworth: Penguin, 1969, 49, 82, 96–7. Naipaul had certainly read a number of Narayan novels prior to the publication of this novel. See above Note 4.

38 Fakrul Alam, 'R.K. Narayan and the End of British India', *South Asian Review*, 23, 1 (2002), 70–85, particularly 71 and 81.

39 Meenakshi Mukherjee, 'The Anxiety of Indianness: Our Novels in English', in Nilufer E.Barucha and Vrinda Nabar, eds, *Mapping Cultural Spaces: Postcolonial Literature in English: Essays in Honour of Nissim Ezekiel*, New Delhi: Vision, 1998, 78–93, 82; quoted in Alam, 'R.K. Narayan and the End of British India', 71.

40 Alam, 'R.K. Narayan and the End of British India', 78.

41 Greene, Introduction, *FE* v-vi.

42 Lakshmi Holmstrom, *The Novels of R.K. Narayan*, Calcutta: Writers Workshop, 1973, 51.

43 *Ibid.*, 50–58.

44 At least one critic, Fawzia Afzal-Khan takes a completely different view of Margayya from first to the last. She concludes her discussion of *The Financial Expert*, which argues for the co-existence of 'myth' and 'realism' in the novel, by saying that 'despite some redemption, [he] remains to the end the small, ignoble character fixated on money, as he was in the beginning', Afzal-Khan, *Cultural Imperialism and the Indo-English Novel*, University Park, PA: Pennsylvania State University Press, 1993, 43.

45 Unlike most of Narayan's novels, the first British edition of *Waiting for the Mahatma* included a glossary, particularly explaining many of the Gandhian terms for its international readership and thereby, it could be argued, contributing to the dissemination of his teachings.

46 *Waiting for the Mahatma*, London: Methuen, 1955, 19. Subsequent references in this chapter cite *WM*.

47 Cf. particularly Krishna in *The English Teacher* and Jagan in *The Vendor of Sweets*.

48 The phrase Naipaul uses to characterize Srinivas in *Mr Sampath*, *India: A Wounded Civilization*, London: André Deutsch, 1977, 22.

49 Cf. the old village temple in *The Dark Room*, the temple across the Sarayu river in *The Financial Expert* and the temple where Raju

takes up residence in the later action of *The Guide*.

50 *Pace* Naipaul's view that 'the novel is a form of social inquiry, and as such outside the Indian tradition', *India: A Wounded Civilization*, London: André Deutsch, 1977, 18–19.

51 Bose was elected leader of the Indian National Congress in 1939, but resigned from this position when he failed to secure Gandhi's support. An advocate of strong, totalitarian leadership, he spent periods in Nazi Germany and Japan, where in 1943 he founded the anti-British Indian National Army, which recruited its soldiers from Southeast Asians of Indian descent, Indian prisoners-of-war and defectors form the Indian army.

52 Naipaul, *India: A Wounded Civilization*, London: André Deutsch, 1977, 18ff.

53 An explanation presumably included for the benefit of Western readers.

54 See my book, *Postcolonial Con-Texts: Writing Back to the Canon*, London and New York: Continuum, 2001, particularly 'Introduction: Parents, Bastards and Orphans' (1–14) for a discussion of ways in which this trope is used in post-colonial writing.

55 Edward Said, *The World, The Text and the Critic*, London: Faber and Faber, 1984, 174.

56 A site 'in which individuals whose behavior is deviant in relation to the required mean or norm are placed', Michel Foucault, 'Of Other Spaces' (1967), <http://foucault.info/documents/hetero-Topia/foucault.heteroTopia.en.html> (Accessed 21 September 2006).

57 E.g. William Walsh, *R.K. Narayan: A Critical Appreciation*, London: Heinemann, 1982, 88.

58 Cf. *MyD* 79–80, where Narayan refers to the station as the location that provided the impulse from which his fictional town took shape: 'Malgudi with its little railway station swam into view, all ready-made, with a character called Swaminathan running down the platform'. See also Susan and N. Ram, *R.K. Narayan: The Early Years*, 105; and a letter to Graham Greene, 10 June 1936, in which Narayan says the ending of *Swami* was the image which came to him first and inspired the whole novel (Greene Papers, John J. Burns Library, Boston College, MS 95–3, D7, Folder I).

59 Cf. the discussion of *The Bachelor of Arts* and *The English Teacher* in Chapter 2 above.

Chapter 4

1 See Warren French with Javaid Qazi, 'Some Notes on "Reluctant Guru"', in *R.K. Narayan: Contemporary Critical Essays*, ed. Geoffrey Kain, East Lansing, MI: Michigan State University Press, 1993, 187–91.

2 R.K. Narayan, *Reluctant Guru*, 1974; New Delhi: Orient paperbacks, n.d., 13. Subsequent references in this chapter cite *RG*.

3 R.K. Narayan, *My Days: A Memoir*, New York: Viking, 1974, 167–9. Subsequent references in this chapter cite *MyD*.

4 R.K. Narayan, 'Gods, Demons and Modern Times', *Barnard Alumnae*, Winter 1973, 4.

5 A work in which he retold stories from *The Mahabharata*, *The Ramayana*, *The Yoga-Vasishta* of 'Devi', *The Shiva Purana* and the Tamil epic *Silapadikharam*, *Gods, Demons and Others*, London: Vintage, 2001, [v]. Subsequent references in this chapter cite *Gods*.

6 See, e.g., Kirpal Singh, 'The Ordinary and Average as Satiric Traps: The Case of R.K. Narayan', in *R.K. Narayan, Contemporary Critical Essays*, ed. Geoffrey Kain, East Lansing, MI: Michigan State University Press, 1993, 84; Chitra Sankaran, *The Myth Connection: The Use of Hindu Mythology in Some Novels of Raja Rao and R.K, Narayan*, Ahmedabad: Allied Publishers, 1993, 215ff; and Geoffrey Kain, 'R.K. Narayan', in *A Companion to Indian Fiction in English*, ed. Pier Paolo Piciucco, New Delhi: Atlantic, 2004, 17.

7 John Lowe, 'A Meeting in Malgudi: A Conversation with R.K. Narayan', in *R.K. Narayan: Contemporary Critical Essays*, ed. Geoffrey Kain, East Lansing, MI: Michigan State University Press, 1993, 181.

8 I am indebted to Robert Cox for this phrasing.

9 R.K. Narayan, *The Guide*, 1958; Harmondsworth: Penguin, 1980, 220. Subsequent references in this chapter cite *Guide*.

10 Lakshmi Holmstrom, *The Novels of R.K. Narayan*, Calcutta: Writers Workshop, 1973, 64, 67; M.K. Naik, 'Two Uses of Irony: V.S. Naipaul's *The Mystic Masseur* and R.K. Narayan's *The Guide*', *World Literature Written in English*, 17, 2 (1978), 654.

11 E.g. Fakrul Alam, 'Narrative Strategies in Two Narayan Novels', in *R.K. Narayan: Critical Perspectives*, ed. A.L. McLeod, New Delhi: Sterling, 1994, 17, who says 'the reader has to decide if Raju has assumed sainthood or just lost consciousness because of hunger and fatigue'.

12   John Lowe, 'A Meeting in Malgudi: A Conversation with R.K. Narayan', in *R.K. Narayan, Contemporary Critical Essays*, ed. Geoffrey Kain, East Lansing, MI: Michigan State University Press,, 1993, 181.

13   'The Writerly Life', *A Writer's Nightmare: Selected Essays 1958–1988*, New Delhi: Penguin, 1988, 200.

14   Narayan talks about his response to the film in 'Misguided Guide', *A Writer's Nightmare: Selected Essays 1958–1988*, New Delhi: Penguin, 1988, 206–17, expressing particular displeasure at its use of locations that displaced the action from South India and the corruption of the 'strictly classical [dance] tradition of South Indian *Bharat Natyam*' (211).

15   Chitra Sankaran identifies this as a reworking of the mythological figure of the trickster sage, *The Myth Connection: The Use of Hindu Mythology in Some Novels of Raja Rao and R.K, Narayan*, Ahmedabad: Allied Publishers, 1993, 214 ff.

16   M.K. Naik, 'Two Uses of Irony: V.S. Naipaul's *The Mystic Masseur* and R.K. Narayan's *The Guide*', *World Literature Written in English*, 17, 2 (1978), 650.

17   See my discussion of *The Mystic Masseur* in *The Web of Tradition: Uses of Allusion in V.S. Naipaul's Fiction*, Aarhus: Dangaroo and London: Hansib, 1987, 34–51.

18   Sura P. Nath's phrase, 'R.K. Narayan's Dialogic Narrative in *The Guide*', in *R.K. Narayan: Critical Perspectives*, ed. A.L. McLeod, New Delhi: Sterling, 1994, 129.

19   Keith Garebian, 'Strategy and Theme in the Art of R.K. Narayan, *ARIEL*, 5,4 (1974), 74.

20   See particularly Sura P. Nath, 'R.K. Narayan's Dialogic Narrative in *The Guide*', in *R.K. Narayan: Critical Perspectives*, ed. A.L. McLeod, New Delhi: Sterling, 1994, 129–36; and Fakrul Alam, 'Narrative Strategies in Two Narayan Novels', also in *R.K. Narayan*, ed. McLeod, 8–21. Also: M.K. Naik, *The Ironic Vision: A Study of the Fiction of R.K. Narayan*, New Delhi, 1983, 63–4; and Syd Harrex, *The Fire and the Offering: The English Language Novel of India, 1935–1970*, Calcutta: Writers Workshop, 1978, Vol. 2, 118–19.

21   Narayan's own remarks on his writing habits are typified by his describing himself to Ved Mehta as 'an inattentive quick writer who has little sense of style', 'The Train Had Just Arrived at Malgudi Station', *New Yorker*, 15 September 1962, 72. However, his manuscripts in the Mugar Memorial Library, Boston University and the

Harry Ransom Humanities Research Centre at the University of Texas in Austin often suggest careful revision.

22 William Walsh, *R.K. Narayan: A Critical Appreciation*, London: Heinemann, 1982, 121.

23 When I met Narayan during the concert season in Chennai in December 1997, questions about particular performances formed his main subject of his conversation. Cf. T.S. Satyan, 'Walking with R.K. Narayan', *Frontline*, 6–19 July 2002, who writes: 'Not many know that music was Narayan's "real passion". He would never miss a good concert. Some of the great musicians were his family friends. Whenever they visited Mysore, they stayed in his home. […] Narayan would often say, "But for the education I received, I think I would have become a Bhagavatar – professional classical musician." Surprisingly, music as a theme and musicians as characters do not figure in Narayan's novels, rues our common friend, H.Y. Sharada Prasad' (< http://www.hinduonnet.com/fline/fl1914/19140670.htm> Accessed 4 September 2006). *The Guide* is a very obvious exception to this. Also cf. Narayan, 'Music in Madras', *The Hindu*, 13 January 1952, where he says 'music becomes the only reality' during the end-of-December music festival. Copy in Special Collections, Mugar Memorial Library, Boston University, No. 737, Box 5.

24 Themes for *Bharat Natyam* are taken from the *Ramayana, Mahabharata* and *puranas*. Estimates of when it originated suggest it evolved between 2,500 years and 1,500 years ago. The term *Bharat Natyam* is compounded from 'bha' (for *bhava* or 'emotional projection'), 'ra' (for *raga* or 'melody') and 'ta' (for *tala* or 'rhythm'), while Natyam means 'the art of dance'. Originally performed by *devadasis* (temple dancers), it was originally a form for solo female performance, though since its twentieth-century revival, group work has also been popular. In contemporary performance it is seen as a system, which encourages experimentation rather than strict adherence to classically prescribed rules. Information taken from <http://www.tamilstar.com/dance/bharat> (Accessed 19 August 2006); and <http://www.exoticindiaart.com/product/CA92 > (Accessed 20 August 2006).

25 <http://www.tamilstar.com/dance/bharat> (Accessed 19 August 2006).

26 See above Note 4.

27 H.L. Seneviratne, 'Food Essence and the Essence of Experience', *The Eternal Food: Gastronomic Ideas and Experiences of Hindus and Buddhists*, ed. R.S. Khare, Albany, NY: State University of New York Press, 1992, 182.

28   *Ibid.*, 179; glosses in square brackets in original.

29   R.K. Narayan, *A Story-Teller's World*, New Delhi: Penguin, 1989, 119–23.

30   Cf. 'This 2000 years-old art is still fresh and fascinating as it must have been when it inspired the brilliant sculptors who have left perennial records of Bharatnatyam in the magnificent temples of Tamil Nadu', <http://www.exoticindiaart.com/product/CA92 > (Accessed 20 August 2006).

31   K. Chellappan, 'The Dialectics of Myth and Irony in R.K. Narayan', in *R.K. Narayan: Critical Perspectives*, ed. A.L. McLeod, New Delhi: Sterling, 1994, 27. There is a possible veiled allusion to this myth in Chapter 5 of the novel, where one of Raju's clients during his period as a tourist guide goes to the source of the Sarayu River and identifies it as the spot where Parvathi, Shiva's consort, 'jump[ed] into the fire; the carving on one of the pillars of the shrine actually shows the goddess plunging into the fire and water arising from the same spot' (*Guide* 49). If so, this would be reliant on equating the fictional Sarayu with the Ganges.

32   See Chapter 3, Note 58.

33   R.K. Narayan, *The Man-Eater of Malgudi*, 1961; Harmondsworth: Penguin, 1983, 15. Subsequent references in this chapter cite *M-E*.

34   Glossary, *Waiting for the Mahatma*, London: Methuen, 1955, 255.

35   Cf. Narayan's reference to Gajendra as 'the Lord of all Elephants in the heavens', *The Painter of Signs*, 1976; Harmondsworth: Penguin, 1982, 62. Subsequent references in this chapter cite *PS*.

36   Cf. Naipaul's view in *India: A Wounded Civilization*, London: André Deutsch, 1977, that Srinivas (in *Mr Sampath*) turns his back on social responsibility for a form of non-violence, which is a travesty of Gandhianism: 'Gandhian nonviolence has degenerated into something very like the opposite of what Gandhi intended. For Srinivas nonviolence isn't a form of action, a quickener of social conscience. It is only a means of securing an undisturbed calm; it is nondoing, noninterference, social indifference' (25).

37   In Hindu mythology, Nataraj is Shiva in his form as the cosmic dancer who begins and ends the world. Cf. Rosie's decision in *The Guide* that 'she'd have a bronze figure of Nataraja, the god of dancers, the god whose primal dance created the vibrations that set the worlds in motion' (*Guide* 107). Although Shiva is characteristically seen as locked in a struggle with Vishnu, there are attempts to reconcile the gods as two sides of a duality, sharing common characteristics. This *may* explain the novel's suggestion that

Nataraj is a putative Krishna and *could* be related to the syzygy that Nataraj and Vasu appear to represent. It certainly helps to account for the attraction that Nataraj feels for Vasu, even when he is most troubled by his behaviour.

38   In addition to producing his own version of the *Ramayana*, Narayan extracted the story of Ravana, the *rakshasa* king of Lanka, from the epic for retelling in *Gods, Demons and Others* (*Gods* 99–124).

39   Cf. *The Painter of Signs*, where the protagonist Raman worries that Daisy may be 'Mohini, who tempted men and fooled them' (*PS* 75).

40   Narayan provided an account of the story in a talk he gave at Barnard College, New York, as a Gildersleeve Visiting Lecturer in the early 1970s; reprinted as 'Gods, Demons and Modern Times' in *Barnard Alumnae*, Winter 1973, 3–7.

41   See Chapter 3, particularly Note 14.

42   E.g. Edwin Gerow, 'The Quintessential Narayan', *Literature East and West*. 10, 1–2 (1966), 1–18; Meenakshi Mukherjee, *The Twice-Born Fiction*, New Delhi: Heinemann, 1971, 150–55; Shirley Chew, 'A Proper Detachment: The Novels of R.K. Narayan', in *Readings in Commonwealth Literature*, ed. William Walsh, Oxford: Clarendon, 1973, 74; Chitra Sankaran, *The Myth Connection: The Use of Hindu Mythology in Some Novels of Raja Rao and R.K. Narayan*, New Delhi: Allied Publishers, 1993, 67–91; Ganeswar Mishra, 'The Novel as Purana: A Study of the Form of *The Man-Eater of Malgudi* and *Kanthapura*', *How Indian is the Indian Novel in English*, Bhubaneswar: Utkal University, 1990, 18–35, repr. in *R.K. Narayan: Contemporary Critical Essays*, ed. Geoffrey Kain, East Lansing, MI: Michigan State University Press, 1993, 9–23; K. Chellappan, 'The Dialectics of Myth and Irony in R.K. Narayan', in *R.K. Narayan: Critical Perspectives*, ed. A.L. McLeod, New Delhi: Sterling, 1994, 28.

43   V.S. Naipaul, *India: A Wounded Civilization*, London: André Deutsch, 1977, 25.

44   Cf. Margayya's devotion to Lakshmi in *The Financial Expert*, discussed above in Chapter 3 and Nirad Chaudhuri's comment, quoted there, that 'every normal Hindu home' has 'a little sanctum [...] devoted to the goddess Lakshmi', *A Passage to England*, New Delhi, Orient Paperbacks, n.d., 114.

45   Types of irony identified by D.C. Muecke in *Irony: The Critical Idiom*, London: Methuen, 1970, 57–62.

46 Nirad Chaudhuri, *A Passage to England*, New Delhi, Orient Paper-backs, n.d., 114–15.

47 R.K. Narayan, *The Ramayana*, 1972, Harmondsworth: Penguin, 1977, xi.

48 *Ibid.*, vii.

49 *Ibid.*

50 Dryden's definition of 'the true end of satire', Preface *to Absalom and Achitophel, The Poems and Fables of John Dryden,* London: Oxford University Press, 1962, 189.

51 Muecke, *Irony: The Critical Idiom,* London: Methuen, 1970, 66.

52 Søren Kierkegaard, *The Concept of Irony, with Constant Reference to Socrates,* trans. Lee M. Capel, London: Collins, 1966, 271; quoted by Muecke, *ibid.,* 67.

53 *Ibid.*

54 Harleen Singh, 'Satirical Freedoms and Myths of Modernity: R.K. Narayan's *The Painter of Signs', South Asian Review,* 23, 1 (2002), 199.

55 *India: A Wounded Civilization,* London: André Deutsch, 1977, 18, 37.

56 *Ibid.,* 13–36.

57 *Ibid.,* 38.

58 *Ibid.,* 18–27. See the discussion of *Mr Sampath* in Chapter 3 above.

59 *The Vendor of Sweets,* 1967; Harmondsworth: Penguin, 1983, 10. Subsequent references in this chapter cite *VS.*

60 Tabish Khair, *Babu Fictions: Alienation in Contemporary Indian English Novels,* New Delhi: Oxford University Press, 2001, 232.

61 *Ibid.,* 233.

62 See the Introduction to John Thieme and Ira Raja, eds, *The Table is Laid: The Oxford Anthology of South Asian Food Writing,* New Delhi: Oxford University Press, 2007, xvii–lv.

63 Judit Katona-Apte, 'Dietary Aspects of Acculturation: Meals, Feasts, and Fasts in a Minority Community in South Asia', in *Gastronomy: The Anthropology of Food and Food Habits,* ed. Margaret L. Arnott, The Hague: Mouton, 1975, 321–2.

64 Author of the *Natya Shastra* or 'Science of Drama'. See my discussion of the episodes devoted to Rosie's dancing career in *The Guide* above and Notes 27 and 28 of this chapter.

65 *Laughing Matters: Comic Tradition in India*, Chicago: University of Chicago Press, 1988, 7–8; quoted in Feroza Jussawalla, "Indian Theory and Criticism", in Michael Groden and Martin Kreiswirth, eds, *The Johns Hopkins Guide to Literary Theory and Criticism*, Baltimore: Johns Hopkins University Press, 1994, 401.

66 Cp. Vasu's practice in *The Man-Eater of Malgudi*.

67 *India: A Wounded Civilization*, London: André Deutsch, 1977, 43.

68 See the discussion in Chapter 1 above.

69 See *VS* 45, 73–4, 97, 104–5.

70 *Ibid*, 28, 76.

71 *Ibid*., 42.

72 *Ibid*., 102.

73 Jonathan Swift, *Gulliver's Travels and Other Writings*, ed. Louis A. Landa, London: Oxford University Press, 1976, 148–50.

74 Cf. *Waiting for the Mahatma*, London: Methuen, 1955, 24–34.

75 Ranga Rao, *R.K. Narayan*, New Delhi: Sahitya Akademi, 2004, 88, sees the end of the novel in these terms, pointing out that 'Jagan is not taking sanyasa, he is going into the penultimate *asrama*, vanaprasthya'.

76 Unlike the exoteric side of the quest, which *was* concerned with the physical transformation of base metal into gold, the esoteric side had a spiritual goal: that of securing a perfect union with God and Jung interpreted this in terms of psychic transformation. In his autobiographical *Memories, Dreams and Reflections* he describes how he realized the link between alchemy and his own ideas on the development of the self, after reading a German translation of the Taoist alchemical treatise, *The Secret of the Golden Flower*, coming to appreciate that 'The experiences of the alchemists were, in a sense, my experiences, and their world my world. This was, of course, a momentous discovery. I had stumbled upon the historical counterpart of my psychology of the unconscious' (*Memories, Dreams and Reflections*, London: Collins, 1963, 196).

77 *India: A Wounded Civilization*, London: André Deutsch, 1977, 18–19.

78 Cf. Tabish Khair, *Babu Fictions: Alienation in Contemporary Indian English Novels*, New Delhi: Oxford University Press, 2001, 226–42.

79 Ranga Rao, *R.K. Narayan*, New Delhi: Sahitya Akademi, 2004, 88.

80 'Making a Map of the Imagination', R.K. Narayan interviewed by Clare Colvin, *Sunday Times*, 23 April 1989, G9.

81 Narayan's, or at least Raman's, chronology is mistaken here. Rani Jhansi (1835–58), a nationalist heroine who died fighting against the British, was a contemporary of the young Queen Victoria.

82 See Sadhana Allison Puranik, '*The Painter of Signs*: Breaking the Frontier', in *R.K. Narayan: Contemporary Critical Essays*, ed. Geoffrey Kain, East Lansing, MI: Michigan State University Press, 1993, 129.

83 'Indira Gandhi', in *A Writer's Nightmare: Selected Essays 1958–1988*, New Delhi: Penguin, 1989, 219.

84 *Ibid.*, 221. There is a parenthetical reference to Laxman in *The Painter of Signs*. A minor figure in the novel, an accountant, is said to be a 'replica of the Common Man created by the cartoonist Laxman, which appeared every morning in a newspaper' (*PS* 125), an analogy which it is tempting to extend to many of the characters who people Malgudi, including protagonists of the novels such as Raman.

85 *Ibid.*, 219. See also Chapter 3, Note 1.

86 Steve Carter, 'Narrative Ostranenie in R.K. Narayan's *Painter of Signs*', *Journal of Commonwealth Literature*, 29, 2 (1994), 109.

87 For a developed feminist reading of Daisy's character, see Shantha Krishnaswamy, 'Daisy Paints Her Signs Otherwise', in *R.K. Narayan: Contemporary Critical Essays*, ed. Geoffrey Kain, East Lansing, MI: Michigan State University Press, 1993, 115–24. Krishnaswamy argues that 'Daisy is a dangerous, disruptive, and fanatical nun wedded to her goal, out to destroy the Malgudian order of things' (115). Arguably, though, any such destruction is incidental to her social activism and desire for personal independence. The novel's use of point of view is, as discussed here, complex, but it remains primarily focused on Raman.

88 One of the eight forms of Hindu marriage prescribed in the *dharmasastras*, including the Law of Manu, and generally viewed as a love marriage. In the novel, Daisy agrees to it after Raman proposes it to her as the most appropriate of the *five* forms of Hindu marriage, saying that it has particular classical authority and is suitable when 'two souls [meet] in harmony [...] and no further rite or ceremony [is] called for' (*PS* 124). Subsequently it is referred to as 'as easily snapped as made' (*PS* 132). Narayan retells one of the best-known mythical accounts of such a marriage in his account of the story of Shakuntala and Dushyanta in *Gods, Demons and Others* (*Gods* 202–13), a story taken from the *Ramayana*.

89   Cf. *PS* 45, 118, 128, for other references to this story.

90   Steve Carter, 'Narrative Ostranenie in R.K. Narayan's *Painter of Signs*', *Journal of Commonwealth Literature*, 29, 2 (1994), 110.

91   In a seemingly anachronistic reference, Raman thinks of behaving like Rudolph Valentino in *The Sheik* (PS 74), a film he has seen as a student. Even allowing for the possibility of this classic 1921 film's continuing to be shown in South India after the coming of sound, the chronology seems more appropriate to Narayan than to Raman, who is in his early thirties in the year of the novel, 1972. Narayan's attraction to the film is confirmed by a very similar reference in *The Vendor of Sweets*, where Jagan imagines himself 'to be the "Sheik" in the Hollywood film in which Rudolph Valentino demonstrated the art of ravishing women (*VS* 127). In this case the reference is less anachronistic, since the elderly Jagan is remembering the early days of his marriage.

92   Cf. her response to his likening himself to King Santhanu in the *Mahabharata*: '"You always find some ancient model"' (*PS* 125). Raman later refers to himself as 'quite prepared to surrender himself completely to her way of thinking and do nothing that might leave him in the plight of Santhanu. No questioning and the wife stays, but any slight doubt expressed, she flies away forever' (*PS* 131). Ranga Rao sees the 'Ganga-Santanu myth' as informing the text in much the same way as the Bhasmasura myth underpins *The Man-Eater of Malgudi*. He explains, 'In the myth, Santanu falls in love with Ganga, a beautiful maiden, in reality the goddess of the sacred river; she marries him on condition he will not question whatever she does. She drowns each child as it comes, until Santanu is unable to bear it and stops her from destroying the latest offspring. Ganga hands over the baby to Santanu and goes back to her world. In Narayan's reworking of the epic story love is pitted against the family', Ranga Rao, *R.K. Narayan*, New Delhi: Sahitya Akademi, 2004, 90–1. Harleen Singh sees this parallel as an instance of 'the ambivalent tonalities of Narayan's treatment of Indian legends and myths, so that, even as one is aware of the virtue of traditional wisdom, the absurdity of the application of that very tradition is equally viable', 'Satirical Freedoms and Myths of Modernity: R.K. Narayan's *The Painter of Signs*', *South Asian Review*, 23, 1 (2002), 199.

Chapter 5

1   John Lowe, 'A Meeting in Malgudi: A Conversation with R.K. Narayan', in *R.K. Narayan, Contemporary Critical Essays*, ed. Geoffrey Kain, East Lansing, MI: Michigan State University Press, 1993, 181; and Ranga Rao, *R.K. Narayan*, New Delhi: Sahitya Akademi, 2004, 110, who says that Narayan expressed this opinion to David Davidar in 1998, adding that Narayan said he would like to be 'A Contemplative Tiger' in his next incarnation.

2   Cf. Narayan's earlier use of this name for the tiger in a story told to schoolchildren in *The English Teacher*, Chicago: University of Chicago Press, 1980, 136–8.

3   On the first occasion it is suggested that his time as a caged circus animal is retribution for his having imprisoned others in a previous incarnation; on the second it is suggested that he may have been a poet, *A Tiger for Malgudi*, 1983; Harmondsworth: Penguin, 1984, 42 and 143. Subsequent references cite *Tiger*.

4   R.K. Narayan, *The Man-Eater of Malgudi*, 1961; Harmondsworth: Penguin, 1983, 52

5   See the discussion in Chapter 4.

6   Jopi Nyman, *Postcolonial Animal Tale from Kipling to Coetzee*, New Delhi: Atlantic, 2003, 39–40.

7   *Ibid*. See 'Mowgli's Brothers' and 'The Law of the Jungle', Kipling, *All the Mowgli Stories*, London: Macmillan/St Martin's Press, 1973, 7–27, 73–4.

8   Sujit Mukerjee, 'Tigers in Fiction: An Aspect of the Colonial Encounter', *Kunapipi*, 9,1 (1987), 12.

9   Margaret Atwood, *Survival: A Thematic Guide to Canadian Literature*, Toronto: Anansi, 1972, 73–4.

10 *Ibid.*, 74.

11 Sujit Mukherjee, 'Tigers in Fiction: An Aspect of the Colonial Encounter', *Kunapipi*, 9,1 (1987), 2–3.

12 See, e.g., *Man-Eaters of Kumaon* (1944) and *My India* (1952). Newspaper clippings in the Narayan holdings in the Harry Ransom Humanities Research Centre at the University of Texas in Austin, Acquisition R12739, Box 11, include items which demonstrate his interest in Raj tiger hunts at the time he was writing the novel. They include reviews of a life of Jim Corbett and an anthology of Indian hunting stories and a copy of an article entitled 'Shikars and Sahibs' by Jug Suraiya (*Times of India*, 17 December 1989, 1 and 4).

13 Sujit Mukherjee, 'Tigers in Fiction: An Aspect of the Colonial

Encounter', *Kunapipi*, 9,1 (1987), 5.

14 Jopi Nyman, *Postcolonial Animal Tale from Kipling to Coetzee*, New Delhi: Atlantic, 2003, 41.

15 It was declared India's national animal in 1972. See Kailash Sankhala, *Tiger! The Story of the Indian Tiger*, London: William Collins, 1978, 130–31.

16 John Lowe, 'A Meeting in Malgudi: A Conversation with R.K. Narayan', in *R.K. Narayan: Contemporary Critical Essays*, ed. Geoffrey Kain, East Lansing, MI: Michigan State University Press, 1993, 182.

17 Narayan, *The Emerald Route*, 1977; New Delhi: Penguin, 1999, 5.

18 *Ibid.*

19 Narayan was familiar with caged tigers from the Mysore zoo. See, e.g., Narayan, *Mysore*, Mysore: Government of Mysore, 1939, 2, where he refers to having seen 'a notice, "Caught in Kadur Forests"', over a tiger cage in the Mysore zoo.

20 The Malgudi of Market Road and the surrounding streets only appears briefly in a carnivalesque episode, in which Raja strikes fear into the townsfolk, after killing his circus-trainer, Captain, and escaping from the confinement of this phase of his life.

21 Now the 'hero' of the world's most widely syndicated comic strip, Garfield was a comparative junior at the time when *A Tiger for Malgudi* was first published. The cool fat cat who loves food and hates exercise made his début in the comic pages on 19 June 1978 and now appears in over 2,570 papers, with an estimated daily readership of 263 million. <http://pressroom.garfield.com/Garfield_bio> (Accessed 2 October 2005).

22 R.K. Narayan, *The South Bank Show*, London Weekend Television, 1983. First televised ITV, 12 March 1983.

23 See *Disgrace* (1999) as well as *The Lives of Animals* (1999).

24 Cf. *Tiger* 108 and 128.

25 Cf. its role as a signifier of the impossibility of fixing meaning in language in *The Painter of Signs*.

26 Geoffrey Kain, 'Eternal, Insatiable, Appetite: The Irony of R.K. Narayan's Baited Hero', in *R.K. Narayan: Contemporary Critical Essays*, ed. Geoffrey Kain, East Lansing, MI: Michigan State University Press, 1993, 101.

27 See Joseph Alter, *Gandhi's Body: Sex, Diet and the Politics of Nationalism*, Philadelphia: University of Pennsylvania Press,

2000 for an account of how Gandhi's dietary regime formed part of his broader ethic of selfless abstinence. I am indebted to Ira Raja for directing me towards this work. Cf. Jagan's first words in *The Vendor of Sweets*: '"Conquer taste, and you will have conquered the self"' (*The Vendor of Sweets*, 1967; Harmondsworth: Penguin, 1983, 5).

28 Though not, as Kain suggests ('Eternal, Insatiable, Appetite: The Irony of R.K. Narayan's Baited Hero', 109) a man-eater. His Master, whom the novel presents as the ultimate authority in such matters, asserts this categorically when he first encounters Raja (*Tiger* 105).

29 Towards the end, in one of the novel's few passages that suggests a broader context by employing a mythic analogue, Narayan briefly alludes to the story of Savitri, Satyavan and Yama, which he had previously drawn on in *The Dark Room*. See *Talkative Man*, 1986; Harmondsworth: Penguin, 1987, 113ff. Here, however, the reference reads as a grafted-on coda rather than as an intertext that is integral to the novel's meaning; and Rann's subsequent desertion of Commandant Sarasa reverses the pattern of triumphant wifely fidelity that is enforced by the Savitri myth. Subsequent references to *Talkative Man* in this chapter cite *Talkative*.

30 Cf. an undated 1935 letter written by Greene to Narayan's friend, 'Kittu' Purna, in which he takes the view that if *Swami* fails to find a publisher it will be because it is 20,000 words short of the ideal length, quoted by Susan and N. Ram, *R.K. Narayan: The Early Years: 1906–1945*, New Delhi: Viking, 152.

31 Geoffrey Kain, '*Talkative Man*: R.K. Narayan's Consummate Performance of Narayan', *South Asian Review*, 23, 1 (2002), 5–21.

32 The character of *Talkative Man* recurs in Narayan's fiction from his earliest work onwards. He is the narrator of the short story 'Garden', published in the second issue of *Indian Thought* (July–September 1941) and of an even earlier, pre-Malgudi story, 'A Night of Cyclone', originally written in 1929 and republished as 'End of the World' in *The Hindu* in October 1938 (Ram and Ram, *R.K. Narayan: The Early Years*, 88–90, 342 and 449, Note 50). Narayan republished 'A Night of Cyclone' in *Old and New: Eighteen Short Stories*, Mysore: Indian Thought Publications, 1981, 125–31, which also includes (89–96) another *Talkative Man* story, 'Lawley Road', one of Narayan's best-known short fictions. 'Lawley Road' is also available in *Lawley Road*, New Delhi: Orient Paperbacks, n.d., 7–12 and *Malgudi Days*, Harmondsworth: Penguin, 1984, 111–16.

33   See Krishna Sen, 'Will the Real Dr Rann Please Stand Up?', *South Asian Review*, 23, 1 (2002), 22–48.

34   I am indebted to Ira Raja for this information.

35   *Gods, Demons and Others*, 1964; London: Vintage, 2001, 7. Subsequent references in this chapter cite *Gods*. Also *A Story-Teller's World*, New Delhi: Penguin, 1989, 7. Narada is also identified as the sage who told Rama's story to Valmiki in an epigraph to Narayan's *Ramayana*, 1972; Harmondsworth: Penguin , 1977, [vii]; and in his narrative of 'Valmiki' in *Gods, Demons and Others*, which uses the wording Narayan would later employ in his *Ramayana* epigraph, *Gods* 133–4.

36   *The World of Nagaraj*, 1990; London: Mandarin, 1991, 3. Subsequent references in this chapter cite *WN*.

37   Krishna Sen, 'Will the Real Dr Rann Please Stand Up?', *South Asian Review*, 23, 1 (2002), 24.

38   Cp. Gilles Deleuze and Félix Guattari, *A Thousand Plateaus: Capitalism and Schizophrenia*, trans. Brian Massumi, 1980: Minneapolis: University of Minnesota Press, 1987, where the emphasis is on the more positive aspects of contemporary nomad thought.

39   See Chapter 3, Note 58.

40   Cf. V.S. Naipaul's use of the similar image of the water-hyacinths, which are clogging up the Zaire (Congo) River in *A Bend in the River* (1979). The local people refer to them as 'the new thing' or 'the new thing in the river' and view them as an enemy to traditional social values and lines of communication, *A Bend in the River*, London: André Deutsch, 1979, 53.

41   Ranga Rao, *R.K. Narayan*, New Delhi: Sahitya Akademi, 2004, comments that 'the upper class is in decline' (99) in *The World of Nagaraj* and notes details such as the descent of a former executive engineer as evidence of 'the degradation of the upper caste in Kabir Street' (100).

42   Confirmation that Nagaraj sees the milestone as a general metaphor for his state of mind comes when he returns to the image at the end of the novel, *WN* 183–4.

43   Cf. Dr Rann in *Talkative Man*.

44   See *WN* 67, 82, 155–6 and 180.

45   Rajini Srikanth, '*The World of Nagaraj*: Narayan's Metanovel', in *R.K. Narayan, Contemporary Critical Essays*, ed. Geoffrey Kain, East Lansing, MI: Michigan State University Press, 1993, 201.

46   Tristram playfully discusses Horace's categories in Chapter 4 of

the first volume of the novel, Laurence Sterne, *Tristram Shandy*, 1759–67; Harmondsworth: Penguin, 2003, 8. See Horace, *Ars Poetica*, lines 146–52.

47 Cf. his remarks in 'What Kind of Literature Do Our Students Need', talk on All India Radio, Bangalore, broadcast on 16 June 1978, in which he said that he wrote in English rather than Tamil or Kannada out of 'personal preference', adding that when he began his career 'no one questioned it, language had not become a sensitive issue. People spoke and wrote any language suited to their needs or circumstances'. Quoted and briefly discussed in Chapter 1 above.

48 Reprinted in *A Story-Teller's World*, New Delhi: Penguin, 1989, 7.

49 Narayan originally published the novella in Mysore on its own, with sketches by his brother R.K. Laxman, as *Grandmother's Tale*, in 1992. In the first British edition (1993), it was published along with the earlier novellas, 'Guru' and 'Salt and Sawdust'. The first American edition (1994) included various short stories. References here are to the British edition, *The Grandmother's Tale: Three Novellas*, London: Heinemann, 1993, subsequently cited in this chapter as *GT*.

50 Annotated by Narayan as an 'An ancient Tamil poetess'.

51 *My Days: A Memoir*, New York: Viking, 1974, 11.

52 Susan and N. Ram, *R.K. Narayan: The Early Years*, New Delhi: Viking, 1996, 17.

53 *Ibid.*, 14–18, 18.

54 See *GT* 3 and 55–6.

55 Cf. another reference to a physical object that provides a tangible link between past and present and further confirms the factual basis of the story: 'He [the narrator's – and Narayan's – great grandfather, Viswanath] sat in a small room in the front portion of his house and kept his wares in a small bureau, four feet high, half glazed. (The heirloom is still with the family; when I was young I was given that little bureau for keeping my school books and odds and ends. I had inscribed in chalk on the narrow top panel of this bureau "R.K. Narayanaswami B.A.B.L. Engine Driver". My full name with all the honours I aspired to' (*GT* 52–3).

56 Susan Ram, Introduction to Susan and N. Ram, *R.K. Narayan: The Early Years*, New Delhi: Viking, 1996, xxvi.

57 *Swami and Friends*, Chicago: University of Chicago Press, 1980, 22.

58 Cf. *Waiting for the Mahatma*. *The Painter of Signs* also contains

a very similar figure in the character of Raman's aunt, who tells a tale that bears a striking resemblance to that of the grandmother of the final novella. In a passage that gives a potted version the main narrative of 'The Grandmother's Tale', Raman's aunt tells him the story of her grandfather's desertion of his young wife, who pursued him years later, found him living with a 'concubine' in Poona and initiated the same series of events, leading to their reconciliation, as is narrated in 'The Grandmother's Tale', *The Painter of Signs*, 1976; Harmondsworth: Penguin, 1982, 31–2.

59   Susan and N. Ram, *R.K. Narayan: The Early Years*, New Delhi: Viking, 1996, 17, 338.

60   Cf. *The Dark Room*, 1938; London: Heinemann, 1978, particularly 115–16; and Narayan's retelling of the mythic Savitri's story in *Gods, Demons and Others* (*Gods* 182–9). She is also cited as an exemplar of wifely devotion in *The Guide*, 1958; Harmondsworth: Penguin, 1980, 136 and in *Talkative Man*: see Note 28 above.

61   John Hawley, '"R.K. Narayanswami [sic] B.A.B.L. Engine Driver": Story-telling and Memory in *The Grandmother's Tale, and Selected Stories*', *South Asian Review*, 23, 1 (2002), 86–105, 97.

62   *Ibid.*

Chapter 6

1   See Note 6 below; and Susan and N. Ram, *R.K. Narayan: The Early Years: 1906–1945*, New Delhi: Viking, 1996, 188–92, for quotes from several contemporary reviews that utilized the Chekhov analogy.

2   Graham Greene, Introduction to R.K. Narayan, *The Bachelor of Arts*, 1978; Chicago: University of Chicago Press, 1980, v.

3   *Ibid.*, x.

4   H.E. Bates, quoted in Ram and Ram, *R.K. Narayan: The Early Years*, 190.

5   William Walsh, *R.K. Narayan*, London: Heinemann, 1982, 1.

6   Viz. his comment that Narayan writes with 'a humour strange to our fiction, closer to Chekhov than to any English writer, with the same underlying sense of beauty and sadness', Graham Greene, *Reflections: 1923–1988*, London: Reinhardt Books, 1990, 56; quoted by Susan and N. Ram, *R.K. Narayan: The Early Years*, 151.

7   William Walsh, *R.K. Narayan*, London: Heinemann, 1982, 168–9.

8   See the comments by these two critics, who did so much to establish the study of Indian writing in English, quoted in the first part of the Contexts and Intertexts chapter of this study.

9   Lakshmi Holmstrom, *The Novels of R.K. Narayan*, Calcutta: Writers Workshop, 1973.

10 Mary Beatina, *Narayan: A Study in Transcendence*, New York: Peter Lang, 1994. See too her essay 'The Guide: A Study in Transcendence', in *R.K. Narayan: Contemporary Critical Essays*, ed. Geoffrey Kain, East Lansing, MI: Michigan State University Press, 1993, 55–77.

11 Tabish Khair, *Babu Fictions: Alienation in Contemporary Indian English Novels*, New Delhi: Oxford University Press, 2001, 232.

12 *Ibid.*, 233.

13 Ranga Rao, *R.K. Narayan*, New Delhi: Sahitya Akademi, 2004, passim, particularly 58–9. Rao explains that the third type is the *tamasic* (angry or wicked). *Gunas* correspond very roughly to the Western notion of Humours, as in the Jonsonian Comedy of Humours, but the correspondences is not exact.

14 See Chapter 4, Note 42 for a listing of several of the numerous discussions of the use of myth in *The Man-Eater*.

15 K. Chellappan, 'The Dialectics of Myth and Irony in R.K. Narayan', in *R.K. Narayan: Critical Perspectives*, ed. A.L. McLeod, New Delhi: Sterling, 1994, 22–32.

16 Susan and N. Ram, *R.K. Narayan: The Early Years, passim*, particularly Chapters 2 and 3.

17 P.S. Chauhan, '*Talkative Man* and the Semiotics of Malgudi Discourse', *South Asian Review*, 23, 1 (2002), 49–69.

18 Steve Carter, 'Narrative Ostranenie in R.K. Narayan's *Painter of Signs*', *Journal of Commonwealth Literature*, 29, 2 (1994), 109–16.

19 Rajini Srikanth, 'The World of Nagaraj: Narayan's Metanovel', in *R.K. Narayan, Contemporary Critical Essays*, ed. Geoffrey Kain, East Lansing, MI: Michigan State University Press, 1993, 197–203.

20 Sura P. Nath, 'R.K. Narayan's Dialogic Narrative in *The Guide*', in *R.K. Narayan: Critical Perspectives*, ed. A.L. McLeod, New Delhi: Sterling, 1994, 129–36.

21 V.S. Naipaul, *India: A Wounded Civilization*, London: André Deutsch, 1977, 18–27 and 37–43.

22 M.K. Naik, *The Ironic Vision: A Study of the Fiction of R.K. Narayan*, New Delhi: Sterling, 1983.

23 John Thieme, 'Irony in Narayan's *The Man-Eater of Malgudi*', *The English Review*, 3, 4 (1993), 13–17.

24 See too K. Chellappan, 'The Dialectics of Myth and Irony in R.K. Narayan', in *R.K. Narayan: Critical Perspectives*, ed. A.L. McLeod, New Delhi: Sterling, 1994, 22–32.

25 See above, Note 13.

26 Usha Bande, 'Validating the Self: The Female Hero in R.K. Narayan's *The Painter of Signs*', in *Women in Indo-Anglian Fiction: Tradition and Modernity*, ed. Naresh K. Jain, New Delhi: Manohar, 1998, 101–13.

27 Shantha Krishnaswamy, 'Daisy Paints Her Signs Otherwise', in *R.K. Narayan: Contemporary Critical Essays*, ed. Geoffrey Kain, East Lansing, MI: Michigan State University Press, 1993, 115–24.

28 Britta Olinder, 'The Power of Women in R.K. Narayan's Novels, in *R.K. Narayan: Critical Perspectives*, ed. A.L. McLeod, New Delhi: Sterling, 1994, 96–104.

29 'The Grandmother's Tale' could be added here, but although there is a female inner narrator who tells her story, the main centre of consciousness is male and the work is only of novella length.

30 K. Radha, 'Mahtama Gandhi in R.K. Narayan and Chaman Nahal', in *R.K. Narayan: Critical Perspectives*, ed. A.L. McLeod, New Delhi: Sterling, 1994, 105–12.

31 Nilufer E. Bharucha, 'Colonial Enclosures and Autonomous Spaces: R.K. Narayan's Malgudi', *South Asian Review*, 23, 1 (2002), 129–53; and Fakrul Alam, 'R.K. Narayan and the End of British India', *South Asian Review*, 23, 1 (2002), 70–85.

32 Feroza Jussawalla, 'Cricket and Colonialism: From *Swami and Friends* to *Lagaan*', *South Asian Review*, 23, 1 (2002), 112–28.

33 K. V. Bapa Rao, 'I Dream I Am Tate: A Tribute to R.K Narayan's Memory', outlookindia.com, 14 May 2001, <http://www.outlookindia.com/full.asp?sid=1&fodname=20010514&fname=bapa> (Accessed 23 May 2001).

34 *Swami and Friends*, 1935; Chicago: University of Chicago Press, 1980, 1.

35 *The Grandmother's Tale: Three Novellas*, London: Heinemann, 1993, 67.

ahimsa	non-violence; ethical belief in non-injury or kindness to other creatures
asrama	a stage (of which there are four) in the life of a twice-born Hindu
Bharat Natyam	form of Indian classical dance, particularly associated with Tamil Nadu
brahmacharya	religious studentship or apprenticeship – the first of four stages into which the life of a twice-born Hindu is divided, according to the *Manusmriti*
charka	spinning wheel
devadasi	temple-servant; dancing girl; temple prostitute
dharma	the complex of religious and social obligations which a devout Hindu is required to fulfil: right action, duty, morality, virtue, justice; customary observances of community or sect; the prescriptions or sanctions of religion; moral law
Gita	The *Bhagavad-Gita* – section of the *Mahabharata* in which Krishna addresses the warrior Arjuna on the eve of battle
grihastya (also *garhastya*)	the stage of being a householder and man of affairs – second *asrama* in the life of a twice-born Hindu, as laid down in the *Manusmriti*
karma	fate – as a consequence of acts in a previous life; action (with its outcomes and implications of merit); duty or obligation
khaddar	thick, coarse, homespun cloth

Mahabharata	'Great Story of India'; Sanskrit epic, centred on the war between two sets of cousins, the Pandavas and the Kauravas
Mahatma	'Great Soul', particularly as applied to Gandhi
Manusmriti	'Law of Manu'; ancient text which prescribes codes of ethical conduct for Hindus
maya	illusion; supernatural power; the world as perceived by the senses (considered as illusory); wealth; woman; feeling
Natya Shastra	classic work on 'The Science of Drama' by Bharat
puja	worship
puranas	a group of voluminous works in Sanskrit, dealing with aspects of ancient Indian history, legend, mythology and theology
rakshasa	demon
Ramayana	Sanskrit epic, centred on the hero Rama's expedition against Ravana, the *rakshasa* king of Lanka, who has abducted his wife, Sita
rasa	taste, flavour; juice, gravy, essence; savour, relish; pleasure, joy; elegance, charm, wit
sadhu	holy man; religious mendicant
sanyasa	fourth stage or *asrama* in the life of a twice-born Hindu; life as a wandering ascetic
sanyasi	person who has entered the fourth *asrama*
shastra	treatise; scripture; a work or book dealing with religion or any branch of ancient Indian learning, which is regarded as of divine authority
swaraj	home rule
vanaprastha	third stage in the *Manusmriti*, in which the householder becomes a forest-dweller or hermit prior to the final renunciation
varna	caste
varnasrama -dharma	right action, particularly as determined by one's caste and *asramas*

Select bibliography

The primary bibliography gives details of Narayan's book-length works. The listings of his novels give their dates of first publication *and* the editions used in this study. Most have been published separately and several times in India, the UK and the USA, as well as in many other countries in translation. Details of omnibus collections are also included.

The secondary bibliography is highly selective. It provides details of books, essays and articles that were influential in the writing of this study, along with other particularly useful works on Narayan's fiction. It can be supplemented by the useful bibliography in Geoffrey Kain, ed. *R.K. Narayan: Contemporary Critical Essays*, East Lansing, MI: Michigan State University Press, 1993, 221–230, an invaluable source of information on Narayan criticism up to the time of its publication

Works by R.K. Narayan

NOVELS

Details refer to the first English edition and, in cases where references in this study are to another edition, also to the actual edition used here.

Swami and Friends, London: Hamish Hamilton, 1935; Chicago: University of Chicago Press, 1980.

The Bachelor of Arts, London: Nelson, 1937; Chicago: University of Chicago Press, 1980.

The Dark Room, London: Macmillan, 1938; London: Heinemann, 1978.

The English Teacher. London: Eyre and Spottiswoode, 1945; Chicago: University of Chicago Press, 1980.

Mr Sampath – The Printer of Malgudi, London: Eyre and Spottiswoode, 1949; London: Heinemann, 1979.

The Financial Expert, London: Methuen, 1952.

Waiting for the Mahatma, London: Methuen, 1955.

The Guide, London: Methuen, 1958; Harmondsworth: Penguin, 1980.

The Man-Eater of Malgudi, London: Heinemann, 1961; Harmondsworth: Penguin, 1983.

The Vendor of Sweets, London: The Bodley Head, 1967; Harmondsworth: Penguin, 1983.

The Painter of Signs, London: Heinemann, 1977; Harmondsworth: Penguin, 1982.

A Tiger for Malgudi, London: Heinemann, 1983; Harmondsworth: Penguin, 1984.

Talkative Man, London: Heinemann, 1986; Harmondsworth: Penguin, 1987.

The World of Nagaraj, London: Heinemann, 1990; London: Mandarin, 1991.

The Grandmother's Tale: Three Novellas, London: Heinemann, 1993.

OMNIBUS EDITIONS

A Malgudi Omnibus, London: Minerva, 1994 (*Swami and Friends*, *The Bachelor of Arts* and *The English Teacher*).

More Tales from Malgudi, London: Minerva, 1997 (*Mr Sampath – The Printer of Malgudi*, *The Financial Expert*, *Waiting for the Mahatma* and *The World of Nagaraj*).

R.K. Narayan Omnibus, Volume 1, London: Everyman's Library, 2006 (*Swami and Friends*, *The Bachelor of Arts*, *The Dark Room* and *The English Teacher*).

R.K. Narayan Omnibus, Volume 2, London: Everyman's Library, 2006 (*Mr Sampath – The Printer of Malgudi*, *The Financial Expert* and *Waiting for the Mahatma*).

SHORT STORIES

Malgudi Days, Mysore: Indian Thought Publications, 1943.

Dodu and other Stories, Mysore: Indian Thought Publications, 1943.

Cyclone and Other Stories, Mysore: Indian Thought Publications, 1945.

An Astrologer's Day and Other Stories, London: Eyre and Spottiswoode, 1947.

Lawley Road and Other Stories, Mysore: Indian Thought Publications, 1956; New Delhi: Orient Paperbacks, n.d.

A Horse and Two Goats and Other Stories, London: The Bodley Head, 1970.

Old & New: Eighteen Short Stories, Mysore: Indian Thought Publications, 1981.

Malgudi Days, London: Heinemann, 1982; Harmondsworth: Penguin, 1984.

Under the Banyan Tree and Other Stories, London: Heinemann, 1985; Harmondsworth: Penguin, 1987.

Grandmother's Tale, Madras: Indian Thought Publications, 1992; *The Grandmother's Tale: Three Novellas*, London: Heinemann, 1993; *The Grandmother's Tale and Selected Stories*, Hopewell, NJ: Ecco Press, 1994

SHORT FICTION with NON-FICTION

A Story-Teller's World, Stories, Essay, Sketches, New Delhi: Penguin, 1989.

Salt & Sawdust: Stories and Table-Talk, New Delhi: Penguin, 1993.

NON-FICTION

Travel Books

Mysore, Mysore: The Government Press, 1939.

My Dateless Diary: An American Journey, Mysore: Indian Thought Publications, 1964; New Delhi: Penguin, 1988.

The Emerald Route, Bangalore: The Government of Karnataka, 1977; New Delhi: Penguin, 1999.

Autobiography

My Days: A Memoir, New York: Viking, 1974.

Essays

Next Sunday, Mysore: Indian Thought Publications, 1956.

Reluctant Guru, New Delhi: Hind Pocket Books, 1974; New Delhi: Orient Paperbacks, n.d.

A Writer's Nightmare, Selected Essays 1958–1988, New Delhi: Penguin, 1988.

Indian Myths Retold

Gods, Demons and Others, New York: Viking, 1964; London: Vintage, 2001.

The Ramayana: A Shortened Modern Prose Version of the Indian Epic, New York: Viking, 1972; Harmondsworth: Penguin, 1977.

The Mahabharata: A Shortened Modern Prose Version of the Indian Epic, New York: Viking, 1978; Harmondsworth: Penguin, 2001.

The India Epics Retold, New Delhi: Penguin, 1995.

Edited Miscellany

Indian Thought: A Miscellany, New Delhi, Penguin, 1997.

Selected Criticism

Afzal-Khan, Fawzia, *Cultural Imperialism and the Indo-English Novel: Genre and Ideology in R.K. Narayan, Anita Desai, Kamala Markandaya and Salman Rushdie*, University Park: Pennsylvania State University Press, 1993.

Alam, Fakrul, 'Narrative Strategies in Two Narayan Novels', in *R.K. Narayan: Critical Perspectives*, ed. Alan McLeod, New Delhi: Sterling, 1994, 8–21.

——, 'R.K. Narayan and the End of British India', *South Asian Review*, 23, 1 (2002), 70–85.

Albertazzi, Silvia, *Translating India: Travel and Cross-Cultural Transference in Post-Colonial Indian Fiction in English*, Bologna: Cooperativa Libraria Universitaria Editrice Bologna, 1993, 11–31.

Almond, Ian, 'Darker Shades of Malgudi: Solitary Figures of Modernity in the Stories of R.K. Narayan', *Journal of Commonwealth Literature*, 36, 2 (2001), 107–16.

Bande, Usha, 'Validating the Self: The Female Hero in R.K. Narayan's *The Painter of Signs*', in *Women in Indo-Anglian Fiction: Tradition and Modernity*, ed. Naresh K. Jain, New Delhi: Manohar, 1998, 101–13.

Beatina, Mary, *Narayan: A Study in Transcendence*, New York: Peter Lang, 1994.

Bharucha, Nilufer E., 'Colonial Enclosures and Autonomous Spaces: R.K. Narayan's Malgudi', *South Asian Review*, 23, 1 (2002), 129–53

Carter, Steve, 'Narrative Ostranenie in R.K. Narayan's *Painter of Signs*', *Journal of Commonwealth Literature*, 29, 2 (1994), 109–16.

Chauhan, P.S., '*Talkative Man* and the Semiotics of Malgudi Discourse', *South Asian Review*, 23, 1 (2002), 49–69.

——, 'The Commonwealth of the Imagination: Narayan and Naipaul', in *Language and Literature in Multicultural Contexts*, ed. Satendra Nandan, Suva: University of the South Pacific, 1983, 89–96.

Chellappan, K., 'The Dialectics of Myth and Irony in R.K. Narayan', in *R.K. Narayan: Critical Perspectives*, ed. A.L. McLeod, New Delhi: Sterling, 1994, 22–32,

Chew, Shirley, 'A Proper Detachment: The Novels of R.K. Narayan', in *Readings in Commonwealth Literature*, ed. William Walsh, Oxford: Clarendon Press, 1973, 58–74.

Dnyate, Ramesh, 'The Hothouse Cactus: A Note on R.K. Narayan's *The Painter of Signs*, in *Image of India in the Indian Novel in English, 1960–1985*, ed. Sudhakar Pandey and R. Raj Rao, London: Sangam Books, 1993, 61–8.

Garebian, Keith, 'Strategy and Theme in the Art of R.K. Narayan, *ARIEL*, 5, 4 (1974), 70–81.

Gerow, Edwin, 'The Quintessential Narayan', in *Considerations: Twelve Studies of Indo-Anglian Writings*, ed. Meenakshi Mukherjee, Columbia, MO: South Asia Books, 1977, 66–83; repr. from *East and West*, 10, 1–2 (1966), 1–18.

Greene, Graham, Introduction to *The Bachelor of Arts*, London: Nelson, 1937.

——, Introduction to *The Financial Expert*, London: Methuen, 1952, v–vi.

Hariprasanna, A. *The World of Malgudi*, New Delhi: Prestige, 1994.

Harrex, S.C. *The Fire and the Offering: The English Language Novel of India, 1935–1970*, Calcutta: Writers Workshop, 1978.

Hawley, John, '"R.K. Narayanswami [sic] B.A.B.L. Engine Driver": Story-telling and Memory in *The Grandmother's Tale, and Selected Stories*', *South Asian Review*, 23, 1 (2002), 86–105.

Holmstrom, Lakshmi, *The Novels of R.K. Narayan*, Calcutta: Writers Workshop, 1973.

Iyengar, K.R., Srinivasa, *Indian Writing in English*, Bombay: Asia Publishing House, revised 2nd. edn., 1973,

Jussawalla, Feroza, 'Cricket and Colonialism: From *Swami and Friends* to *Lagaan*', *South Asian Review*, 23, 1 (2002), 112–28.

Kain, Geoffrey, 'Eternal, Insatiable, Appetite: The Irony of R.K. Narayan's Baited Hero', in *R.K. Narayan, Contemporary Critical Essays*, ed. Kain, East Lansing, MI: Michigan State University Press, 1993, 101–13.

——, 'R.K. Narayan', in *A Companion to Indian Fiction in English*, ed. Pier Paolo Piciucco, New Delhi: Atlantic, 2004, 1–31.

——, '*Talkative Man*: R.K. Narayan's Consummate Performance of Narayan', *South Asian Review*, 23, 1 (2002), 5–21.

——, ed., *R.K. Narayan: Contemporary Critical Essays*, East Lansing, MI: Michigan State University Press, 1993.

Khair, Tabish, *Babu Fictions: Alienation in Contemporary Indian English Novels*, New Delhi: OUP, 2001.

Krishnaswamy, Shantha, 'Daisy Paints Her Signs Otherwise', in *R.K. Narayan: Contemporary Critical Essays*, ed. Geoffrey Kain, East Lansing, MI: Michigan State University Press, 1993, 115–24.

McLeod, Alan, ed., *R.K. Narayan: Critical Perspectives*, New Delhi: Sterling, 1994.

Mishra, Ganeswar, 'The Novel as Purana: A Study of the Form of *The Man-Eater of Malgudi* and *Kanthapura*', *How Indian is the Indian Novel in English*, Bhubaneswar: Utkal University, 1990, 18–35.

Mishra, Pankaj, 'R.K. Narayan', in Arvind Krishna Mehrotra, ed., *A History of Indian Literature in English*, London: Hurst, 2003, 193–208.

M'Marete, Gideon Nteere, 'Krishnan's Jasmine-Scented Quest', in *R.K. Narayan: Contemporary Critical Essays*, ed. Geoffrey Kain, East Lansing, MI: Michigan State University Press, 1993, 37–47.

Mukherjee, Meenakshi, 'The Anxiety of Indianness: Our Novels in English', in *Mapping Cultural Spaces: Postcolonial Literature in English: Essays in Honour of Nissim Ezekiel*, ed. Nilufer E. Bharucha and Vrinda Nabar, New Delhi: Vision, 1998, 78–93.

——, *The Twice-Born Fiction*, 1971; repr. New Delhi: Pencraft, 2001.

Naik, M.K., *The Ironic Vision: A Study of the Fiction of R.K. Narayan*, New Delhi: Sterling, 1983.

——, 'Two Uses of Irony: V.S. Naipaul's *The Mystic Masseur* and R.K. Narayan's *The Guide*', *World Literature Written in English*, 17, 2 (1978), 646–55.

Naipaul, V.S., *India: A Wounded Civilization*, London: André Deutsch, 1977, 18–27 and 37–43.

Nath, Sura P., 'R.K. Narayan's Dialogic Narrative in *The Guide*', in *R.K. Narayan: Critical Perspectives*, ed. A.L. McLeod, New Delhi: Sterling, 1994, 129–36.

Olinder, Britta, 'Reality and Myth in R.K. Narayan's Novels', in *Language and Literature in Multicultural Contexts*; ed. Satendra Nandan, Suva: University of the South Pacific, 1983, 286–96.

——, 'R.K. Narayan's Short Stories: Some Introductory Remarks', *Commonwealth Essays and Studies*, 8, 1 (1985), 24–30.

Pousse, Michel, *R.K. Narayan: A Painter of Modern India*, New York: Peter Lang, 1995.

Puranik, Sadhana Allison, '*The Painter of Signs*: Breaking the Frontier', in *R.K. Narayan: Contemporary Critical Essays*, ed. Geoffrey Kain, East Lansing, MI: Michigan State University Press, 1993, 125–39.

Radha, K., 'Mahtama Gandhi in R.K. Narayan and Chaman Nahal', in *R.K. Narayan: Critical Perspectives*, ed. A.L. McLeod, New Delhi: Sterling, 1994, 105–12.

Ram, Susan and Ram, N., *R.K. Narayan: The Early Years: 1906–1945*, New Delhi: Viking, 1996.

Rao, Ranga, *R.K. Narayan*, New Delhi: Sahitya Akademi, 2004.

——, 'R.K. Narayan: An Indian Perspective', *Journal of Commonwealth Literature*, 36, 2 (2001), 117–21.

Sankaran, Chitra, *The Myth Connection: The Use of Hindu Mythology in Some Novels of Raja Rao and R.K, Narayan*, Ahmedabad: Allied Publishers, 1993.

Sen, Krishna, 'Will the Real Dr Rann Please Stand Up?', *South Asian Review*, 23, 1 (2002), 22–48.

Shankar, D.A., 'Caste in the Fiction of R.K. Narayan', in *R.K. Narayan: Critical Perspectives*, ed. A.L. McLeod, New Delhi: Sterling, 1994, 137–46.

Srikanth, Rajini, '*The World of Nagaraj*: Narayan's Metanovel', in *R.K. Narayan, Contemporary Critical Essays*, ed. Geoffrey Kain, East Lansing, MI: Michigan State University Press, 1993, 197–203.

Sundaram, P.S., *R.K. Narayan*, New Delhi: Arnold-Heinemann, 1973.

Thieme, John, 'Irony in R.K. Narayan's *The Man-Eater of Malgudi*', *The English Review*, 3, 4 (1993), 13–17.

Vanden Driesen, Cynthia, *The Novels of R.K. Narayan*. Nedlands, WA: Centre for South and Southeast Asian Studies, University of Western Australia, 1986.

——, *Centering the Margins: Perspectives on Literatures in English from India, Africa, Australia*, New Delhi: Prestige, 1995, 1–9.

Walsh, William, *R.K. Narayan: A Critical Appreciation*, London: Heinemann, 1982.

——, *A Manifold Voice: Studies in Commonwealth Literature*, London: Chatto and Windus, 1970, 11–23.

Interviews

Narayan interviewed by Andrew Robinson, *The Independent*, 24 October 1986, 14.

'Making a Map of the Imagination', R.K. Narayan interviewed by Clare Colvin, *Sunday Times*, 23 April 1989, G9.

Lowe, John, 'A Meeting in Malgudi: A Conversation with R.K. Narayan', in *R.K. Narayan, Contemporary Critical Essays*, ed. Geoffrey Kain, East Lansing, MI: Michigan State University Press, 1993, 179–85.

General works

Alter, Joseph, *Gandhi's Body: Sex, Diet and the Politics of Nationalism*, Philadelphia: University of Pennsylvania Press, 2000.

Atwood, Margaret, *Survival: A Thematic Guide to Canadian Literature*, Toronto: Anansi, 1972.

Chaudhuri, Nirad, *A Passage to England*, New Delhi, Orient Paperbacks, n.d.

Cronin, Richard, *Imagining India*, London: Macmillan, 1989.

Ezekiel, Nissim, *Collected Poems*, New Delhi: Oxford University Press, 2nd edn., 2005, 237–40.

Foucault. Michel, *The Foucault Reader*, ed. Paul Rabinow, Harmondsworth, Penguin: 1991, 252.

——, 'Of Other Spaces', trans. Jay Miskowiec *Diacritics*, 16, 1 (1986), 22–27.

——, *Power, Knowledge: Selected Interviews and Other Writings*, Brighton: Harvester, 1980.

Gilbert, Sandra M. and Susan Gubar, *The Madwoman in the Attic*, 1979; New Haven: Yale University Press, 1984.

Joyce, James, *A Portrait of the Artist as a Young Man*, 1916; Harmondsworth, Penguin: 1960, 15–16.

Jung, Carl, *Memories, Dreams and Reflections*, London: Collins, 1963.

Khare, R.S., ed., *The Eternal Food: Gastronomic Ideas and Experiences of Hindus and Buddhists*, Albany, NY: State University of New York Press, 1992.

Kipling, Rudyard, *All the Mowgli Stories*, London: Macmillan/St Martin's Press, 1973.

MacLeod, K.M., *Derry and Co.*, London: Pickering and Inglis, 1934.

Massey, Doreen, *Space, Place and Gender*, Cambridge: Polity Press, 1994.

Muecke, D.C., *Irony: The Critical Idiom*, London: Methuen, 1970.

Mukerjee, Sujit, 'Tigers in Fiction: An Aspect of the Colonial Encounter', *Kunapipi*, 9, 1 (1987), 1–13.

Naipaul, V.S., *An Area of Darkness*, Harmondsworth: Penguin, 1968.

Narasimhaiah, C.D., *'N for Nobody': Autobiography of an English Teacher*, Delhi: B.R. Publishing Corporation, 1991.

——, *The Swan and the Eagle: Essays on Indian English Literature*, Simla: Indian Institute of Advanced Study, 1968.

Nyman, Jopi, *Postcolonial Animal Tale from Kipling to Coetzee*, New Delhi: Atlantic, 2003.

Randall, Don, 'Kipling's *Stalky & Co.*: Resituating the Empire and the "Empire Boy"', *Victorian Review*, 24, 2 (1998), 163–74.

Rao, Raja, Foreword, *Kanthapura*, 1938; New Delhi: Orient Paperbacks, 1992.

Said, Edward, *The World, The Text and the Critic*, London: Faber and Faber, 1984.

Sankhala, Kailash, *Tiger! The Story of the Indian Tiger*, London: William Collins, 1978.

Soja, Edward, *Postmodern Geographies: The Reassertion of Space in Critical Social Theory*, London: Verso, 1989.

Thieme, John, *Postcolonial Con-Texts: Writing Back to the Canon*, London and New York: Continuum, 2001.

——, *The Web of Tradition: Uses of Allusion in V.S. Naipaul's Fiction*, Aarhus: Dangaroo and London: Hansib, 1987.

Thieme, John and Ira Raja, eds, *The Table is Laid: The Oxford Anthology of South Asian Food Writing*, New Delhi: Oxford University Press, 2007.

Walsh, William, *Indian Literature in English*, London and New York: Longman, 1990.

Index